Information, Freedom and Property

This book addresses issues on the nexus of freedom of and property in information, while acknowledging that both hiding and exposing information may affect our privacy. It inquires into the physics, the technologies, the business models, the governmental strategies and, last but not least, the legal frameworks concerning access, organization and control of information. It debates whether it is in the very nature of information to be either free or monopolized, or both. Analysing upcoming power structures, new types of colonization and attempts to replace legal norms with techno-nudging, this book also presents the idea of an infraethics capable of pre-empting our pre-emption. It discusses the interrelations between open access, the hacker ethos, the personal data economy, and freedom of information, highlighting the ephemeral but pivotal role played by information in a data-driven society. This book is a must-read for those working on the contemporary dimensions of freedom of information, data protection and intellectual property rights.

Mireille Hildebrandt is a tenured Research Professor of 'Interfacing Law and Technology' at the Faculty of Law and Criminology at Vrije Universiteit Brussel. She also holds the parttime Chair of Smart Environments, Data Protection and the Rule of Law at the Science Faculty of Radboud University.

Bibi van den Berg is an associate professor and research director at eLaw, the Centre for Law and Digital Technologies at the Law School of Leiden University, the Netherlands.

Information, Freedom and Property

The philosophy of law meets the philosophy of technology

Edited by
**Mireille Hildebrandt and
Bibi van den Berg**

Routledge
Taylor & Francis Group

a GlassHouse book

First published 2016
by Routledge
2 Park Square, Milton Park, Abingdon, Oxon, OX14 4RN

and by Routledge
711 Third Avenue, New York, NY 10017

a GlassHouse book

Routledge is an imprint of the Taylor & Francis Group, an informa business

British Library Cataloguing in Publication Data
A catalogue record for this book is available from the British Library

Library of Congress Cataloging-in-Publication Data
Names: Hildebrandt, Mireille, editor. | Berg, Bibi van den, editor.
Title: Information, freedom and property : the philosophy of law meets the philosophy of technology / edited by Mireille Hildebrandt and Bibi van den Berg.
Description: Abingdon, Oxon ; New York, NY : Routledge, 2016. | "A GlassHouse book." | Includes bibliographical references and index.
Identifiers: LCCN 2015049695 | ISBN 9781138669130 (hbk) | ISBN 9781315618265 (ebk)
Subjects: LCSH: Information technology—Law and legislation | Technology and law. | Data protection—Law and legislation. | Internet—Social aspects. | Law—Philosophy.
Classification: LCC K564.C6 I544 2016 | DDC 343.09/99—dc23
LC record available at http://lccn.loc.gov/2015049695

ISBN: 9781138669130 (hbk)
ISBN: 9781315618265 (ebk)

Typeset in Baskerville by
Keystroke, Station Road, Codsall, Wolverhampton

Contents

Acknowledgements

This volume emerged from the Philosophers' Reading Panel that was organized by the editors of this volume at the 2013 international Conference on Privacy and Data Protection (CPDP) in Brussels. The Philosophers' Reading Panels at CPDP aim for slow and public thinking, probing the depth and the surface as well as the boundaries of law in the era of high tech information and communication technologies. It was the third of its kind, after the 2009 and 2011 panels, which resulted in the first and second volumes in the Routledge series of 'The Philosophy of Law Meets the Philosophy of Technology', entitled *Law, Human Agency and Autonomic Computing*, co-edited by Mireille Hildebrandt and Antoinette Rouvroy in 2011, and *Privacy, Due Process and the Computational Turn*, co-edited by Mireille Hildebrandt and Katja de Vries in 2013.

The Philosophers' Reading Panel was hosted and funded by CPDP and by eLaw, the Center for Law and Digital Technologies, at Leiden University. Many thanks to Paul de Hert, Serge Gutwirth, Rocco Bellanova, and Rosamunde van Brakel of the research group for Law Science Technology & Society studies at Vrije Universiteit for enabling the synergy of a reading panel that actually practises 'slow thinking', operating in the midst of the larger conference that entails an incredibly broad and informative set of panels from around the globe on the nexus of law, social theory and computer science, focusing on privacy and data protection. We are equally grateful to Simone van der Hof of eLaw in Leiden, for generously co-funding and supporting the undertaking.

Special gratitude is due to Antoinette Rouvroy, who co-edited the first volume and inspired the initiative with her groundbreaking insights and mind-boggling analyses. We would like to extend our gratitude and appreciation to the authors who participated in the third Philosophers' Reading Panel, providing a first draft of their papers well in advance to enable a high level of discussion, and for working with us on the chapters of this volume: Gary Marx, Julie Cohen, David Koepsell and Luciano Floridi. We also are highly indebted to Alexandra Couto and Linnet Taylor who joined the volume at a later stage with crucial contributions, thus providing a more complete picture of what is at stake between information, freedom and property.

Finally, we thank Routledge's editorial assistant, Laura Muir, who suffered our delays and turned our typescript into a printed volume, thus making our ideas propertizable assets (though not all authors would agree this is what information wants). And, to put the icing on the cake, let us express our sincere gratitude to our publisher at Routledge, Colin Perrin, who convinced Routledge to take the risk of commodifying our work and thus bringing it to its audience.

Mireille Hildebrandt, Bibi van den Berg

Notes on contributors

Bibi van den Berg is associate professor at Leiden University. She works in two different departments: within the Law School at eLaw, the Centre for Law and Digital Technologies, and within the Faculty of Governance and Global Affairs at the Institute for Security and Global Affairs. At the latter institute, Van den Berg runs the cybersecurity group. She is also acting scientific director of the Cyber Security Academy, a professional Master's programme run by Leiden University, together with Technical University Delft. Van den Berg has an MA and PhD in philosophy, both from Erasmus University in Rotterdam. Van den Berg's research and teaching focus on several themes: (1) cybersecurity; (2) regulating human behaviour through the use of technologies (techno-regulation and nudging); (3) regulation and governance of/on the internet; (4) privacy and identity; and (5) robotics and artificial intelligence.

Van den Berg is a member of the Dutch Cyber Security Council, a Council that advises the Dutch cabinet on how to improve cyber security in the Netherlands.

Julie E. Cohen is the Mark Claster Mamolen Professor of Law & Technology at the Georgetown University Law Center. She teaches and writes about copyright, information privacy regulation, and the governance of information and communication networks. She is the author of *Configuring the Networked Self: Law, Code, and the Play of Everyday Practice* (Yale University Press, 2012), and a co-author of *Copyright in a Global Information Economy* (Aspen Law & Business, 4th edn, 2015). Professor Cohen is a member of the Advisory Board of the Electronic Privacy Information Center.

Alexandra Couto is a Postdoctoral Research Fellow at the Centre for the Study of Mind in Nature, Oslo University. She holds an MPhil and a DPhil in Political Theory from Oxford University. Her recent research focuses on the three following topics: the role of responsibility in luck egalitarianism, the conditions for the justifiability of interpersonal forgiveness and issues relating to the Beneficiary Principle, a principle according to which we might accrue remedial duties by benefiting (innocently) from injustices. Her recently published book

Liberal Perfectionism: The Reasons that Goodness Gives (Walter De Gruyter Inc, 2014) defends a minimal form of liberal perfectionism.

Luciano Floridi is Professor of Philosophy and Ethics of Information at the University of Oxford, where he is the Director of Research and Senior Research Fellow of the Oxford Internet Institute, Governing Body Fellow of St Cross College, Distinguished Research Fellow of the Uehiro Centre for Practical Ethics in the Faculty of Philosophy, and Research Associate and Fellow in Information Policy of the Department of Computer Science. Outside Oxford, he is Adjunct Professor of the Department of Economics, American University, Washington DC. His most recent books are: *The Fourth Revolution: How the infosphere is reshaping human reality* (Oxford University Press, 2014), *The Ethics of Information* (Oxford University Press, 2013), *The Philosophy of Information* (Oxford University Press, 2011), *The Cambridge Handbook of Information and Computer Ethics* (Cambridge University Press, 2010), and *Information: A Very Short Introduction* (Oxford University Press, 2010). He is Editor in Chief of *Philosophy & Technology* and of the Philosophical Studies book series (Springer). He is currently Chairman of Ethics Advisory Board of the European Medical Information Framework, member of Google's Advisory Board on 'the right to be forgotten' and member of the Advisory Board of Tencent's Internet and Society Institute. Among his recognitions, he has been elected Fernand Braudel Senior Fellow by the European University Institute; awarded the Cátedras de Excelencia Prize by the University Carlos III of Madrid; and was the UNESCO Chair in Information and Computer Ethics and Gauss Professor of the Academy of Sciences in Göttingen. He is a recipient of the MEA's J. Ong Award, the APA's Barwise Prize, the IACAP's Covey Award, and the INSEIT's Weizenbaum Award. He is an AISB and BCS Fellow, and a Fellow of the Académie Internationale de Philosophie des Sciences.

Mireille Hildebrandt is a Research Professor of Interfacing Law and Technology at Vrije Universiteit Brussels, with the research group for Law Science Technology and Society Studies (LSTS). She is also a part-time Professor of Smart Environments, Data Protection and the Rule of Law at the Institute for Computer and Information Sciences (ICIS) at Radboud University, Nijmegen. She has been associate editor of *Criminal Law and Philosophy*, and editor-in-chief of the *Netherlands Journal of Legal Philosophy*. Hildebrandt publishes widely on the nexus of philosophy of technology and of law, focusing on the issues around profiling technologies, security policies and criminal law. She co-edited with Serge Gutwirth, *Profiling the European Citizen: Cross-Disciplinary Perspectives* (Springer, 2008), co-authored with 28 authors from the fields of law, computer science and legal philosophy. She initiated the seminars and book series on Philosophers of Law Meet Philosophers of Technology and co-edited and co-authored two previous volumes in the series: *Law, Human Agency and Autonomic Computing* (with Antoinette Rouvroy; Routledge, 2011) and *Privacy, Due Process and the Computational Turn* (with Katja de Vries; Routledge, 2013). She has also written *Smart Technologies and the End(s) of Law: Novel Entanglements of Law and Technology* (Edward Elgar, 2015). For other publications, see http://works. bepress.com/mireille_hildebrandt/.

David Koepsell is an author, philosopher, attorney (retired), and educator whose recent research focuses on the nexus of science, technology, ethics and public policy. He has provided commentary regarding ethics, society, religion and technology on MSNBC, Fox News Channel, *The Guardian*, *The Washington Times*, NPR Radio, Radio Free Europe, Air America, The Atlanta Journal Constitution and the Associated Press, among others. He has been a tenured Associate Professor of Philosophy at the Delft University of Technology, Faculty of Technology, Policy and Management in the Netherlands, Visiting Professor at UNAM, Instituto de Filosoficas, Mexico, and Director of Research and Strategic Initiatives at Comisión Nacional de Bioética in Mexico. For further information, see http://davidkoepsell.com.

Gary T. Marx is Professor Emeritus from MIT and he has also taught at Harvard, the University of California Berkeley (from where he received his PhD) and many other schools in the US, Europe and Asia. He has worked in the areas of race and ethnicity, collective behaviour and social movements, law and society and surveillance studies. His work has appeared in both academic and popular media and has been widely reprinted and translated. In articles and books (e.g. *Undercover: Police Surveillance in America* (University of California Press, 1992); and *Windows Into the Soul: Surveillance and Society in an Age of High Technology* (University of Chicago Press, 2016)), he illustrates how and why surveillance is neither good nor bad, but context and comportment make it so. He has sought to create a conceptual map of new ways of collecting, analysing, communicating and using personal information. Explanation and evaluation require a common language for the identification and measurement of surveillance's fundamental properties and contexts. The richness of the empirical must be disentangled and parsed into categories which can be measured. The work argues for the need to understand current surveillance practices within specific settings in light of history, culture, social structure and the give and take of interaction and to appreciate (if not necessarily welcome) the ironies, paradoxes, trade-offs and value conflicts which limit the best laid plans. Mushrooms do well in the dark, but so does injustice. Sunlight may bring needed accountability through visibility, but it can also blind and burn. Articles at www.garymarx.net illustrate his approach.

Philip Serracino Inglott (1976–2013) was a geek and a tinkerer at heart. As a student of philosophy, he derived his greatest pleasure from helping engineering students fix their bikes. He came from Malta where he graduated in Philosophy and IT. While working for an NGO, he participated in the Virtual University of the Small States of the Commonwealth, which aimed at using open software technology to aid education in developing small states. After that fulfilling experience, Philip returned to philosophy. He obtained his Master's in Philosophy of Science, Technology and Society from the University of Twente in 2010. His thesis dealt with Wikipedia, Open Source Software and their relationship to Deliberative Democracy. At TU Delft, Philip was looking at the effects of Web2.0 and related technologies on the moral frameworks of the internet-native generation. He wanted to uncover the common moral thread that ties WikiLeaks and Anime Music Videos to Open Source and Open Access. Philip was intrigued by how the internet feeds actions like the Occupy Movement and the Arab Spring. Beyond its use as a tool to facilitate and promote such movements, does the practice of using the internet shape our moral frameworks to be less tolerant of authoritarian rule? Philip was married to Victoria. His eclectic interests varied from all things technical to cooking, music and carpentry, politics to gardening, philosophy and anything related to IT. He also liked cats a lot. He passed away in December 2013, ten days after his first academic publication. He was 37 years old.

Linnet Taylor is an Assistant Professor at the Tilburg Institute for Law, Technology and Society (TILT). Her research focuses on the use of new types of digital data in research and policymaking around issues of development, urban planning and mobility. Previously, she was a researcher at the Oxford Internet Institute on the project 'Accessing and Using Big Data to Advance Social Science Knowledge'. Linnet studied a DPhil in International Development at the Institute of Development Studies, University of Sussex, where she was also part of the Sussex Centre for Migration Research. Her doctoral research focused on the adoption of the internet in West Africa. Before her doctoral work she was a researcher at the Rockefeller Foundation, where she developed programmes around economic security and human mobility.

Introduction: information, freedom and property

Mireille Hildebrandt

The confrontation of philosophy of law with that of technology, which is crucial to this volume, aims to test how technology affects law's normativity.[1] This could be paraphrased as the question: how does the physical condition the cultural? For those versed in social theory this may be the less obvious question, but in an extended cyberspace that steadily incorporates the offline world, this may instead be the more urgent question. More concretely, this volume aims to inquire how data-driven technologies such as smart glasses, self-driving cars and smart energy grids impact the right to informational self-determination, the operations of copyright protection and the freedom of information. Even more specific, the question is raised how the technologies of internet filtering, blocking and other forms of surveillance (deep packet inspection, remote hacking), and/or identification and authentication (walled gardens) impact on the freedom and the property of information. The idea is that *it matters how* surveillance or identification is enabled or mediated, while the subsequent question of *how it matters* cannot be answered in the abstract. It requires an investigation of the scale, scope, coerciveness and distribution of the effects of particular socio-technical surveillance infrastructures.[2] Such an investigation inevitably links up with an inquiry into the accessibility of information about individual persons, depending on the material and cultural affordances of its embodiment and its institutionalization.

The book consists of four parts. In the first, titled 'The matrix of information', we discuss some of the properties of information, presenting a taxonomy of its accessibility. The distributed character of this accessibility entails knowledge asymmetries that raise questions around 'The powers of information', which heads the second part of the book. In the third part, we confront the potential empowerment generated by information and communication technology (ICT), testing the proposition that ICT has an inherently liberating force that should be fostered instead of frustrated. This is framed as the question of 'What freedom of which information?' Lastly, in the fourth part, we are invited to reflect upon an infrastructure that is conducive to deliberate(d) choice, based on informed reflection. This should lead to 'An infraethics for an information society', taking to heart that we live in times of abundance, as far as information (or at least data) is concerned. The need to learn how to cope with this abundance ignites debates on the distribution of agency and responsibility, thus returning to the question of who gains access to what information and who are capable of assessing its value.

Part I The matrix of information

This volume kicks off with a chapter by the Nestor of surveillance studies, emeritus MIT professor Gary T. Marx. In his chapter, he undertakes the rare and contrarian task of unbottling some of the genies of data or information, initiating what he coins a sociology of information. While computer scientists are developing a sociology of multi-agent systems,[3] engaging in large scale simulations of emergent behaviours of societies composed of artificial agents, Gary Marx discusses 'the role that communication and data exchange/use play as *universal* aspects of human society' (emphasis added),[4] paradoxically demonstrating the relational, contextual and empirical nature of the properties of information. In the opening move for this volume, Marx tackles accessibility as a property of information. He develops a matrix of the physical and cultural aspects that co-determine accessibility, highlighting a series of components that play out in every nook and corner of the matrix, perhaps even disrupting its dividing lines: awareness, collection, understanding, a record, sharing, private property and usage. For a lawyer, such a diversity of categories is infuriating, as they cut across the domain at different levels, overlapping, mixing and excluding each other as a series of wild cards in a poker game. For a philosopher, the exercise is thought-provoking but frustrating, as the reader is not taken by the hand for some 'proper' conceptualization or argumentation. Marx does not stand still, his analyses form a moving target, showing that information wants to be free, while underlining that, in the end, it all depends.

Gary Marx's ingenious exercise of summoning a series of properties of information whilst focusing on accessibility invites a train of thought about the *universality of the relational, empirical and contextual nature of information* and the myriad ways in which accessibility, appropriation and appropriateness of information intersect and accumulate.

In the second chapter, Hildebrandt follows-up on Gary Marx's matrix of what he calls physical and cultural barriers against access to information.[5] She challenges the idea that information exists as a non-material good with universal properties, and inquires how – and to what extent – the materiality of information co-determines its properties, while taking note of the cultural constraints that reinforce, block or transform these properties. As to the materiality of information, Hildebrandt notes that this refers to the retention of information. In human society, this retention takes the form of primary and secondary retention (perception and memory) and tertiary retention (inscriptions on external carriers, such as papyrus, paper or silicon chips). Based on an investigation into the materiality of information, this chapter investigates three distinct but interrelated 'properties' of information: accessibility, propertizability and appropriateness. The main point of the chapter is to inquire into how these properties may be transformed in the era of digital data and machine learning, notably by arguing that digital data make accessing and assessing the information that is retained more difficult. Basically, the claim is that 'reading' the data requires additional technological mediation, which creates novel asymmetries.

Part II The powers of information

In the third chapter, opening the second part of the volume, Julie E. Cohen addresses the issue of knowledge and power asymmetries, as generated by new types of information flows. She maps the problem of control over information in terms of transformations in: (1) the domains of; (2) the legal discourse within; and (3) the power relationships generated by copyright and information privacy/ data protection law. Already in her previous work, *Configuring the Networked Self: Law, Code, and the Play of Everyday Practice*,[6] Cohen undertook the task of interrelating these two domains of positive law, by showing how they configure the modulations triggered by data-driven and networked applications, whilst simultaneously being re-configured by them. In this chapter, Cohen targets both the traditional legal narratives and the institutional arrangements that should enable the vindication of authorship and privacy. She highlights how emergent global networks of neoliberal governance afford invisible circumvention of traditional legal and institutional safeguards, facilitating rent-seeking behaviours for those capable of controlling the flows of information in upcoming personal data ecosystems.

In the fourth chapter, the challenge of global power asymmetries is taken up from the perspective of lower-income countries. Linnet Taylor, an anthropologist with a track record in research on these issues in sub-Saharan Africa, introduces the 2012 data analysis competition organized by Orange on call records of all its Ivorian subscribers. She traces the way this competition was first labelled a development project, heralded by the United Nations and the World Economic Forum. Taylor shows how the anonymity of the data sets may seem to protect individuals against being identified, whereas in point of fact the mobility patterns derived from the data would enable profilers to target ethnic communities, thus creating a potentially life-threatening detection mechanism – endangering the freedom of movement and the integrity of individual members of these communities. The chapter thus addresses two pivotal issues of data protection that have received little attention so far: (1) the implications of big data analytics in countries without data protection law; and (2) the emerging privacy harms that threaten groups rather than individuals, while paradoxically thereby threatening the lives and fundamental rights of individuals profiled as members of such groups.

Part III What freedom of which information?

Under the heading of 'ICT's architecture of freedom', David Koepsell and Philip Serracino Inglott take the lead in advocating the radical position that the emerging architecture of ICT necessarily favours freedom of information. Whereas Marx and Hildebrandt mapped how, and under what conditions, information may be accessible, and Cohen and Taylor pinpoint the growing power asymmetries that come with control over information, Koepsell and Inglott argue that the matter of ICT has an 'inherently liberating potential'.[7] Their chapter contains a captivating history of technological development, where they argue that though current ICT is not really different from previous technologies, it nevertheless renders the potentially liberating effects of technology more visible, more inevitable and more powerful. They ruminate against the purportedly mistaken ontological assumptions of legal positivism, which they claim infects most lawyers. These assumptions concern the dichotomy between copyright and patent, expression and invention, aesthetics and functionality. According to the authors, these dichotomies are meant to enable monopolies that go against the grain of the values inherent in ICT.

In her response to Koepsell and Inglott, Alexandra Couto takes issue with the approach developed in the previous chapter, inquiring into the legal and moral grounds for protecting intellectual property as well as freedom of expression. Her main point is that the authors seem to adhere to a mild form of technological determinism, while they also move from the empirical claim that intellectual property (IP) goods are increasingly hard to regulate to the normative claim that these goods should not be regulated by IP law at all. In fact, Couto finds that Koepsell and Inglott reject any regulation of expressions and information, whereas she believes that considering the harms that may be caused by either requires at least some form of protection. Lastly, Couto investigates the moral grounds for a right to IP, arguing for the need to attribute appropriate rewards for creators, even if only with an eye to the societal benefits.

Part IV An infraethics for an information society

In the last part of this volume, Luciano Floridi takes the floor with a cogent argument to design what he calls an *infraethics*, meant to detect and institutionalize the norms that enable and oblige people to make informed ethical choices. His move towards infraethics is meant to introduce the ethical and political aspects of freedom and property in relation to a new role of information. This new role is explained in the context of the current transition from history (based on ICTs that record and transmit information) to what Floridi terms *hyperhistory* (based on ICTs capable of new types of data processing). His distinction between history and hyperhistory concerns the fact that the ICTs of the current and upcoming era inform much of the critical infrastructure of our society in a way that makes societal welfare, personal well-being and intellectual flourishing contingent upon these ICTs. The transition is then placed in the context of nation states and – other, non-governmental – 'multi-agent systems', acting as information agents and hyperhistorical players at the global level. Floridi finds that the playing field of political decision-making has been transformed by globalization, de-territorialisation and fluidification, requiring a sustained effort to re-design environments in such a way that they are conducive to ethical choices, actions or processes. Instead of proposing another version of *ethics by design*, he proposes a *pro-ethical design* or *infraethics*, meant to 'privilege the facilitation of reflection' on ethical choices, actions and processes. The enforcement of rights that involve the accessibility and assessibility of information, such as IP rights, freedom of information and data protection, directly affect the infrastructure of the ethical domain. Considering the network effect of their implications, Floridi points out that these rights urgently require reconfiguration or at least reconsideration in view of whether, and how, they enable reflection on the ethical choices, actions and processes they afford.

In the last chapter of this volume Bibi van den Berg responds to Floridi's call for an infraethics. Infraethics should steer people towards reflection on the choice they make, making sure that the decisions they take are based on conscious deliberation instead of habit, fear or ignorance. This, however, presents us with an embarrassment of choice, confronting politicians, experts, citizens and consumers with an information overload that causes anxiety instead of liberation. Van den Berg investigates two ways of dealing with such overload: (1) employing artificial intelligence capable of optimizing search results and individual or aggregate preferences and (2) the use of behavioural economics as a tool to nudge people into desirable behaviours, based on the irrational bias that informs strategies of coping with uncertainty or information overload. Putting the two together and investigating their assumptions and implications is an important step forward, considering how they enable each other and are often engaged to pre-empt, steer or nudge the behaviours of a population. Van den Berg finds that under the label of 'decision support', people are actually surreptitiously influenced behind their backs, even if with the best of intentions. She notes that this type of decision support system actually diminishes our agency under the guise of contributing to it; we are helped to make better informed choices in a way that is entirely intransparent and thus bypasses our autonomy. It is in this light that she returns to Floridi's infraethics. Although she finds his proposal to force people to make deliberate choices to be paternalistic, she qualifies this particular type of paternalism as emancipatory, because it does not diminish reflection but increases freedom.

Notes

1 See Hildebrandt (2008) on legal and technological normativity, and Hildebrandt (2015) on novel entanglements of law and technology.
2 See for an elaboration of scale, scope, coerciveness and distribution, the reports of the EU-funded research project SIAM (Security Impact Assessment Measure), available at http://cordis.europa.eu/project/rcn/97990_en.html (accessed 19 January 2016).
3 Pentland (2014); Helbing (2012). More intriguing, Meister et al. (2007); Rammert (2011).
4 This volume, at [10] of Chapter 1.
5 See also the ground breaking work of Ihde (1990, 2008) on the nexus of technology and culture.
6 Yale University Press, 2012.
7 This volume, at [118] of Chapter 5.

References

Helbing, D. (2012) *Social Self-Organization: Agent-Based Simulations and Experiments to Study Emergent Social Behavior*. Berlin: Springer.

Hildebrandt, M. (2008) 'Legal and Technological Normativity: More (and Less) than Twin sisters'. *Techné: Journal of the Society for Philosophy and Technology* 12(3): 169–183.

——. (2015) *Smart Technologies and the End(s) of Law: Novel Entanglements of Law and Technology*. Cheltenham: Edward Elgar.

Ihde, D. (1990) *Technology and the Lifeworld: From Garden to Earth*. Bloomington, IN: Indiana University Press.

——. (2008) *Ironic Technics*. Copenhagen: Automatic Press.

Meister, M., Schröter, K., Urbig, D., Lettkemann, E., Burckhard, H.-D. and Rammert, W. (2007) 'Construction and Evaluation of Social Agents in Hybrid Settings: Approach and Experimental Results of the INKA Project'. *Journal of Artificial Societies and Social Simulation* 10(1), available at http://jasss.soc.surrey.ac.uk/10/1/4.html (accessed 19 January 2016).

Pentland, A. (2014) *Social Physics: How Good Ideas Spread – The Lessons from a New Science*. New York, NY: Penguin Press.

Rammert, W. (2011) 'Distributed Agency and Advanced Technology. Or: How to Analyse Constellations of Collective Inter-Agency'. *Working Paper TUTS-WP-3-2011*. Technical University Technology Studies. Berlin: Technical University Berlin.

Part I

The matrix of information

Chapter 1

Genies: bottled and unbottled

*Gary T. Marx**

Figure 1.1 Free Smells: Jimmy John's Restaurant, Seattle

You can look, but you can't touch.

– Sign in a ceramics shop

Once the toothpaste is out of the tube, it's hard to get it back in.

– H.R. Haldeman (1974) on *Watergate*

Free Smells

– Sign in Jimmy John's Restaurant, Seattle

Introduction

In the introduction to the seminar that inspired this volume, Mireille Hildebrandt asked, 'How does the architecture of the internet afford and constrain transformations in the substance of copyright and or privacy?' A reverse question lurks as well, 'How does the nature and setting of what is to be afforded or constrained affect the architectures (physical, social and legal) that appear?' The electronic copyright and privacy issues treated in this volume, as important as they are, form a relatively small strand in the role that communication and data exchange/use play as universal aspects of human society (and maybe aspects of animal society as well, given their taking in and giving off of data/signals).[1] Electronic information and data,[2] as topical as they are, need to be seen within a broader context, which far transcends the latest newsworthy *crise du jour*.

The relative accessibility or inaccessibility of information is central to many current and enduring conflicts over communication and surveillance: from WikiLeaks, to discovered DNA; from censorship, gag rules, confidentiality and classification policies, to free speech zones, disclosure statements and freedom of information policies; and from warnings and laws about copying DVDs, sharing music files, using cell phone cameras in athletic clubs or videotaping in theatres, to requirements that police interrogations be videotaped and rules protecting a citizen's right to make video and audio recordings in public (even of police who might be videotaping citizens at the same time).[3] Controversies over the use of a hidden device to jam loud cell phone conversations in public or to remotely destroy information on a computer or illegally interpreted satellite TV signals, offer other illustrations of current contestation.[4] A factor related to some of the above involves controversies over the legality and accessibility of the various material tools used to obtain and to block information.

The eternal conflicts involved with efforts to free up or to restrict accessibility are central to the concerns of this book – whether this involves pursuing the former in the name of freedom of information, free speech and democratic accountability or the latter on behalf of national security, law enforcement, diplomacy and property rights and its curious bedfellow, privacy.[5]

The presence or absence of various kinds of borders, which may include or exclude the flow of information, persons, goods, resources and opportunities, are central to the topic (Zuriek and Salter 2005; Andreas and Nadelmann 2006). The borders or barriers which, depending on their permeability, make information available or block it, can be physical, logistical or cultural. Examples of the former are distance, darkness, time, dense undergrowth, disaggregated data and the face (which may mask true feelings, but a masked face is an even better example). In the absence of a physical/technical blockage, some data are immediately available to anyone with normal senses and cognition, for example, seeing a person's unmasked face or observing apparent gender, height and age. But we should also note the existence of rules that attempt to alter this initial availability-unavailability. Some obvious examples of rules to inhibit or facilitate the flow of data are those protecting privacy and confidentiality or those requiring informed consent or freedom of information.

Like the proverbial sound of the forest tree falling in the absence of a listener, the potential reception of the data depends on the senses of the receptor. '*Naturally*' available visual and oratory data are not accessible to the blind and deaf, absent mechanical supports that amplify or convert data and one must know something of the sounds of a language to put it to use. Yet some data does have a relatively more literal quality as with certain signals in sign language. Contrast the seemingly more inherent meaning of indicators for '*I*' and '*You*', when pointing at oneself and another person with the sound for the words or their appearance in different scripts. Some Japanese and some other written pictograph inspired languages have remnants of a more ostensive reference. The relationships between properties of the physical world and the presence of rules and hard technologies – which become part of the physical world as a result of human actions – are understudied. Some natural conditions mean that there is no need for a protective rule (when protection is desired), at least until technology manages to pierce protective borders (note the nineteenth century development of photography or the current claims of brain wave reading technology used for lie detection). In other cases, this very protection can create a perceived need to have a rule and/or technology that overcomes the protective border.[6] Rules (whether legal, administrative, or informal as with manners) are aspects of culture intended to direct behaviour. Table 1.1 combines the physical and cultural variables in order to yield a typology of types of information control or outcome with respect to the two kinds of border.

Table 1.1 highlights four situations that result from considering the presence or absence of cultural and physical borders with respect to the flows of personal information.

An example of where both cultural and physical borders are present is a prison (D). In the absence of either border, only manners and limits on the senses prevent seeing and making inferences about a person encountered on the street or overhearing the conversation of nearby persons (A). Anti-stalking laws and

Table 1.1 Borders and information

		PHYSICAL BARRIER to CROSSING	
		No (Soft)	Yes (Hard)
CULTURAL (NORMATIVE) BARRIER to CROSSING	No (Open/free)	A. Looking at a person speaking to you, city borders	B. Sense limitations (darkness, distance, walls)
	Yes (Closed/ unfree)	C. Staring, backstage regions, privacy and confidentiality expectations, religious and sacred areas, DVD, music file sharing	D. Convents, military bases, vaults

manners, such as 'don't stare', illustrate cultural borders in the absence of a physical border (C). B illustrates the case of being beyond the range of another's unaided seeing or hearing, which protects information even in the absence of rules.

Of course, physical and cultural barriers are not independent, although in general more attention is given to how the latter alters the physical than how the physical conditions alter the culture.[7] This chapter first considers the initial presence or absence of physical barriers or supports to data access. The latter part of the chapter considers how culture often subsequently creates or undermines barriers to data access. Relative to the givens (or at least starters) of the physical and temporal worlds, culture provides a more artificial kind of prop for information control. It tells us what data means (for instance, private or public) and in offering directives for behaviour such as for the freedom or protection of data, culture may seek to alter the givens of the natural world. My goal here is to categorize types of information about persons and to specify connections between the physical and the cultural, with a particular interest in how the former may condition the kinds of rules that appear.

As is now so well known, gigantic industries and state organizations (not to mention employers, parents and the curious) use ever more sophisticated tools to access others' information and to a lesser extent provide tools to protect information. The qualitative and quantitative changes in surveillance in recent decades triggered my interest in the topic with respect to questions of privacy, information protection and resistance (Marx 2003, 2009, 2015c (forthcoming)). Since finishing a book on undercover police several decades ago, I have been concerned with issues involving secrecy and the revelation and concealment of information. This has involved empirical studies of topics such as work monitoring, caller-id, informers, whistle blowers, hotlines, freedom of information acts, notice and informed consent. Much of that prior work dealt with the uncovering of information that is relatively *inaccessible*, while not thinking much about information that is *accessible*.[8] In contrast, this chapter begins with data that are relatively accessible, particularly as it involves the initial conditions around what comes to be information. Accessibility will be seen as a property of data, and after assessing this particular property, the chapter turns to the meaning of other properties that are used to characterize the person. It does this by identifying descriptive and analytic attributes of the kinds of data that can be attached to persons. My goal is to contribute to the creation of a more systematic sociology of information, which can bring some conceptual unity to the discovery and protection issues and related questions.

The sociology of information

There is need for a situational or contextual approach, which, while not denying some commonalties across communication and surveillance behaviour, emphasizes patterned differences. Such an approach offers a systematic account of the empirical variations whose causes, processes and consequences need to be organized to be better understood.

Amidst the sweeping claims (whether of dystopians, utopians, ideologues, commercial entrepreneurs, single case study over-generalizers, or one trick pony theoretical reductionists), we need to specify. Conclusions, whether explanatory, evaluative or for public policy, require identifying the dimensions by which the richness of the empirical world can be parsed into dissimilar or similar analytic forms in the hope of revealing patterns amongst the seeming chaos. The emerging field of the sociology of information provides an approach to the topic (Marx 2007; Marx and Muschert 2007). Using the method of analytic induction (Robinson 1951), I draw from myriad empirical examples to generate concepts that can contain the major sources of variation.

Key elements in this approach are that we should attend to:

1. a family of distinct yet related concepts relating to information (for instance, privacy and publicity, public and private, personal and impersonal data, surveillance and surveillance neutralization, secrecy, confidentiality, anonymity, pseudo-anonymity, identifiability, and confessions) (Marx 2001, 2005, 2011);
2. the characteristics of the data-gathering technique (contrast the unaided and aided sense, for instance, directly overhearing a conversation or intercepting electronic communication on the internet, or a written account by a third party of an event versus the same event revealed by a hidden video camera);
3. the goals pursued (contrast collecting information to prevent a health epidemic with the spying of the voyeur or spying for national security);
4. role relationships and other social structural aspects (for instance, contrast parents gathering personal information on children with an employer or merchant gathering information on employees or customers, and contrast these with the reciprocal and equivalent watching of industrial espionage agents or poker players);
5. space/location/time (contrast personal information in a home or office with that on a public street or in cyberspace, or the past versus the future);
6. cultural themes which provide meaning and direction in telling us why communication and surveillance are needed, or why they are themselves the problem, and how they should be experienced by subjects, agents, senders and receivers of information and broader audiences;
7. the dynamic aspects viewed over time, as groups and individuals struggle to make the accessible inaccessible or the reverse;
8. the characteristics of the data. What are the characteristics of the datum in its most basic form? What social meanings are attached to this and to the subsequent forms and categories that are constructed (contrast a general characteristic such as gender or age or anonymity with a more specific characteristic that provides a unique and locatable identity, or with the assignment of a particular pattern of data points to a category such as

credit worthy). How are these characteristics affected by the form in which the data are gathered and presented?

In this chapter, I give particular attention to the questions in point 8 above, and to the character of the data gathering or presentation technique in point 2 above.

Information's accessibilities

A central contribution of social studies of science and technology is, of course, to document the role of interests and culture in the design and application of technology. Culture and interests affect what gets ground out of the sausage machine and officially counts as food (if not food for thought, then at least data for analysis). Technical structures (whether hardware or software) and what subsequently emerges from the data they make it possible to collect involve elements of choice and there is much cross-cultural variation. But the structures do not set the terms of their birth environments, nor (at least initially) of the raw material they deal with. What Karl Marx (1994: 188) said of history might be paraphrased to apply to information control, 'humans make their own information control policies and technologies; however, they do not make them as they please, but under circumstances already given in the world both natural and cultural'.

While I am not suggesting an 'essentialist' or unduly deterministic position, elements of the initial *accessibility* and assessments of what *kind* of material is present (what I refer to as its properties) need to be considered. In spite of the heights of human inventiveness, neither the tools of data collection nor culture are fully determinative in the face of the prior conditions existing in the empirical/physical/material world. These conditions, in conjunction with the unaided senses, result in the material that may become data and can have an effect in how the data will be defined.[9]

These initial properties help structure a central dynamic, as humans struggle over how they should be viewed, and seek to alter the conditions (whether this concerns efforts of the holders of information to make it more or less accessible, or of potential discoverers or recipients of information, to obtain or avoid obtaining it).[10] The way information is treated (both re how it is labelled and in actors' subsequent behaviour) must be viewed as a game with players (roles), resources (rules, material tools, strategies and tactics), moves and a variety of serious goals beyond fun.[11] My point is hardly to deny that vital, emergent dynamic, but to call for mindfulness because some elements on the game board transcend culture and politics.

As suggested, in the beginning there are some 'natural' limits and 'facilitants' to the use of information. I use the word 'natural' with some trepidation and simply mean the state prior to intentional alteration or supplement. While numerous attributes can be identified, in this section I am particularly interested in whether in some raw or initial state the material is relatively accessible or inaccessible with respect to various components to be discussed. I use the term 'access' here to name a broad variable that goes from inaccessible to accessible with various points between and a number of subtypes within. The access properties question complements a long-standing interest in the empirical and ethical aspects of information discovery. Accessibility is a multi-dimensional construct. Below I identify some key components. The connections among these can be path dependent in either a natural or a logical sense; a blockage such as darkness is usually present before a tool or rule appears to overcome this and if it is not known that the raw material for data creation exists (the fact that there is a secret is itself a secret) then efforts to create/discover data are unlikely. But other components can come together in a variety of configurations such as whether or not a reproducible record can be made and whether or not results can be, and actually are, accessed and used. This empirical richness and indeterminacy are at the core of the topic and what makes it so challenging. Hereunder, I sum up seven key components of accessibility: accessibility lies in the relationship between data and whoever may access the data, depending on the context, the technological mediation used to access the data, and the cultural mediations that constrain or enable access.

1. *Awareness*
    Is the would-be data gatherer/user aware that material for data/information exists in a given case, or in general? The fact that data or the potential to create it exists is often not known. In many settings there is so much hay and there are so few needles that, unless the interested agent is prescient or lucky, or an accident or whistle blower reveals the data's existence, it will be unlikely to be known. Requirements for notice and informed consent are 'awareness' elements. But mere awareness that data exists is distinct from the other components.

2. *Collection*
    Can the actor access the content of data? 'Can' may refer to the initial condition of the data, apart from rules permitting, limiting or prohibiting access. Are the data initially or potentially available, whether as a result of their natural state or rules and technology? For example humans cannot see in the dark even if no rule prohibits it, without a techno-boost; but humans can stand outside a door and eavesdrop even if they should not.[12] However, to be aware of the datum and even to 'have' it as in being able to see, read or hear it, of course need not mean comprehending it.[13]

3. *Understanding*
    Even where access is not naturally or rule restricted, can the actor make sense of it? Data may be universally available to anyone with normal senses in the data flow and may or may not be comprehensible because of some limitation on the part of a potential recipient or some form of border or other restriction. An example of the former on the part of the receptor would be blindness or not understanding the language of a communication. Encryption, a subscription service or eligibility requirements illustrate the latter.

4. *A record*
   Is the data in such a form or can a record (whether as a right or at least a possibility) be made of the transaction or behaviour in question such that it is reviewable by those it pertains to and/or to others? If so, is what is reviewable an original, a copy or a facsimile and how well does the data lend itself to record creation? Reproduction can be a strategic resource with the possibility of endless re-use and exchange, it can offer evidence and a standard by which rival claims can be judged and the record can be used for influence and even blackmail. Signs prohibiting photography in museums or recording concerts or films fit here, as would rules requiring that police record interrogations.

5. *Sharing*
   Can the information be legitimately communicated to others (or selected others)? This involves the ability to provide the information, apart from the form the communication may take. Secrecy policies, particularly in national security, law enforcement, business and personnel matters (e.g. confidentiality and privacy) can prohibit or limit sharing, or even forbid indicating that one has possession of certain information, apart from revealing its content. Depending on the form, reproduction may be permitted for limited purposes as with the fair use doctrine associated with copyright law or it may be prohibited under any circumstances. Amateur (ham) radio operators are a fascinating case here. In the United States for example, they can listen, but they cannot record or tell and they must have a renewable licence. The borderless quality of the airwaves is conducive to rules across jurisdictions as with treaties. An interesting issue is whether the rules change if one gives the information away rather than sells, or otherwise personally profits from it. Definitions of personal property and materiality apply here.

6. *Private property*
   Does access to the data entail the right (or ability) to treat it as private personal property subject to distribution, alteration or destruction as the owner desires? To simply orally recount the words that were said or to draw a picture of something that happened may be treated differently than to more directly (literally?) capture it via a digital image or sound recording. A book or a newspaper comes with the expectation that the owner can do with it whatever he or she wishes (even as we recoil from book burning). A bound book contains two kinds of property – the cover, paper and ink, and the less tangible ideas contained within it. Different rules may apply to the two types. Note how some software licensing restricts what the 'owner' can do with his or her property with respect to reverse engineering the source code or to combining it with other software, or, in the case of hardware, like a smartphone, contracting with other service providers. This also can get muddied with respect to historic buildings and even works of art, for instance raising the question of whether the current owner has an obligation to the community or to the artist to maintain the work in its original condition.[14]

7.   *Usage*
     May the person (or group) with data access take actions based on the information (apart from
     how the data itself is treated)? It is easier to think of prohibitions on acting than
     legally mandated examples of freedom to act, since that is the default state.
     But among the former, consider laws against insider trading. You can know
     but you cannot do anything about it (even though as a practical matter one
     really could act and such violations are not uncommon, given the temptations
     and low visibility). The ban on card counting in gambling casinos is an
     interesting case with respect to the difficulty of enforcement, at least initially.
     The patent system (based on the Latin term *patere* – to lay open) nicely
     illustrates the uncoupling of access to information from the right to use it
     (while ironically making possible the potential to use it, unlike with trade
     secrets).

Some information (as hackers claim) wants to be free, like the commons: open for
the grazing of speechmaking and comprehending to all members. Information
can be a free good in the economist's sense of the term in being available to all
without conventional costs. It can be like a river that not only runs free, but is freely
used by those who can get to it. However, free flowing data like a river can be
dammed or polluted. In a politically, legally and socially stratified world with
private property and our concern for the dignity of the person, access is often
restricted, beyond the limits of the senses and cognition noted above.

If you are poor and have no livestock to graze on the commons, the freedom is
empty, the same goes for the quip (from before the internet): 'yes, freedom of the
press is a great thing, just ask the person who owns a printing press!'[15] The opposite
claim that information wants to be controlled is equally valid, given the contemporary importance of secrecy and privacy and logistical limits of scale, dispersal
and time. Perhaps it is better to take the middle ground and claim that information
wants to (or normatively at least should) be selective or discrete, seeking a flashing
yellow, 'it depends' light.[16]

It would be interesting to compare air and information as free goods. Air as a
free good is of course made up of various industrial and other pollutants. Access
to information can bring a variety of costs beyond the need to pay money for it,
for instance, an unwanted obligation to report, information overload and
the destruction of functional illusions. Information shows varying degrees of
intention and artifice, contrast a given such as height or mathematics with
propaganda. In human environments, air is often far from 'natural', think of the
air in front of a bakery or restaurant altered by fans spreading inviting smells;
work environments that may pump in jasmine as a calming means; casinos that
pump in oxygen to keep people awake. Contrary to the sign in Jimmy Joe's
restaurant at the beginning of this chapter, one must pay for aroma therapy and
perfumes, and in some petrol stations for tyre air. In some places, such as Berkeley
in California, wearing perfume at public meetings is frowned upon in order to
protect the allergic.

There appears to be a tilt toward viewing the natural as ethically superior to the constructed. That certainly applies with respect to using the unaided senses to obtain information, as we tend to trust what is perceived with our own sense better than what is mediated or given second hand from others. In the United States this involves the assumption of the muddled concept of a reasonable expectation of privacy. It is deemed that one cannot have a reasonable expectation of privacy when the personal information is readily available (whether in its natural state or because a veil is lifted or not lowered by the actor).

Descriptive and analytic aspects of data involving persons

Thus far our concern has been with aspects of the accessibility of data, with a particular interest in the implications of the initial presence or absence of physical barriers to data access. I argue that this is one factor conditioning how data are initially viewed that offers an axis around which to think about the kinds of rules and tools that attach to data under varied conditions of accessibility. But in itself, this tells us relatively little about the cultural content of data and how they are evaluated. For that we need a system to organize the cultural attributes of the data. I offer two kinds of concepts, descriptive and analytic. I focus on the important category of information attachable to individuals and identify several kinds of descriptive (substantive) information with respect to 10 questions (these vary from the 'Who is it?' to 'When?' and 'Where?'), see Table 1.2. Table 1.3 deals with the analytic properties of the information. Table 1.4 offers a way to organize the presence or absence of a border as this bears upon whether information is personal or impersonal.

Table 1.2 Types of descriptive information connectable to individuals

1. Individual (the who question)
   Ancestry
   Legal name
   Alpha-numeric
   Biometric (natural, environmental)
   Password
   Aliases, nicknames
   Performance

2. Shared (the typification-profiling question)
   Gender
   Race/ethnicity/religion
   Age
   Education
   Occupation
   Employment
   Wealth
   DNA (most)

General physical characteristics (gender, blood type, height, skin and hair colour) and appearance
Health status
Organizational memberships
Folk characterizations by reputation – liar, cheat, brave, strong, weak, addictive personality

3. Geographical/locational (the where, where from/where to and beyond geography, how to reach question)
    A. Fixed
        Residence, residence history
        Telephone number (land line)
        Postal address
        Cable TV
    B. Mobile
        Email address
        Mobile phone
        Vehicle and personal locators
        Wireless computing
        Satellites
        Travel records

4. Temporal (the when question)
    Date and time of activity

5. Networks and relationships (the who else question)
    Family members, married or divorced
    Others the individual interacts/communicates with, roommates, friends, associates, others co-present (contiguous) at a given location (including in cyberspace) or activity including neighbours

6. Objects (the which one and whose is it question)
    Vehicles
    Weapons
    Animals
    Communications device
    Contraband
    Land, buildings and businesses

7. Behavioural (the what happened/is happening question)
    A. Communication
        Fact of using a given means (computer, phone, cable TV, diary, notes or library) to create, send, or receive information (mail covers, subscription lists, pen registers, email headers, mobile phone, GPS)
        Content of that communication
    B. Economic behaviour – buying (including consumption patterns and preferences), selling, bank, credit card transactions
    C. Work monitoring
    D. Employment history
    E. Norm and conflict related behaviour – bankruptcies, tax liens, small claims and civil judgments, criminal records, suits filed

8. Beliefs, attitudes, emotions (the inner or backstage, presumably 'real' person question)

(Continued)

Table 1.2 (Continued)

9. Measurement characterizations (past, present, predictions, potentials) (the kind of person, predict your future question)
   Opinions of others, reputation
   Credit ratings and limits
   Insurance ratings
   SAT and college acceptability scores
   Intelligence tests
   Civil service scores
   Drug tests
   Truth telling (honesty tests, lie detection – verbal and non-verbal)
   Psychological inventories, tests and profiles
   Occupational placement and performance tests
   Medical (HIV, genetic, cholesterol, etc.)

10. Media references (the what was said about the person question)
   Yearbooks
   Newsletters
   Newspapers
   TV
   Internet

Table 1.3 Dimensions of individual information

1. Accessible		
	No (private)	Yes (public)
2. Personal		
	Yes	No (Impersonal)
3. Intimate		
	Yes	No
4. Sensitive		
	Yes	No
5. Unique identification		
	Yes (distinctive but shared)	No (anonymous)
	Core	Non-core
6. Locatable		
	Yes	No
7. Stigmatizable (reflection on character of subject)		
	Yes	No
8. Prestige enhancing		
	No	Yes
9. Reveals deception (on part of subject)		
	Yes	No
10. Strategic disadvantage to subject		
	Yes	No

11. Multiple kinds of data (extensive and intensive)		
	Yes	No
12. Documentary (re-usable) record		
	Yes (permanent?) record	No
13. Attached to or part of person		
	Yes	No
14. Biometric		
	Yes	No
15. 'Naturalistic' (reflects reality in obvious way, *prima facie* validity)		
	No (artefactual)	Yes
16. Information is predictive rather than reflecting empirically documentable past and present		
	Yes	No
17. Enduring shelf life		
	Yes	No (transitory)
18. Alterable		
	Yes	No
19. Individual alone or radiates to others		
	Yes (e.g. olfaction)	Radiate (e.g. communication taps)

Table 1.4 The person and information types

		Accessibility (as in easily available)	
		Public	Private
Connection to individual	Personal	A. Scent, DNA, Facial image, voice, gait	B. Religious beliefs, sexual preference, health status
	Impersonal	C. Height, native language, right-handed	D. Blood-type, car mileage

Means of information protection, discovery and communication: blocked and unblocked

Apart from the classification of types of access and of kinds of data, we need to consider how individuals evaluate the data settings they encounter. Those in possession of information and those seeking to obtain it, those with information who wish to communicate it and those without it who do not want the communication are on the same dance floor, even as the steps are often different. The dance may be solitary, conflictual or co-operative. A variety of tools and counter-tools can be noted that gain access or guard against it; that communicate or avoid communication. This is a dynamic game with moves and counter-moves.

Efforts to tighten or loosen the collection and flow of data may involve positive and negative incentives such as financial and other rewards or legal penalties (fines, torts), regulatory devices such as licences, copyrights and patents, and material artefacts (tools that extend the senses or garble the data) and strategies such as coercion, threat, persuasion and subterfuge. Much energy and invention go into developing impermeable or permeable borders and various points in between, in an effort to hide what would otherwise be in plain sight or easy to discover, or to reveal what is not, depending on the role played. Regarding revelation, consider infra-red technology that enables night vision; X-rays that 'see' through barriers such as clothes, skin and luggage; cutting trees and foliage to increase visibility; designing buildings for defensible space; merging data widely dispersed in time, place and form; and even having a lip-reader with binoculars intercept communication too far away to be overheard, whether for law enforcement or in sports.[17] A bank's prohibition of wearing sunglasses, hats and masks also fits here, as do prohibitions on carrying concealed weapons, requirements for see-through school backpacks and uniforms without pockets, and standards for how technologies are to be made.[18] In other cases the easy availability of information may create incentives for protecting it, involving rules, tools and tricks to that end. High walls, encryption for communication, and masks, plastic surgery, elevator shoes, and false IDs for individuals are examples of protecting what otherwise could be seen. Interesting examples of blocking what would otherwise be available include witness protection programmes or testifying behind a screen and having voices altered or having an audition for a symphony orchestra behind a screen hiding their appearance in order to work against discrimination based on gender or race. Even when the environment provides information or an opportunity to express it, self-control, manners, concern over reciprocity and a sense of honour or an oath may result in forgone opportunities to observe or share information in the absence of laws, for instance averting the eyes not to embarrass others, speaking softly in public, suppressing a cough during a performance, or not gossiping.

So what?

The distinctions noted above and the tables and figures are one thing, explanations and policy arguments are another. The next step, after making conceptual distinctions, is to seek their correlates and consequences and to suggest hypotheses. In the context of this chapter, I go no further than to briefly illustrate the kind of speculation or theory that is desirable. I will do this with respect to Table 1.3, which lists accessibility and a variety of other properties of information that can be used to characterize persons and their data.[19] Attitudes towards the appropriateness of data availability are related to these characteristics. To the extent that the values involved on the left side of Table 1.3 are present (other factors being equal), greater protections are likely.[20] Conversely, to the extent that the values on the right side of Table 1.3 are present, there will be fewer or no restrictions. The variables in Table 1.3 can be combined in a variety of ways and show some patterns, for example, that stigmatizing information is more likely to be private, and anonymous information to be public.[21] The variables might also be ranked relative to each other; that is, the potential for a negative critique regarding information collection seems much greater for some items (for instance, if it discredits or diminishes a person, as with item numbers 7–10) than for others (for instance, where the information is from multiple or single sources). But for now, let us simply note that the variables have an additive effect, and the more (both in terms of the greater the number and the greater the degree) the values on the left side of the table are present, the more likely it is that the data about an individual will be deemed worthy of being protected.

Specific judgments about access to data on individuals of course will depend on the context and when, where and what is involved. The intensity of a negative judgment is likely to be greater to the extent that a uniquely identified and locatable person is involved and when information is personal, private, intimate, sensitive, stigmatizing, strategically valuable, extensive, biological, artefactual, predictive,[22] reveals deception,[23] is attached to the person, and involves an enduring and unalterable documentary record. These variables may have contradictory impacts, and the values in the preceding sentence can vary independently of each other. Moreover, under some conditions, those attributes may support favourable assessments, and it is their absence that will be associated with criticism, even when means and ends are appropriate. Thus, being unable to identify and locate a subject can be a sign of failure and wasted resources. The lack of extensive data may mean less confidence in results. The collection and availability of naturalistic forms of information about persons may be seen as too invasive.[24] But whether or not the kind of data collected leads to positive or negative judgments, the important point is that each kind can play an independent role in how surveillance is judged.

It is one thing to predict characteristics likely to be associated with attitudes toward personal information practices. Proof and explanation are a different matter. The assertions above drawn from Table 1.3 are hypotheses to be empirically assessed. If this patterning of indignation (or conversely acceptance) is found to be correct, what might account for it? Does a common thread or threads traverse the judgments that are reached? I believe the answer is yes, as follows. Tools with an invasive potential that break the natural borders protecting private information maintain a taint, no matter how lofty the goal. In the absence of appropriate regulation, they are likely to be negatively viewed. For information that is not naturally known, norms tend to protect against revealing information that reflects negatively on a person's moral status and legitimate strategic concerns (for instance, safety or unreasonable discrimination in employment, banking, or insurance). The policy debate is about when it is legitimate to reveal and conceal (for instance, criminal records after a sentence has been served, unpopular or risky but legal lifestyles, contraceptive decisions for teenagers, genetic data given to employers or insurers, or credit card data passed to third parties). It is also about the extent to which the information put forth may be authenticated, often with the ironic additional crossing of personal borders to gather still more personal information.

The greater the distance between the data in some presumed original or initial form and their '*artefactuality*' as conditioned by a measurement device, the stronger is the need to explain how the tool works and to validate non-self-evident claims.[25] Contrast a claim about deception based on a polygraph exam with a videotape of a shoplifter. The seeming realism and directness of visual and audio data make them easier to understand and believe than more disembodied data appearing from unseen and generally poorly understood tests and measurements.[26] Another factor affecting indignation or acceptance can be the extent to which the information is unique, characterizing only one locatable person or a small number of persons. This is one version of the idea of 'safety in numbers', apart from the potentially negative aspects of anonymity.[27]

It is a truism to note that rules are related to motivations and literal possibilities to behave in ways that the rules seek to control. Yet rules also show some realism in not trying very hard to regulate things that are almost impossible to regulate. Note the hollowness of a judge telling a jury to ignore something it has just seen and heard (a frequent feature of the US *Perry Mason* television series). In our culture, there are fewer rules about information gained through overt, direct (non-technologically aided) hearing and seeing, although if present they are more likely to involve rules about recording, sharing, or using such data rather than controlling the initial access. Rules, manners and even softer expectations that culture provides are means of control. Consider deference rules such as not looking the ruler in the eye or messages such as:

> This information is being released upon receipt of a valid written authorization or as otherwise prescribed by law. The information contained in this document is *confidential* and may also be *legally* protected. Further disclosure by the recipient without additional written authorization may be in violation of several federal regulations. If you are not legally entitled to read this document, stop reading at once.

Of course, unenforceable laws (such as those against suicide) have a symbolic and educational role indicating what the ideal is from a standpoint of those making the laws, apart from the likelihood of successful implementation. Ideals matter, but so does the rational allocation of scarce social resources where needs are always greater than what is available. In that regard, a Washington State anti-anonymity (pro-access to identification information) law that requires written political advertising to clearly identify 'the sponsor's name and address' exempts 'sky-writing, inscriptions', and other forms of advertising 'where identification is impractical'.[28]

Ignoring this view, there also are anti-graffiti statutes that hardly put a stop to the phenomenon; it seems far better to build with graffiti-resistant materials as on some subways.

Further questions

With this initial effort I have considered some aspects of how the properties of information may affect subsequent offensive and defensive patterns of behaviour on the part of groups with conflicting interests and goals. I end with some related questions.

I have focused on an actor either desiring to protect or to access forms of information in various ways. In particular, I have been interested in the conflict where the implicit goal of one party is to keep or limit access by the possessor from the information-deprived whose goal is to obtain the information. This broad category includes citizens wanting to protect the privacy of their internet searches, communication and purchases, as well as corporations and governments wanting to learn about each other and citizens, but not to share their 'own' information (or better to carefully control and benefit from any release of that information), irrespective of whether they collect the information externally or within their internal operations.

The directionality of information flows is a related and neglected factor that also needs consideration. In the privacy realm for example, most attention is on the questionable taking information *from* the person. But consider the contrasting case that was given only brief consideration, namely that of impositions *upon* the person, whether unwanted written messages, sound, images or smells.[29] In such cases, the possessor of information seeks to deliver it, as with mailshots, TV and phone ads, spam, and loud mobile phone conversations (or even regular conversations in an enclosed space such as a restaurant or train), or public black lists intended to stigmatize, damage reputations and otherwise restrict the labelled party. What are the means and processes present when the access or communication that an individual or an organization provides is unwanted by the potential recipient and/or is socially harmful (a nice contrast to settings where information is desired but protected by its possessor)? What means are used to *avoid* access, collecting and knowing or at least experiencing?[30] Are the means of blocking or otherwise neutralizing communication inward, that is toward an eager receptor, the same as blocking data flows outward, that is toward a potential recipient who does not want to receive the communication at all? A full analysis would integrate this into the more common struggles over access sought and denied rather than access unwanted and rejected. Consideration also needs to be given to the co-operative or symmetrical cases where the goals of givers and receivers can be shared or at least mesh (for instance, in many professional settings of care, between buyers and sellers and to a degree between workers and employers). Another aspect of the direction question I have been concerned with is under what conditions do individuals feel that a personal information border has been *wrongly crossed*, or that there has been a *failure in not crossing* a border in relation to the collection of information? The latter is particularly interesting and neglected, but see Etzioni (1999) and Allen (2003). There is an imbalance in studies of privacy invasion as against the paucity of studies of the failure to discover or publicize information when that is appropriate.

As noted, one variable condition regarding rules about information is whether it involves an identifiable individual and the nature of that identification, and another is the kind of information (Tables 1.2 and 1.3). But apart from substance, the form the data appears in, or is gathered or presented in, needs consideration. Control and perception are related to whether data initially are in visual, auditory, olfactory, numerical, or narrative form, conditioning the kind of rule and tool used in collection and to a lesser degree reproduction, analysis and communication.[31]

People may know things about themselves that others do not, and the contours of the rules about whether or not they can or must inform others needs to be understood, as do equivalent questions for organizations. Apart from whether the information involves an identifiable person, the question of whether some form of permit or permission is required is important and becomes even more complicated when transactional data is involved and/or the data involves multiple persons, some of whom may agree while others do not (a group photo posted on social media). Just 'whose' data is it? What about third parties that are not even involved in the interaction but happen to be within the data flow? What of subjects deemed incompetent or unable to grant required permission?

Control of the subject's information may reside with authorized intermediaries. That is the case when a person's co-operation or permission is needed for access to information about *another*, for instance, a minor, a trustee, in case of the exhumation of a relative's grave, or the releasing of papers of the deceased. Second party reporting for birth and death records fits here. In neither case is the subject of the information responsible for reporting. Questions related to the issue of whose data is at stake can be those that involve issues of scale or scope and whether the information is about a single individual or many others. Is it the case that the wider the circle of intimate contacts involved, the more likely it will be that restrictions are present? As an example, contrast the lesser standard for searching an individual person than for a wiretap warrant that involves repetitive monitoring (at least initially) of communication with a large number of persons in the subject's circle. Over time, greater restrictions seem likely to appear where there is a tar brush effect, that is, where data collection on one person leads inevitably to include many others who may not be proper subjects for personal border crossing. Beyond information picked up from family members' innocuous calls if a phone is tapped, consider how DNA reveals some information about families as well as the initial subject.

Value conflicts endure

Interdisciplinary exchanges, as in this volume, are vital to bring a little light to issues that can be clouded and tilted by power (whether resting on tradition or unequal resources). The field of information technology with respect to social implications and trends suffers from an abundance of sweeping generalizations and a surfeit of conceptual definition, nuance and evidence for claims, and a clear justification for the values underlying a position.

With respect to where society is headed and its moral evaluation, current technologies are too often thought to be harbingers of either a new utopia or the old nightmares of Kafka, Huxley and Orwell. They are seen to involve qualitative, even revolutionary changes or simply minor shifts in enduring aspects of human society and personality. Freedom and privacy are far from dead, although they might be catching their breath. From some vistas things can be seen to be getting better, and from others, getting worse. The ironies, paradoxes, trade-offs and value conflicts which limit the best-laid plans must be observed and analysed, even if not always welcomed. I end with another list, enumerating some common value conflicts. Given their enduring presence, even with an abundance of good discussion, good will, intelligence and competence, these issues will – and should – remain at least somewhat contentious. Given the inherent value conflicts, we must face the fact that someone's ox is always going to be gored, and that all solutions come with costs. Some of the relevant value and goal conflicts are:

1. Liberty and order.
2. Communalism and individualism.
3. Aggregate (often statistical) rationality and efficiency against due process, justice, and fairness for each case.
4. Universalism (equality) versus particularism (differentiation).
5. Information control as repression/domination/colonization/homogenization or as responsible management/oversight/care/guidance.
6. The desire to be noticed and the desire to be left alone.
7. Prevention versus response after the fact.
8. Deterrence versus apprehension.
9. Information as a human rights issue or as a variable contextual, local conditions issue (e.g. privacy).[32]
10. Publicity/visibility and transparency as needed for accountability, but also serve as unwanted deterrents to creativity, civility and diplomacy.
11. Control of personal information (privacy) as central to selfhood, intimacy and group borders, but also to suspicion and hiding dishonesty, violations, conspiracies.
12. Freedom of expression as necessary for various kinds of truth, but also as protective of defamation/harassment/slander/irresponsible and mendacious speech, unwanted encroachments on person.

Conclusions: questions and answers

I would never be one to disrespect the Talmudic wisdom which asks, 'Why spoil a good question with an answer?' Far easier to state the question(s) and suggest concepts and methods that can point toward answers, even if the latter will often be opaque, fragmented, contradictory and paradoxical. So I simply summarize an approach to some answers.

The goal of this chapter has been to develop a more systematic sociology of information that can contribute to understanding the broad social contexts within which information is controlled (whether by being available or by being restricted). Of eight key elements noted here, I emphasize the social structural aspects such as types of role played and the characteristics of the data as these are related to the way data is defined and treated. Types of social setting and other variables impacting the social control of information are identified. Among these are settings in which there are both cultural and physical borders to information, neither, or one or the other.

A cross-cutting theme involves the key variables around data's initial accessibility and how rules and hard and software tools impact this. Accessibility is to be found in the connections between the basic data, the kind of setting, those who may access it and the technological and cultural mediations that constrain or enable access. Seven basic components of accessibility are identified: awareness, collection, understanding, records, sharing, private property and usage.

The cultural meaning of the personal data that is subject to control can be approached via its descriptive or its analytic aspects. Understanding these is central to the kinds of rules and tools found with information control and controversies over privacy, surveillance, confidentiality and secrecy.

With respect to the descriptive aspects, 10 forms were identified: individual (the who question); shared (the typification-profiling question); geographical/ locational (the where, where from/where to and beyond geography, how to reach question); temporal (the when question); networks and relationships (the who else question); objects (the which one and whose is it question); behavioural (the what happened/is happening question); beliefs, attitudes, emotions (the inner or backstage, presumably 'real' person question); measurement characterizations (past, present, predictions, potentials) (the kind of person, predict your future question); media references (the what was said about the person question).

With respect to the analytic dimensions, 19 forms are suggested: accessible; personal; intimate; sensitive; unique identification; locatable; stigmatizable; prestige enhancing; reveals deception; or strategic disadvantage to subject; multiple kinds of data; re-usable record; attached to person; biometric; naturalistic; predictive; shelf life; alterable; alone or radiates. It is one thing to predict characteristics likely to be associated with attitudes toward personal information practices. Proof and explanation are a different matter. Based on these distinctions, a number of hypotheses to be empirically assessed are suggested.

Four types of information setting are identified based on combining the public-private accessibility and personal-impersonal dimensions. The discussion above offers the empirical material out of which explanatory and normative views are or could be based. But even with clear empirical evidence, interpretation is another matter. I noted that assessing the meaning of data was made more difficult by conflicts in values. A number of such conflicts were noted such as between liberty and order. Many disagreements involve conflicts between competing goods rather than a simple struggle between good and evil. The chapter concludes with additional questions that the concepts offered in the chapter suggest.

Notes

* Paper prepared for conference on Internet Freedom, Copyright and Privacy, CPDP, Brussels, 2013. I am most grateful to Mireille Hildebrandt for her insightful comments facilitating communication across disciplines and continents.

1 For animals there are functional (if not necessarily cognitive) equivalents of trade secrets and related forms in their use of secrecy and deception (Mitchell and Thompson 1986).

2 For convenience, I will use the terms information and data interchangeably. Of course for some purposes it is useful to note the progression from data to information to purported knowledge and then even to kinds of validity and truth. The time period, context, goals of conceptualization and skill of the agent will condition what the 'stuff' is called.

3 This depends on the tool, however – in the US even in a 'public' public park using a parabolic mike to make a recording is likely illegal (even for law enforcement absent a warrant), but should the mere possession of it also be illegal? Can such a tool cleanly differentiate sound from public as against legally protected 'private' places (that also are of course public in one sense) (Nissenbaum 1998; Marx 2001) and what of the private person's data easily accessible in public places, for instance because it broadcasts to anyone with the proper receptor; what aspect should be protected and realistically, what aspect can be protected? The reverse question is equally important and slighted: by what standards should relatively inaccessible personal information (whether because it is in a private place or because of its low visibility properties) be revealed? Consider, for example, spousal and child abuse within the home or a person with a contagious disease with no external indicators.

4 A small phone jammer that can block cell phone transmissions within a 30 foot radius is for sale, see www.jammer4uk.com/portable-cell-phone-jammer-3g4gwifigpslojack-8-powerful-antennasband-control-switch-p-49.html (accessed 2 February 2016). Consider also the delicious irony in Amazon's zapping copies of *1984* and *Animal Farm* from its Kindle after customers had purchased them (*New York Times*, 17 July 2009). The fact that the purchaser's electronic location and ownership are personal information apparently did not transcend the company's belief in its ownership rights.

5 With respect to this last concern, consider the justification of a widely circulated email intended to protect privacy on social media through evoking the United States Uniform Commercial Code (UCC 1-103 1-308), which is, however, irrelevant in this case:

> WARNING: Any person and/or institution and/or Agent and/or Agency of any governmental, public or private structure including but not limited to the United States Federal Government also using or monitoring/using this website or any of its associated websites, you do NOT have my permission to utilize any of my profile information or any of the content contained herein including, but not limited to . . . my photos, and/or the comments made about my photos or any other 'picture' art posted on my profile. You are hereby notified that you are strictly prohibited from disclosing, copying, distributing, disseminating, or taking any other action against me with regard to this profile and the contents herein. The foregoing prohibitions also apply to your employee(s), agent(s), student(s), or any personnel under your direction

or control. The contents of this profile are private and legally privileged and confidential information, and the violation of my personal privacy is punishable by law.

(See http://gizmodo.com/5915875/your-facebook-privacy-notice-is-unenforceable-nonsense (accessed 19 January 2016))

6 Marx 2015b deals with broader efforts to engineer social control.

7 A nice example of this interaction concerns the violations of confidentiality and non-disclosure agreements as seen in an apparent increase in tell-all books such as *Game Change* (Heilemann and Halperin 2010). According to one account, 'discretion is on the wane and disclosures on the rise' as a result of new markets created by internet communication (*New York Times*, 17 January 2010). The formal rules may be buttressed by, and reflective of, the culture as well as undermined by it, with a little help from technology.

8 One form is the 'dirty data' of organizations, that is, hidden discrediting information that usually stays secret. But not always; such information may be revealed as a result of means such as legal requirements, experiments, whistle blowers, accidents, trace elements, undercover police and new surveillance technologies (Marx 1984, 1988). There are also 'clean data' of low visibility, even on the part of those individuals with nothing to hide. Much day-to-day activity occurs here, such as using the bathroom or the routine processing of bureaucratic requests such as for a building permit. The initial unavailability of such data to wider audiences is more likely to reflect logistics, not secrecy and cover-ups.

9 Of course as Lisa Gitelman (2013) and her colleagues nicely demonstrate, there is no such thing as raw data. Of course, that does not mean that any imaginable construction can be sustained indefinitely in the face of some push back from what *is* out there, before human constructions are applied. Indeed, a key question is what within our sense of the world is culturally variable (and even then what is the range of that variability) and what is more universal across cultures and time periods. The stuff out of which meaning is made has some obdurate and determining qualities. But wending one's way through those mirages, sand traps and landmines is eternally challenging.

10 Framing the issue in this way makes it possible to note the parallels between organizations concerned with secrecy or limiting the flow of information and individuals concerned with protecting their privacy. However, the former is better thought of as organizational secrets or intellectual property rather than as privacy.

11 Classic statements here are by Schelling (1960) and Goffman (1969), but my emphasis in this chapter is on the conditions which the players encounter at the start of the games.

12 An additional factor is what people choose to do given the situation they face, thus the question is: are the rules honoured, are technologies used to overcome or create data access blockages?

13 Whether actors take advantage of the data's availability or honour rules and protective technologies intended to protect it, is yet another issue.

14 Although they entail data taken in by the senses, art or the façade of a building are not information in the sense used here, but there they offer material to which meaning may be assigned.

15 The internet, while evening things up a bit, generally still requires significant resources in order to continuously release information that garners attention and to cull the vast amount that is continually available.

16 Contradiction, paradox, irony and conflict are pronounced and a lot depends on how the kaleidoscope is turned. Note that businesses generally want to rein in information by commodifying it, while privacy advocates also seek to limit it but for other reasons, civil liberties advocates stress the role of freedom of information and freedom of speech

in unleashing it. But the transparency and visibility which can be good for democracy may not be good for the dignity of the too naked person. Dysfunctions and inefficiencies are likely greatest at the extreme ends of the continua.

17 Consider the famous (infamous?) case of the 1951 play off game between the New York Giants and the Brooklyn Dodgers in which the home run hitting batter (Bobby Thomson) apparently learned what pitch to expect based on radioed communication from a coach with binoculars in the bleachers, who read the catcher's signal to the pitcher (Prager 2006).

18 The 1994 Digital Telephony Act also known as CALEA (103-414, 108 Stat. 4279, codified at 47 USC 1001-1010) for example, required that digital communication devices be built to permit eavesdropping. More recently, there has been an effort to create new legislation that would require internet companies that provide communication such as Gmail, Facebook, Blackberry and Skype to be technically capable of quickly complying with a wiretap order (*New York Times*, 23 October 2010).

19 The discussion of Table 1.3 draws from Marx (2015a).

20 There is an obvious need to study cultural variation, not only within national subcultures, but across societies as well. In China, to judge from the questions I was asked when I taught there, it is appropriate and perhaps even a sign of respect to ask how old a person is, and there seems no inhibition on asking a stranger how much money he earns. In Europe, it is much less common than it is in the US to ask those one has just met about their family status such as whether they are married, divorced or whether they have children. The information that is required or prohibited from an employment curriculum vitae offers another striking contrast with Europe. A nice comparative study could be (and most likely has been) done in the vein of Miss Manners-type books across cultures and the emergence of global commonalities within subcultures such as business, diplomacy and entertainment.

21 Table 1.3 can also be used to explore the patterning of rules about information with respect to revelation, discretion and withholding.

22 Claims about the past are at least subject to an empirical standard, however musty the memories and degraded the material artefacts. Past failings may also be more excusable than those predicted for the future (for instance, 'she has learned her lesson', 'he has grown up', or 'that mistake was paid for'). Disagreements about an individual's future are more speculative. In professional contexts, this often involves the claims of rival experts representing different interests under a mantle of neutrality and scientific expertise.

23 Here it is not only that the content offered by the subject is erroneous, but also that the person is revealed to be dishonest.

24 The logic here is that the unwarranted taking of information in actually reflecting the person, would be seen as worse than an abstract category applied by others for which the individual can say, as did novelist Orhan Pamuk (2007) about the data presented in his first passport: 'that's not me'. However, one could as well argue the opposite. The latter in being artificial and less realistic, or at least less self-evident, while still claiming to represent the person, is worse than the seemingly more real 'natural' information. A relevant factor, of course, is whether the characterization supports or undermines the individual's interests or persona. This is an aspect of backstage behaviour. The individual's sense of a unique self is partly found in the less than perfect fit between cultural expectations and the situation (regarding both attitudes and behaviour). Goffman's (1959) concept of role distance and his idea of distinctive identity lying partly in the cracks of the roles played, fit here.

25 As noted earlier, at the most abstract level the imposition of language and meaning on what we perceive means that everything is in a sense an artefact of the interventions of the observer. Yet a central point of this chapter is to argue that the stuff with

which cognition and manipulation work has some implications for the work that they do.

26 Of course, appropriate scepticism is needed precisely because this tilt toward such data creates rich opportunities for deception. The Chinese expression, 'a picture is worth a thousand words' must be tempered with attentiveness to whether and when 'seeing is believing' or 'believing is seeing' or when they should be disconnected. The same holds for not questioning the assumption that using numbers to convert disembodied raw data is necessarily more objective and reliable than the interpretive work of humans, granted that humans may discriminate and cover their mistakes and rule-violations.

27 Beyond lack of accountability, there also can be a lessened likelihood of bystander intervention as anonymity increases (Darely and Latané 1968).

28 See http://apps.leg.wa.gov/rcw/default.aspx?cite=42.17A.320 (accessed 19 January 2016). Of course as with neutralization it is easy to imagine ways of blocking skywriting, such as with another plane distorting what the first wrote, but then the self-destructive quality of skywriting would make that impractical as well, let alone the other risks it would bring.

29 These, of course, can be joined as with Orwell's telescreen, note the monitoring of internet behaviour leading to marketing solicitations.

30 Of course, whether smell and touch are information or convey information can be debated, and for many purposes differ from communication involving words. Yet smell can communicate meaning (of a fire) and touch served the blind persons (if badly) in identifying different parts of an elephant in the Indian fable.

31 Note conversion to numerical or chart form or the blocking of faces in a visual image or distorting of voices.

32 The issue of whether (and which) human rights are (or ought to be) universals as against the honouring of local traditions that contradict them is an enduring question.

References

Allen, A.L. (2003) *Why Privacy isn't Everything: Feminist Reflections on Personal Accountability*. New York, NY: Rowman & Littlefield.

Andreas, P. and Nadelmann, E. (2006) *Policing the Globe*. Oxford: Oxford University Press.

Etzioni, A. (1999) *The Limits of Privacy*. New York, NY: Basic Books.

Darley, J.M. and Latané, B. (1968) 'Bystander intervention in emergencies: Diffusion of responsibility'. *Journal of Personality and Social Psychology* 8(4): 377–383.

Gitelman, L. (ed.) (2013) *'Raw Data' Is an Oxymoron*. Cambridge, MA and London: MIT Press.

Goffman, E. (1959) *The Presentation of Self in Everday Life*. Garden City, NY: Doubleday.

——. (1969) *Strategic Interaction*. Philadelphia, PA: University of Pennsylvania Press.

Heilemann, J. and Halperin, M. (2010) *Game Change*. New York, NY: HarperCollins.

Marx, G.T. (1984) 'Notes on the discovery, collection, and assessment of hidden and dirty data'. In J. Schneider and J.I. Kitsuse (eds) *Studies in the Sociology of Social Problems*. Norwood, NJ: Ablex Publishing Corporation: 78–113.

——. (1988) *Undercover: Police Surveillance in America*. Berkeley, CA: University of California Press.

——. (2001) 'Murky Conceptual Waters: The Public and the Private'. *Ethics and Information Technology* 3(3): 157–169.

——. (2003) 'A Tack in the Shoe: Neutralizing and Resisting the New Surveillance'. *Journal of Social Issues* 59(2): 369–390.

——. (2005) 'Some Conceptual Issues in the Study of Borders and Surveillance'. In E. Zureik and M.B. Salter (eds) *Who and What Goes There? Global Policing and Surveillance*. Devon: Willan Publishing: 11–35.

——. (2007) 'Desperately Seeking Surveillance Studies: Players in Search of a Field'. *Contemporary Sociology* 36(2): 125–130.

——. (2009) 'A Tack in the Shoe and Taking off the Shoe: Neutralization and Counter-neutralization Dynamics'. *Surveillance and Society* 6(3): 295–230.

——. (2011) 'Turtles, Firewalls, Scarlet Letters and Vacuum Cleaners: Rules about Personal Information'. In W. Aspray and P. Doty (eds) *Privacy in America: Interdisciplinary Perspectives*. Lanham, MD: Scarecrow Press: 271–294.

——. (2015a) *Windows into the Soul: Surveillance and Society in an Age of High Technology*. Chicago, IL: University of Chicago Press.

——. (2015b) 'Technology and Social Control: The Search for the Illusive Silver Bullet Continues'. In J.D. Wright (ed.) *International Encyclopedia of the Social & Behavioral Sciences*, 2nd edn. Philadelphia, PA: Elsevier: 177–124.

——. (2015c) 'Coming to Terms: The Kaleidescope of Privacy and Surveillance'. In B. Roessler and D. Mokrosinska (eds) *Social Dimensions of Privacy: Interdisciplinary Perspectives*. Cambridge: Cambridge University Press (forthcoming).

Marx, G.T. and Muschert, G.W. (2007) 'Personal Information, Borders, and the New Surveillance Studies'. *Annual Review of Law and Social Science* 3: 375–395.

Marx, K. (1994) *The Eighteenth Brumaire of Louis Bonaparte*. New York, NY: International Publishers.

Mitchell, R.W. and Thompson, N. (1986) *Deception: Perspectives on Human and Nonhuman Deceit*. New York, NY: SUNY Press.

Nissenbaum, H.F. (1998) 'Protecting Privacy in an Information Age: The Problem of Privacy in Public'. *Law and Philosophy* 17(5): 559–596.

Pamuk, O. (2007) 'My First Passport'. *The New Yorker*. 16 April 2007.

Prager, J. (2006) *The Echoing Green*. New York, NY: Pantheon Books.

Robinson, W.S. (1951) 'The Logical Structure of Analytic Induction'. *American Sociological Review* 16(6): 812–818.

Schelling, T.C. (1960) *The Strategy of Conflict*. Cambridge, MA: Harvard University Press.

Zuriek, E. and Salter, M. (2005) *Who and What Goes There? Global Policing and Surveillance*. Devon: Willan Publishing.

Chapter 2

Properties, property and appropriateness of information

Mireille Hildebrandt

Introduction

In this chapter, I challenge the idea that information exists as a non-material good with universal properties, and inquire how – and to what extent – the materiality of information co-determines its properties, while taking note of the cultural constraints that reinforce, block or transform these properties. In the next section, I inquire into the issue of what constitutes 'culture', after which I investigate what is information. Based on the finding that information is a relational and relative notion, I test how the materiality of information co-determines three distinct but interrelated properties of information: accessibility, propertizability and appropriateness. I understand these properties as depending on the technological embodiment and the cultural framing of information. By embedding the question on access, appropriation and appropriateness in a plurality of material and cultural constraints, I also – though briefly – confront the related issue of whether 'freedom' is something like a 'natural' property of information, as others may argue in this volume. Lastly, I investigate how accessibility, propertizability and appropriateness fare in the era of big data, notably in the case that information is retained by data-driven artificial agency.

What is the matter of culture?

Of what stuff is culture made: norms, patterns of behaviour, social interaction, speech acts? Or, should we admit that the technological mediation that prevails in a particular culture stands for the backbone that determines what norms and behaviours can emerge at all? Is the stuff of culture thereby fundamentally and foremost material? The easy answer, based on current scholarship, would be that the matter of culture is structure and agency (Giddens 1986), systems and actions (Luhmann 1995; Habermas 1996), institutions and norms or patterns of mutual expectations built around shared and contested values (Ricoeur 1973; Glenn 2007); maybe adding that culture is always emergent (Durkheim 2012) and seldom homogeneous (Geertz 2010a). In his chapter, Marx hints that he is using the concept of culture as providing '[r]ules, manners and even softer expectations', which he understands as 'means of control'.[1] He clearly indicates that culture is what constrains or empowers people to either access or block information about themselves or others, over and above the 'natural' accessibility of information. His use of the term 'natural' refers to how things are organized before intentional human action intervenes, and his use of the term 'physical' refers to the natural or technical 'hardness' of the constraints that enable or disable access of information. Whereas nature and technology supposedly share this 'hardness', culture and technology clearly share their artificial character, as they are both made by human intervention, even though we tend to associate culture with organically grown and value-oriented ways of doing things, and technology with intentionally constructed functional artefacts. So, it seems that nature and technology are hard, whereas culture is soft; while technology and culture are artificial, whereas nature is natural. Maybe these are indeed universal properties of human reality, in the sense that what makes us human is the artificiality of our world (De Mul 2015), taking into account that even our natural world is a construction based on how the use of language frames and mediates what we call nature, reality, or the material environment. We cannot discuss nature outside the boundaries of language, though we can no doubt experience the world in silent engagement.

Perhaps, then, culture is made out of language in the double sense of language systems (*langue*) and language usage (*parole*) where system and usage co-shape each other in a pertinent and permanent process of referring to the world outside language. This is done through the use of language symbols that, however, simultaneously refer to other language symbols (De Saussure 1915; Ricoeur 1973). This is where a web of meaning emerges, grows, gets disrupted and reconfigures, always under the double influence of the systematic character of the internal structure of a language and the events, resistance and transformations of the world to which those who *use* a language refer. Clifford Geertz (2010b: 312) proposed that:

> Culture, here, is not cults and customs, but the structures of meaning through which men give shape to their experience;

Structures of meaning may sound vague, but it was also Clifford Geertz (2010b: 215) who wrote about the precision of vagueness:

> This is doubtless more than a little vague, but as Wittgenstein, the patron saint of what is going on here, remarked, a veridical picture of an indistinct object is not after all a clear one but an indistinct one. Better to paint the sea like Turner than attempt to make of it a Constable cow.

So, what matters in culture are the structure of meaning and the shaping of experience. Here we can turn back to information along a double track: first, we could say that culture *informs us of* what to expect, how to respond, and when to refrain from whatever intervention; second, culture allows us to learn about *what information is open to scrutiny and which information should remain shielded from overexposure.* The concept of information plays a double act here, because culture is in part information about information.

What is information?[2]

So what is information? Is it a property or an attribute of things, people or environments? Or is it about things, people or environments? Or, taking the big view, is anything ultimately information, that is, the growth of complexity that challenges the second law of thermodynamics? Does thinking in terms of information imply that we move 'from a materialist to an informational metaphysics', as Floridi (2010: 12) contends, where:

> objects and processes are de-physicalized in the sense that they tend to be seen as support-independent (consider a music file). They are typified, in the sense that an instance of an object (my copy of a music file) is as good as its type (your music file of which my copy is an instance).

What does it mean when information is defined in terms of well-formed data (put rightly together), while being meaningful (in terms of some form of semantics) (cf. Ibid.: 20–21)? How does data relate to information, and how does thinking in terms of data 'inform' the idea that information is support-independent? I would argue that data is discrete, electronic and physical, and though identical information can be supported on different platforms or architectures this does not make it support-independent; it merely indicates that a plurality of embedded systems can support identical information. Other than data, information itself is not necessarily discrete. This raises the question of what 'identical information' means, when comparing information inscribed on paper with supposedly identical information inscribed in an integrated circuit on a silicon chip that requires digital bits and bytes to capture, store and manipulate information. In what sense can it be identical? Is it identical or similar? And, if information is not the inscription on paper or silicon, is it in the mind of those capable of reading the inscriptions – and what if those readers are computers?

Can we discuss information as either a property of something or the essence of everything without assuming or integrating a discussion of communication? Can information exist that is not communicated, not sent and received, stored, retrieved, combined or removed? Is a heap of electronic data stored in a data server information, or is it something that merely has the potential of becoming information, once it is 'read' by a being that is capable of acting upon it? Is a library stuffed with books a warehouse of information even if nobody can read the language in which the books have been written? Might the content of these books have been information to the native speakers until the last one passed away, whereas it is noise to all others? Is the content still information if I am a native speaker, but have already read all the books several times (is information necessarily new, whereas knowledge need not be new to count as such)? And, even if the qualification of something being information would not be dependent on something being communicated, should we not admit that a mere heap of signs, data or things cannot be seen as information until structure has been attributed, turning the noise of unstructured data into something informative? Could it be that what is informative for a bat is not so for a human, depending on distinct sensory capacities, and on the distinct kinds of environment both require due to distinct embodiments and concomitant needs?

Clearly, information is a relational and relative concept. It points to an exchange or a transfer between agents, or at least a 'reading' by an agent and its environment, for instance consisting of other agents. Even reading the weather from the clouds, the winds and the temperature, is a way of being informed, although no other agent deliberately provided the information. Perception (sensing), cognition (categorizing, associating, abducting) and subsequent action (moving, manipulating, feeding, speaking) all seem involved in the reiterant process of munching, interpreting, filing, remembering, anticipating or sharing information. This allows me to make a double move. On the one hand, information is contingent upon a sensing, acting and cognizing agent whose embodiment and survival in a particular environment matter. Information is agent-dependent. On the other hand, the information that is read from the environment, which includes other agents, can be translated into a code, language or sign system that enables sharing what has been learnt in the process of acting upon the information that was detected. This code or sign system has a certain abstraction as compared to the initial confrontation between an agent and its environment, a certain 'aboutness' or second-order nature that is facilitated by its material externalization in for instance the script or digital data. Abstraction, from this point of view, is an affordance of the material support that extends the human mind (to my knowledge other animals do not employ technologies to inscribe their communications in order to transfer information). As Gleick (2010: 37) notes:[3]

> The written word – the persistent word – was a prerequisite for conscious thought as we understand it. It was the trigger for a wholesale, irreversible change in the human psyche [. . .].

In fact, Maryanne Wolf (2008) has investigated to what extent such a wholesale change can be traced in the neuronal pathways of the reading brain, demonstrating that the ardent process of learning to read and write transforms both the morphology and the behaviours of the human brain. If we return to the double track of the previous section, and recall that *culture is – also – information that co-determines how we access (and assess) information,* we can now conclude that neither culture nor information are disembodied dimensions of reality, but partly artefactual constraints that enable increasingly complex, viable and mutual expectations that co-constitute both individual persons and their society.

About properties of information

The conclusion of the preceding section should be that information is not a property of something, while whether 'something' is information is agent-dependent in a number of ways (for instance, depending on the environment in which the agent finds herself, the timing, the context, the anticipation of the behaviours of other agents and more). Information was also found to operate at – at least – two levels: first, information plays out between an agent and her environment, enabling the agent to be selective in her choice of what perception is critical, relevant or simply useful in view or her anticipated actions; second, information that has been found critical, relevant or simply useful can be retained, as it may come in handy or even be crucial for future occasions. This retention plays out within the agent's mind and – inspired by Husserl – can be called secondary retention,[4] because it follows the initial retention of what is critical, relevant or simply useful within the plethora of perceptions that could otherwise flood the agent. Secondary retention constitutes the individual human memory. However, information can also be retained outside the mind of the individual agent; she can find ways to inscribe the information on an external support, such as paper or silicon chips. This can be termed 'tertiary retention', as suggested by Stiegler (2013). In between, we have language and speech, which enable the sharing of information with others, thus retaining it beyond the individual agent's mind without necessarily inscribing it on an external carrier (unless one defines another's brain as an external carrier). I would suggest that language and speech change the manner in which secondary retention takes place, that is, how the information is stored and retrieved. Written language and computer code determine how tertiary retention takes shape, whether on paper or on silicon. Since most people do not speak or think in terms of computer code, I have doubts about whether this should be called a human language. Computer code is special, also, because it is not merely used to store information, but also to give instructions to manipulate stored information, for instance in order to operate a car, a smartphone or whatever. Computer programs might be understood as a specific type of information, but they are not merely about what is critical, relevant or useful as they contain instructions that automate machine behaviours that are deemed critical, relevant or useful in specific situations. Here we move beyond the 'aboutness' of secondary and previous forms of tertiary retention, to 'automation' and 'intervention'. Is this quaternary retention? It seems more in the realm of action or behaviour, rather than retention.

My contention is that the properties of information depend, first, on the level at which the information plays out. This concerns primary retention, between an agent and her environment, which is fundamentally ephemeral; secondary retention, within the mind of the individual agent that needs to retain the information for future usage, taking into account that we do not only have a memory but *we also are our memory*; and, tertiary retention, which takes place on the external support that contains coded information, which can be seen and held and passed on to another. Second, in the case of tertiary retention, the properties of information depend on the affordances of the support that carries information. Paper has different affordances than silicon, notably with regard to accessibility (including comprehensibility). Apparently, discretization on integrated circuits enables not only the retention of unprecedented amounts of coded information, but also affords the coding of instructions that operate the automation of all kinds of behaviours. These affordances will impact the properties of information, because such automation manipulates the data that may 'carry' information, even if we might not qualify computer programs themselves as information.

Before checking on how the properties of information vary depending on these levels of engagement, we must pay attention to the nature of information that is 'kept in' tertiary retention and to what happens when it is retrieved from its external support. As we know, information that is kept in secondary retention undergoes a host of changes beyond our conscious awareness; memories disappear, they are transformed by subsequent experience, associated with specific sensory or motor capacities, they align with similar or other types of memories and these alignments are continuously reconfigured in the course of the life of the agent (cf. Zimmer, Mecklinger and Lindenberger 2006; Hoerl and McCormack 2001). In the case of tertiary retention, we can discriminate between the script, the printing press, and digitization as the most recent format of tertiary retention. In case of the script, copies had to be made by hand and changes from the original text were abundant, due to errors or attempts to improve the text or even to change the content. Other than in the case of secondary retention, these changes are in principle visible and traceable, since they are retained outside the human body. Written text thus enables us to reflect on the information that is retained, and this reflection is often expressed in secondary literature that comments upon a primary text. This is what has enabled abstraction, according to many scholars of the history of writing technologies (cf. Gleick 2010; Ong 1982; Goody and Watt 1963; Wolf 2008). The advent of the printing press accelerated this process, while at the same time the process of retention was automated; changes to the text were no longer possible once the typesetting was final. All subsequent copies are truly identical. This type of tertiary retention thus functions in an altogether different fashion than our 'normal' (Marx would say 'natural') individual human memory, which is continuously reconfigured. However, reading, commenting, secondary literature and more, do enable transformation of the information. In contrast with the memory inscribed in the wetware of individual minds, these transformations are in principle both explicit and traceable due to their externalized retention.

Under the influence of the mathematical theory of information, usually called cybernetics or simply information theory, information retained on silicon chips is meant to remain identical with itself, just like in the case of printed text (Gleick 2010; Hayles 1999). The main concern of information theory was not the meaning (semantics) of information but its integrity, transfer and computability. Information theory was concerned with messages and with how to prevent a breach of confidentiality without distortion of the data (think of encryption). The integrity of information, a critical concept in digital security, refers to the fact that information is not meddled with, changed, deleted or enhanced, but remains identical during capture, storage and transfer as well as during any calculations performed upon the data. Since information theory thinks in terms of discrete digital data, data is easily confused with information. Wrongly so. If data is stored or processed within a computing system, for instance, based upon the instructions of a computer program, there is no cognizing agent involved who 'introjects' the information into her individual mind for some purpose or another.[5] Until the data is introjected we could say that it is potential information, depending on an agent gaining access and employing it as critical, relevant or simply useful for her life's projects. This probably entails that an interface is available to retrieve or infer structured data sets in a way that is readable for the agent, because merely looking around in the average data server would not provide a human agent with intelligible information. That raises the interesting question, already touched upon, whether what is stored outside individual human minds is indeed information before it is introjected and employed as such. If we must conclude that it is at the most potential information, we should also admit that all depends on the agent that may access and assess it. Information is thus both relative (to context, purpose) and relational (agent dependent).

Here we can also return to the matter of culture. As pointed out, culture is constituted by human language that enables the sharing of information, for instance about what is to be known and what is to be ignored. This type of information comes in the form of norms, rules, principles and values that are more or less explicit about what is expected of those who identify with the culture. After establishing that the properties of information are co-determined by whether we are speaking of primary, secondary or tertiary retention, we can now flesh out the role of culture in co-determining these properties. It would be tempting to restrict the role of culture to adding or undoing properties constituted by the material support that enables tertiary retention. Although this is certainly the most obvious role of culture, we should pay attention to the fact that culture as such is instituted by means of primary, secondary and tertiary retentions, taking into account the pivotal role of language on and between these three levels. The extent to which culture is possible and how it operates is thus contingent upon the interplay between human language and the triple retentions. For example, Japanese culture may have specific rules for wearing a kimono, depending on the marital status and the age of the wearer, the time of day, a particular celebration such as a tea ceremony, and on whether one is at home, with family, at the office or in another public, social or private place. The nature of these rules (for instance, whether they are strict, explicit, public, secret or local) depends on whether they are communicated orally, within a face-to-face culture, via hand-written manuscripts, printed books or shared via an online social network. It may be that the latter simply does not afford the kind of rules that previously guided the wearing of a kimono; keeping them secret or local may be difficult, while engaging in social networks may change the time people have to spend on dressing up for a tea ceremony. The affordances of the wetware (the human brain and body), human language, paper, the printed page and silicon chips thus co-determine the properties of information in human society – obviously and always depending on the human agent that employs the information in her planning, behaviours and interactions. Information is relational and relative.

Three properties of information

Accessibility of information

Let us now test what it means to say that the properties of information depend on its technical support, focusing on accessibility, 'propertizability' and appropriateness, noting that the latter two relate directly and indirectly to accessibility.

We could begin with discussing whether non-living things, such as stones, molecules or planets somehow perceive information and act on it, perhaps even moving into quantum entanglement (Vedral 2014). Instead, for obvious reasons, I restrict the discussion to human society, taking into account that technological mediation is an inherent part – in the sense of being constitutive – of human society. This makes life slightly easier, because if information is agent-dependent, we have to determine what kind of agent we have in mind before deciding on the properties. If we were to refrain from this restriction, we would have to move into the properties of information for all kinds of plants, animals plus different types of artificial agents. The latter may, however, become relevant in the section on the properties of information in the era of big data.

Information picked up in the phase of primary retention is ephemeral and there is no direct access. However, it is accessible for other human beings who can see, hear, smell or touch whatever the agent who is capturing the information sees, hears, smells, or touches. The other agent basically observes the interaction and, based on her own secondary retention, deduces what is critical, relevant or useful for the agent that is picking up the information. So, though there is no access to the mind of the agent, there is some form of deduction or inference that provides something that could be called indirect access. All depends on whether the other agent is in the same environment, absent walls, distance and other factors that could block access.

Information that is taken up in secondary retention depends on the particular biography of the agent; she will not necessarily integrate and consolidate whatever she encounters in primary retention into the various types of memory that human beings have or operate. As mentioned above, the human wetware is constantly in the process of reconfiguring the architecture of our memory and realigning what we call memories within the confines of their neuronal and bodily architecture. Many memories are stored in the body that seamlessly responds to a certain situation; when the hand of a pianist touches the keys it is the hand that remembers how to act without further ado (Koch et al. 2012). Just like other agents have no direct access to what goes on in primary retention, they have no direct access to what goes on in secondary retention. In this case, indirect access does not depend on being in the same environment and observing an interaction, but on being familiar with the 'memory architecture' of the particular person. This will depend on her biography, on what language she uses and – here it comes – on what cultural incentives are at work. Secondary retention already involves the integration of whatever is perceived into the web of meaning that is constituted by language, which means that another agent has a better chance of making inferences about the information if she shares the cultural constraints and enablers of the agent. This implies that even primary retention is infused with the attribution of meaning, based on the individual experience and the language and culture of the agent. This should not come as a surprise: a new-born infant without much secondary retention experiences its world differently from a toddler or an adolescent. Primary retention is contingent upon the extent to which information is formatted in accordance with the language(s) by which the child learns to communicate, taking into account that, initially, primary retention will have to do without language – which explains the hardship to access this part of our memory with our conscious mind.

We can conclude that other agents have no direct access to the information that is retained in primary and secondary retention, but they can infer, guess and recognize the information to the extent that they share similar experiences (this may depend on age, context, professional background), speak the same language (though a native speaker may still have a different understanding of the same phrasing) and share the same culture (which is, however, seldom homogeneous). The fact that access to information of primary and secondary retention is always indirect implies protection of the life of the mind of an individual person, which is connected to both privacy and freedom of thought.[6] This is what Floridi has called 'ontological friction', and what Marx would probably qualify as 'natural' blocking of access. We should, however, not be surprised that at some point this protection may be overruled by technologies that mediate more direct access to what goes on in the brains. It is unlikely, however, that such access could ever mean that others have direct access to the individual mind of the agent, as the access will always be technologically mediated. Nevertheless, we might start to interpret even our own minds in terms of the machine-readable results of such brain-readers. This is an interesting consequence for the properties of information in the era of big data.

Tertiary retention means that information is written down or printed. Other forms of tertiary retention are analogue or digital audio or visual recording. First, we investigate the accessibility of hand-written text. The inscription this involves is accessible for anybody who can get her hands on the support. Second, access to the content depends on whether the agent is capable of reading, and on whether she understands the language used. Neither is obvious. Third, the text may have been written down many centuries ago, or in another cultural environment; this may hamper the proper understanding of the text, if 'proper' means understanding the author's intention.[7] What we see here is that accessibility is connected with interpretation and with the whole conundrum around the author's intention, the readers' response and the issue of whether a text has an autonomous meaning that depends on how it should be understood, considering both the author's and the readers' backgrounds and contexts. A computer scientist may be tempted to assume that access to the written text coupled with a dictionary or another 'code-breaker' constitutes access, whereas a scholar of Sanskrit may be persuaded to assume that access requires the study of secondary literature on history, cultural anthropology and other information, such as the study of archaeological sites. Interestingly, in the case of tertiary retention, access to the information seems to be direct, but may have to be mediated by study of the relevant language, history and cultural background of the author. Does this challenge our understanding of direct access? Direct access to the information carrier can obviously be blocked by turning off the light, putting the text in a vault, behind closed doors or by burning or otherwise destroying it. Unless copies have been made, the information is lost in the case of destruction, unless it is available in secondary retention.

The printing press makes a substantial difference for several reasons. The proliferation of printed text as compared to hand-written manuscripts makes it more difficult to disable or restrict access, since people can turn to other copies of the same text. Because printing implies identical copies, it also becomes more difficult to lie about the content, because people can more easily find another copy and check the precise wordings. Official record keeping, which may interfere with the privacy of a person, provides direct access to information about a person's name, gender, place and date of birth, residence and about things such as income (for the purpose of taxation). Other types of information can be recorded, for example to enable the operations of the welfare state that aims to redistribute income and guarantee certain minimum standards for housing, healthcare, education and more. Under the rule of law, constraints are installed; in principle, the information must have a legitimate purpose and its usage should be proportional in view of the purpose, and it should not be accessible to anyone other than the government officials who need it to achieve the legitimate purpose, while the competence that allows this particular tertiary retention must be attributed by law (the legality principle, not to be confused with legalism). Because information is supported by paper it takes time and effort to distribute the information (ontological friction again), so whereas the accessibility of text is extended exponentially in the era of the printing press, it is still dependent on the operations of human or mechanical transport (walking, mules, cars, trains, boats and planes). Once tertiary retention moves to digitization, the accessibility is again transformed.

If its code can be broken and the culture studied, written and printed information can be accessible across geographical distance, and across multiple centuries. This means that access no longer depends on interaction between the author and the reader, between the sender and the receiver of information.[8] Access depends on getting one's eyes on the carrier (paper, books) and on having access to secondary information to reconstruct the meaning of the signs that are 'carried'. For the text to be seen as information it must be critical, relevant or simply useful to the person who receives it, which clarifies why merely reconstructing the intention of the author is not necessarily the point, while access to the author's intention is per definition always indirect as it is part of the secondary retention that occurs while writing a text.

Lastly, we look into the accessibility of digital data. Here we encounter a new universe; getting one's eyes on the carrier (silicon) will not be much help. Even an electrical engineer will not learn much about the data by checking the hard disk. To access the data we need to talk to the computer, using computer languages such as source code (reasonably close to human language), a compiler (that translates the source code into machine code), and machine code, to make sure the computer can execute instructions to retrieve the data. A computer scientist or programmer may access the data this way, but most people will need software that enables smooth interaction, for instance in the form of a graphical user interface (GUI). Most digital data, however, are stored in databases that are stored in data-servers, often managed by cloud-providers that enable efficient and thus cheap storage by using a so-called virtual machine. Direct access to the data is therefore improbable on two grounds: first, the silicon inscription does not mean anything to the person interested in the data; and, second, the data is usually stored in a computer system architecture that determines what other systems have access for which types of operations. In principle, most data will not be accessed by human agents, who will, instead, be looking at the aggregated data, perform specific queries, or seek to detect patterns in the data. The aggregation, query and pattern detection are done by the system, which forms a series of layers and instructions between the data-user and the data. In many cases, data can be monetized without any human agent having access to the data, for instance, when auctioning advertising space on a website that is visited by a person with a specific profile. In a commercial environment, access to personal data is mostly a matter of machine-to-machine communication. In that sense, one could say that in the case of information retained as digital data, accessibility is cumbersome and often meaningless. Studying the culture, history or archaeology of the relevant computing system will not help much; being savvy in the field of computer engineering, information science and current business models may be necessary to gain meaningful understanding of the consequences of having one's data processed within a particular architecture. Physical access to one's data will not help to gain such understanding and neither will a listing of the personal data processed by a specific company. What matters here is, for instance, the linkability of the data, the possibility that one's data is being sold or shared, the profiles built from massive amounts of behavioural data that match one's data points. Much of this cannot be accessed because the data is anonymized and the profiles kept shielded behind trade secret or intellectual property rights; as long as the profiles concern categories instead of a particular person they fall outside the scope of data protection. But, once applied, EU law requires transparency and a right to object to being profiled, if the consequences are significant. However, most people are not at all aware of the profiling that goes on, while companies are not interested in explaining how the backend of the system works.

Propertizability of information

Propertization is relevant for copyright, data protection and for freedom of information. The latter suggests that propertization is either impossible or undesirable, while copyright assumes that propertization is at least possible. Some privacy scholars advocate the propertization of personal data, hoping this will provide individuals with increased control over their data (Lessig 2006; Schwartz 2000; Prins 2006; Novotny and Spiekerman 2013). What does the exercise on access teach us about propertizability of information? Can we only propertize what is commodified or commodifiable, and what does it mean? Let us start with a simple and not necessarily legal definition of propertizable, by requiring that something can be possessed by an individual person, whether or not this results in legal ownership. For something to be in the possession of a person, it must at least be identifiable (stable borders), exclusive (possession enables excluding others from having, holding or using it) and rivalrous (if one person has it, another person cannot have it also). We will see that exclusiveness and rivalrousness may not be properties of information, unless we apply certain legal standards that create exclusive rights to different copies of the same information. We shall have to look into whatever 'the same information' means here, but let us already note that the possibility to create such exclusive rights does depend on the possibility to possess rivalrous copies of information. The latter depends on the support, that is, the carrier of the information.

The information that is captured in primary retention is not directly accessible to another human agent, though it may be inferred if the other agent is around and has a similar background (language, culture). As long as the information is not integrated by means of secondary retention it is hardly identifiable as a particular piece of information, though the agent or another agent could speak or write about the experience and this could make it available as an identifiable piece of information. As long as we are in the realm of speech, hearing the information shares the ephemeral character of primary retention, and – if remembered – the dynamics of secondary retention. If the information is expressed by means of written text, we enter the realm of tertiary retention. To the extent that the secondary retention can be inferred, for instance because a person talks about it, some piece of information may be identifiable as such, but we would need spoken or written text to actually identify it, and possessing it would certainly require tertiary retention (written text). This means that I do not consider a memory to be a possession unless the stuff of the memory is written down, filmed or taped. The memory of an individual person is constitutive of that person; she does not merely 'have' a memory, but to a large extent 'is' her memories.[9] I believe it does not make sense to propose that we can 'possess' who we are.

Tertiary retention retains information by means of external storage. Copyright, for instance, provides an exclusive right to the expression of an idea, just like a patent provides an exclusive right to an invention that is based on an original (novel) idea that is useful in the sense of being susceptible to industrial application.

This is interesting because it highlights that ideas cannot be protected by means of intellectual property rights, only their embodiment in an expression or invention. It seems that the embodiment makes the idea identifiable, while it also enables us to demarcate the entity that can be possessed. An idea is formed in the mind of an individual person, even if it emerged after much discussion or other collaboration with others and even if two people had the same idea during the same discussion. An idea seems to be the result of secondary retention, meaning that direct access and possession are not possible. Once the idea is transported, transformed and materialized in the form of a tangible expression or invention, it can be demarcated and protected. One could counter that an oral composition (of a presentation, a choreography or music) is in principle open for copyright, but this is only the case if it is somehow recorded – otherwise it cannot be established what expression is protected. Still, what is protected is not one particular copy of the expression, but 'the expression itself'. This nourishes the temptation to think in terms of an immaterial good that can be dissected from both its material support and the embodied mind of the agent. My take is that this is incorrect. Not because the expression or the invention only exists as a copy on a material carrier or solely exists in the neuronal pathways of an individual creator, but because the expression emerged, developed and consolidated in the interplay between individuals, pen and paper, discussions and experiments that helped to finalize a particular expression or invention. The question where the propertizable form of information is situated is not a very interesting question, but for the sake of propertization the law situates it between the embodied mind of a particular person and the result of the tertiary retention she initiated. One could say that the tertiary retention – a process of inscription – is the basis of the right, while the inscription itself is proof it its existence. The relevant information becomes accessible – in principle – as soon as the tertiary retention is performed, which renders it identifiable as such, and enables possession (exclusion). We must, however, admit that possession is not a natural property of information; once the information is identifiable it can, in principle, be copied and disseminated. We need cultural constraints to block access. At the same time, however, we must admit that if information results from secondary retention but is not expressed and has not led to an invention, it cannot be possessed. Problems emerge from the in-between of idea and expression or invention, when a person has an idea that she shares with others, without finalizing it as an expression or invention, enabling others to develop the expression or invention and thus claiming the property right. This in-between of idea and expression/invention stands for the timespace where information as idea transforms into information as expression/invention, which in turn reconfigures the idea until it consolidates in alignment with its final tertiary retention; this timespace nourishes on the meeting of minds and experimental processes of tertiary retention and forms the middle ground for creativity and innovation. Idea and expression/invention are thus mutually constitutive.

What about propertization of personal data? For instance, the name of a person is a personal data. When an infant is born, she is addressed by means of her name, which she will start associating with – hopefully – pleasant attention, or feeding and which will slowly consolidate as the critical information that is co-constitutive of the self. This takes place in the interplay between primary and secondary retention, while composing the architecture of an individual biographic memory. The name, in this context, is accessible but forms a part of the person to whom it applies and cannot be possessed. It is not rivalrous or exclusive because one person using the name to address the infant does not exclude others from using the same name to address that particular child. As such, the name cannot be propertized, it does not make any sense to imagine it as an identifiable, exclusive and rivalrous good. However, once the name is registered in the civil registry, we have entered the realm of tertiary retention, where the name is inscribed on paper or a silicon chip, and open to copying and sharing. When speaking of written records, such copying and sharing implies indexing and systemization to guarantee retrieval, but the searchability and correlatability are limited. If we are speaking of digital records, a personal data is an inscription on a silicon chip that can be manipulated in a number of ways: copied, correlated, disseminated, deleted or even changed. While it sits in the database, we cannot be sure it is information, as this is agent-dependent. However, government agencies and commercial service providers who keep name records in digital form will probably keep it with the assumption that it might be critical, relevant or useful at some point. This regards not only name records, but any type of information relation to an identified or identifiable person, for instance, the clickstream behaviours of a particular web user. Once the holder of the data retrieves it, for instance to sell it to the highest bidder, it will probably become information for whoever gains access to it, though in the case of behavioural advertising it may be that the data is used to advertise a product to a particular user without the advertiser gaining access to the data. Is propertizability a property of personal data that has been retained in the form of digital data? Obviously, I cannot sell or alienate my name. But I could, for instance, license the use of a name record, under data protection law, based on the fact that whoever wants to use the record requires my consent or a contract to justify lawful use of the digital data. This cannot mean that another person, company or government agency now possesses my name, or my click-stream behaviours. It could entail that another agent gains the possibility to use the digitized name or click-stream behaviours for a specific purpose. I would even suggest that this does not mean that the information inscribed on the chip can be used without further qualification, as it may not even be clear whether the data qualifies as information. The licence would regard the digital data, taking into account that the properties of database systems (notably, the searchability and correlatability of the data they contain) are radically different from those of paper records.

This relates directly to the issue of freedom of information. The notion can be understood in different ways. First, it may refer to the opinion that information cannot be contained and will travel where it wants, ultimately becoming available for all human agents. Some may argue that this is a universal property of information, though I would emphasize that all depends on how you understand information and which retention is at stake. Second, freedom of information can be seen as a normative issue, basically amounting to freedom of movement for information. This could, for instance, add another freedom to the four freedoms of the internal economic market of the European Union: goods, capital, services and people. Third, it can refer to the fundamental right of access to information, which hopes to create a strong civil society, provide transparency about government operations and help individual persons to make informed decisions and to flourish based on this. Whichever meaning is given to the freedom of information, I would claim that all depends on the material constraints of tertiary retention and the cultural prohibitions that are at stake. As mentioned above, digital data is not easily accessible without the necessary interfaces; so, even if digital data travels with the speed of electronic communication systems, freedom of information in the sense of universal accessibility is not a 'natural' property of digitized information.

Appropriateness of information

In her seminal work on privacy as contextual integrity, Helen Nissenbaum speaks of the appropriateness and distribution of information flows, within identifiable contexts (Nissenbaum 2010; Hildebrandt 2014). In this brief excursion into appropriateness as a property of information, I again follow the three levels of retention to determine whether, and if so, how, each level relates to appropriateness of information or information flows. If we follow Nissenbaum, appropriateness implies that we take a normative stance as to what is fitting in a particular context, which seems to be determined by the culture within which the context plays out.

Information involved in primary retention is appropriate if it helps the agent to survive and to flourish in her environment. Appropriate here would be critical, relevant or simply useful for the agent. The same goes for secondary retention. One could, however, take the point of view that information that causes mental or physical pain or disrupts the life of the agent is inappropriate, meaning that the environment of the person should behave in a way that avoids causing harm as this would cause her to retain inappropriate information. This may seem a rather complicated way to formulate a moral appeal to not cause harm, but it is important to acknowledge how traumatic experiences operate at the level of bodily memory (secondary retention), often forcing a person to relive the horrors of the initial experience over and again. Obviously, speaking of 'appropriate' assumes an element of choice on the side of the environment that offers the information; appropriate information assumes agency.

In the context of this volume, we focus on the appropriateness of information retained on external supports. In the era of the written manuscript, access to written information was limited to the class of scribes, who held a *de facto* monopoly. The information inscribed on, for example, clay tablets and papyrus was usually concerned with commercial transactions, deeds, distribution of land and religious and scientific texts. Under what conditions the information itself should be termed inappropriate is difficult to establish in hindsight, but some may find the monopoly on accessing the information that was inherent in the limited alphabetization that characterized the era of the script inappropriate. Of course, the Catholic Church has a long history of banning particular content; the inquisition engaged in book burning, execution and torture to stop the dissemination of heresy. What should interest us here is the fact that the qualification of appropriateness was decided by a person holding office, speaking from a position of authority. The printing press generated a proliferation of text, resulting in subsequent attempts by governments to control the flow of information that was thus enabled. Censorship was the predecessor of copyright, since governments provided licences to specific publishers to achieve the control over what they deemed inappropriate content (Rose 1995). As with the Catholic Church, the decision on appropriateness was made by the authorities, attempting to restrict the free flow of information. Whereas the era of the script, when access to written information was limited to a class of scribes, was conducive to control over information flows in line with authoritarian decisions on appropriateness, the era of the printing press demonstrates the victory of the free flow of information. This can be explained by pointing to the explosion of identical text, which was hard to contain and monitor, and by the fact that the monopoly of the clerks was broken; at some point all citizens could access (read) the information printed in books and journals, making their own judgement about its appropriateness. Simultaneously, however, governments recruited a bureaucracy capable of collecting large amounts of information, notably required for purposes of taxation, conscription and, later, for sustaining the welfare state. Ultimately, the notion of appropriateness of recording information on individual citizens became part of the complex balancing operation of, for instance, Article 8 of the European Convention for the Protection of Human Rights and Fundamental Freedoms 1950, and Articles 7 and 8 of the Charter of Fundamental Rights of the European Union. The issue hinges on the proportionality between gaining insights into the private life of citizens and the need to achieve public goods such as national security, public safety and correct redistribution of income. The most obvious example of inappropriate information is where access to information constitutes an infringement upon the privacy of an individual person.

Notably with regard to personal data, the question is: (1) under which conditions the *existence* of specific information that relates to an identified or identifiable agent is appropriate; and (2) under what conditions the *sharing* of information that is inscribed on, or saved to, a specific support is appropriate. One could propose that information that is incorrect or incomplete is inappropriate, though in some cases incorrect or incomplete information may be desirable and offer the best protection one could think of (González Fuster 2010). This connects with Nissenbaum's (2010) theory on contextual integrity. Her focus is not on individual data but on information flows, which shifts the attention from the appropriateness of information to the appropriateness of sharing. The latter is about making information accessible for other agents and it seems pivotal to evaluate the appropriateness of *making* them accessible, instead of merely the appropriateness of them *being* accessible. The better wording is 'available' rather than accessible; as discussed, data can be monetized without being accessed by a human agent. Surely, availability is again a relational and relative concept; information can be available to some, but not to others and it can be available in a specific context but not in another. This entails that in relation to some agents availability may be inappropriate, while similarly in relation to some contexts revealing information pertaining to another context may be inappropriate. This confirms that appropriateness is not a property of information as such, but agent- and context-dependent.

The move from written and printed text to digitization has enormous implications for the appropriateness of information. This is visible in the legal restrictions on the processing of personal data that complement the right to informational privacy. The most important question, however, regards how access, property and appropriateness of information fare when the accessibility of digital data is restricted to artificial agents that access and assess what data is critical, relevant or useful. This raises new questions about the meaning of information in the era of data-driven environments.

Properties, propriety and appropriateness of big data

Big data is now seen by many as the panacea to any problem one can think of. A semi-religious belief in the wonders of big data analytics has taken over science, commercial enterprise, governments and education. There seems little awareness that patterns found in databases are not necessarily evidence of similar patterns outside the database. Translating problems from the analogue world into digital machine-readable formats can create numerical problems that are unrelated to the problems that need attention. Investing all available funding in collecting, storing and processing big data at the cost of investing in domain expertise and professional attention is nonsensical and dangerous. This is related to the properties of digitized information. The most obvious property is the relative inaccessibility of digital data, discussed above, and the complexities of safeguarding the confidentiality, integrity and availability of digital data and critical infrastructures based on large quantities of machine-readable behavioural data.

More important, however, is the advance of artificial agency that builds on data-driven architectures. Data-driven agents have other affordances than all other types of tertiary retention (script, printing press, audio-visual recordings, digital data). It is not even clear that such agents fit the notion of tertiary retention, because they are not about inscribing digital data on silicon, but about machine learning, feedback mechanisms and about relatively independent detection of critical, relevant or useful information.

Concluding remarks

When Gary Marx decided not to define information he took a wise decision. Information is a moving target. If information differs from knowledge in being novel, it will exhaust its own existence; after the information is accessed it stops qualifying as information. However, although once retained in secondary retention it is no longer information (as it is already known), once retained in tertiary retention it may reappear as information for another agent who accesses it (and to the extent that an agent forgot the information she inscribed as tertiary retention, it may reappear as information even to her, when she retrieves it). If we are dealing with information in the form of digital data, an agent may detect relevant patterns after correlating the data with other data, thus gaining information from the database that is both novel and non-trivial. This way, the outcome of machine learning provides a novel type of information, which may be information to both humans and other machines.

When assessing the accessibility of information we need to pay keen attention to the role of tertiary attention. This chapter argues that human language has different affordances as far as information is concerned than those of computer languages; this has far-reaching implications for the accessibility of the data that inform data-driven infrastructures. We should stop taking for granted that digital data is information and inquire into the consequences of further datafication, notably for critical fundamental rights such as privacy and data protection. To assess whether networking, linking and opening up data is appropriate, we must pay keen attention to how the data is turned into information for which human or artificial agent. This is obviously connected with issues of power, as becomes clear in the next part of the book.

Notes

1 Marx, this volume, at [24] of Chapter 1.
2 In my Chorley Lecture (Hildebrandt 2016) I have developed the argument that the mathematical theory of information 'informs' the explosion of data-driven agency, with huge implications for the mode of existence of modern law.
3 See also on the reading brain, Wolf (2008).
4 I am leaning on the shoulders of Husserl (1964) here, though in a rather liberal manner.
5 The term 'introjection' is from Stiegler (2013).
6 This is not science fiction, see e.g. Randall (2015).
7 On whether this is the most interesting feat of an interpretation, see e.g. Ricoeur (1976).
8 Ibid.; Lévy (1990).
9 While taking into account that this individual memory is contingent upon the collective memory, i.e. culture, that co-constitutes the secundary and primary retentions. See Ricoeur (2004).

References

de Mul, J. (ed.) (2015) *Plessner's Philosophical Anthropology: Perspectives and Prospects*. Amsterdam: Amsterdam University Press.
de Saussure, F. (1915) *Cours de Linguistique Générale*. Paris: Payot.
Durkheim, E. (2012) *The Division of Labor in Society*. Transl. by George Simpson. Eastford, CT: Martino Fine Books.

Floridi, L. (2010) *Information: A Very Short Introduction*. Oxford: Oxford University Press.

Geertz, C. (2010a) *Local Knowledge*. London: Fontana Press.

——. (2010b) *The Interpretation of Cultures*. London: Fontana Press.

Giddens, A. (1986) *The Constitution of Society: Outline of the Theory of Structuration*. Cambridge: Polity Press.

Gleick, J. (2010) *The Information: A History, A Theory, A Flood*. New York, NY: Pantheon.

Glenn, H.P. (2007) *Legal Traditions of the World*. Oxford: Oxford University Press.

González Fuster, G. (2010) 'Inaccuracy as a Privacy-Enhancing Tool'. *Ethics and Information Technology* 12(1): 87–95.

Goody, J. and Watt, I. (1963) 'The Consequences of Literacy'. *Comparative Studies in Society and History* 5(3): 304–345.

Habermas, J. (1996) *Between Facts and Norms: Contributions to a Discourse Theory of Law and Democracy*. Studies in Contemporary German Social Thought. Cambridge, MA: MIT Press.

Hayles, N.K. (1999) *How We Became Posthuman: Virtual Bodies in Cybernetics, Literature, and Informatics*. Chicago, IL: University of Chicago Press.

Hildebrandt, M. (2014) 'Location Data, Purpose Binding and Contextual Integrity: What's the Message?' In L. Floridi (ed.) *Protection of Information and the Right to Privacy – A New Equilibrium?* Heidelberg, New York, NY, Dordrecht and London: Springer: 31–62.

Hildebrandt, M. (2016) 'Law as Information in the Era of Data-Driven Agency'. *The Modern Law Review* 79(1): 1–30.

Hoerl, C. and McCormack, T. (2001) *Time and Memory: Issues in Philosophy and Psychology*. Oxford: Oxford University Press.

Husserl, E. (1964) *Phenomenology of Internal Time Consciousness*. Edited by M. Heidegger. Transl. by J.S. Churchill. Bloomington, IN: Indiana University Press.

Koch, S.C., Fuchs, T., Summa, M. and Müller, C. (2012) *Body Memory, Metaphor and Movement*. Amsterdam and Philadelphia, PA: John Benjamins Publishing Company.

Lessig, L. (2006) *Code Version 2.0*. New York, NY: Basic Books.

Lévy, P. (1990) *Les Technologies de L'intelligence. L'avenir de La Pensée à L'ère Informatique*. Paris: La Découverte.

Luhmann, N. (1995) *Social Systems*. Stanford, CA: Stanford University Press.

Nissenbaum, H.F. (2010) *Privacy in Context: Technology, Policy, and the Integrity of Social Life*. Stanford, CA: Stanford Law Books.

Novotny, A. and Spiekerman, S. (2013) 'Personal Information Markets and Privacy: A New Model to Solve the Controversy'. In M. Hildebrandt, K. O'Hara and M. Waidner (eds) *Digital Enlightenment Yearbook 2013: The Value of Personal Data*. Washington, DC: IOS Press: 102–120.

Ong, W. (1982) *Orality and Literacy: The Technologizing of the Word*. London and New York, NY: Methuen.

Prins, C. (2006) 'When Personal Data, Behavior and Virtual Identities Become a Commodity: Would a Property Rights Approach Matter?' *SCRIPT-Ed* 3(4): 270–303.

Randall, D. (2015) 'Neuropolitics, Where Campaigns Try to Read Your Mind'. *The New York Times*, 3 November 2015.

Ricoeur, P. (1973) 'The Model of the Text: Meaningful Action Considered as a Text'. *New Literary History* 5(1): 91–117.

——. (1976) *Interpretation Theory*. Austin, TX: Texas University Press.

——. (2004) *Memory, History, Forgetting*. Transl. by K. Blamey and D. Pellauer. Chicago, IL: Chicago University Press.

Rose, M. (1995) *Authors and Owners: The Invention of Copyright*. Cambridge, MA: Harvard University Press.

Schwartz, P.M. (2000) 'Beyond Lessig's Code for Internet Privacy: Cyberspace Filters, Privacy-Control and Fair Information Practices'. *Wisconsin Law Review*: 743–788.

Stiegler, B. (2013) 'Die Aufklaerung in the Age of Philosophical Engineering'. In M. Hildebrandt, K. O'Hara and M. Waidner (eds) *Digital Enlightenment Yearbook 2013: The Value of Personal Data*. Washington, DC: IOS Press: 29–39.

Vedral, V. (2014) 'Quantum Entanglement'. *Nature Physics* 10(4): 256–258.

Wolf, M. (2008) *Proust and the Squid: The Story and Science of the Reading Brain*. Cambridge: Icon Books.

Zimmer, H., Mecklinger, A. and Lindenberger, U. (eds) (2006) *Handbook of Binding and Memory: Perspectives From Cognitive Neuroscience*. Oxford: Oxford University Press.

Part II

The powers of information

Chapter 3

Between truth and power

Julie E. Cohen

We speak to *power* in three senses: To those who hold high places in our national life and bear the terrible responsibility of making decisions for war or peace. To the American people who are the final reservoir of power in this country and whose values and expectations set the limits for those who exercise authority. To the idea of Power itself, and its impact on Twentieth Century life.
– American Friends Service Committee,
Speak Truth to Power: A Quaker Search for an Alternative to Violence (1955)

Introduction

The call to 'speak truth to power', now employed most frequently as a banal protest trope or a generalized call to action, originates in the title of a pamphlet in which intellectual leaders of the Quaker faith opposed the ongoing Cold War and advocated its peaceful resolution. They offered an account of the polarization of the geopolitical landscape that moved beyond the continuing threat of horrific violence to reckon with what a contemporary economist might call the opportunity costs of militarization. Those costs were both moral and material; resources devoted to the production and strategic deployment of expensive weapons were resources that could not be devoted to improving standards of living for the world's neediest people. For the writers, the most important kind of power was the power to choose between using American might to achieve military domination and using it to advance the cause of human wellbeing.

The pamphlet authors' appeal to the power to choose between domination and human flourishing remains fundamental, and yet their conceptions of both the exercise of domination and the exercise of principled resistance now seem dated in one critical respect. To understand both domination and resistance in the twenty-first century, we must take account of the ways that networked information technologies mediate the ongoing dialogue between truth and power. That relationship cannot be understood via simple deterministic equivalencies. Arguments about the freedom-enhancing potential of the network too often rely on a conception of networked information technologies as inherently connective and egalitarian in their operation, but they are neither. Between truth and power is the code – the technical infrastructures that facilitate information flows between people, and between people and the entities that wield power in their lives – and the code has fractal effects on both power and truth. Code can become a means for resisting domination or a vehicle for embedding it, but even that formulation is too simple. Through its capacities to authorize, exclude and modulate information flows, code can become a means for multiplying and extending power, and for privatizing and fragmenting truth.

The problem of control over information flows thus emerges as an important vantage point from which to interrogate 'the idea of Power itself, and its impact on [twenty-first] century life'. Although states do attempt to control information flows in various ways, this problem does not map neatly to the exercise of state power, nor does it map to traditional conceptions of power as (capacity for) physical force. Questions about the extent of private control of information flows also have become flash points for public anger about the capacity for self-determination, or lack thereof, enjoyed by ordinary people. Such anger is not frivolous; access to information and control of information are intimately related to the choice between domination and flourishing. Debates about state censorship are highly visible, but they represent only one piece of a larger puzzle, which concerns the extent to which global circuits of information flow are settling into patterns that serve larger constellations of economic and political power. Law and legal institutions are intimately involved in this process, and not only as a means of representation and resistance. Law too stands between truth and power, and code and law together have become tools for structuring contests over the material conditions of understanding, participation and self-determination.

This chapter uses the evolving landscape of law and policy in the areas of copyright and information privacy/data protection to explore the issues of control and power in the emerging networked information society. It considers three inter-related sets of developments. The second section describes patterns of information flow in the domains of copyright and information privacy/data protection, and considers the distinctive kinds of power relations that they are producing. The third section explores the evolving conceptualization of legal rights in the two domains, and traces the ways that the ongoing production and reproduction of private economic power are reshaping shared understandings of what the law guarantees. We see there that both copyright law and information privacy/data protection law have become entry points for neoliberalization within narratives about fundamental rights of authorship, cultural participation, and privacy. In the fourth section, we see that processes of neoliberalization do not involve only concepts. Pressures to reinforce private control of information flows are catalysing far-reaching changes in the structure of governance institutions, altering not only the interpretation of fundamental legal guarantees but also the mechanisms by which legal rights and obligations are defined and enforced. A more systematic integration of questions about control over information flows within traditional legal narratives about fundamental rights and human development is urgently needed, but I argue that it is also important to consider the ways that established institutional pathways for defining and vindicating rights and promoting development agendas are being circumvented by emerging networked governance institutions.

The global realignment of information flows

At its inception, the internet was conceived as the inevitable servant of truth – as a 'technology of freedom' (de Sola Pool 1984) that would enable both political and economic self-determination. The classic form of this claim is John Gilmore's assertion that the internet 'interprets censorship as damage and routes around it'.[1] We have known for some time now that this rather deterministic view of technology is too simple. As Lawrence Lessig (1998) explained, code is not a given but rather a modality of regulation that can be designed this way or that, and its plasticity affords points of regulatory leverage to both state and private actors. Code invites tinkering but also efforts at control.

Informed by Lessig's characterization of code as regulatory, deterministic claims about the way that code 'is' evolved into normative claims about the way that it should be. For the last decade or so, a loose coalition of social movements, non-governmental organizations (NGOs) and academics, joined at one time or another by various state actors, has promoted a vision of code as a tool for advancing freedom from political oppression – a tool for speaking truth to power. In these new claims about the relationship between truth and power, however, a different kind of technological essentialism has persisted, which may be located in the formulation of claims about rights to internet access and use. Such claims seem to presume that tools for censorship of information flows are afterthoughts or hostile add-ons, and that market forces will route around them, incentivizing the development of networked information technologies in ways that are connective and egalitarian. That view is mistaken on a number of levels. As Rebecca MacKinnon (2012) explains, technology companies motivated by the allure of new markets often have complied with censorship demands made by authoritarian governments. But even the technologies in use in democratic societies increasingly incorporate, at their core, capabilities for interdiction and differentiation of information flows.

Here I want to tell two stories: one about copyright and protocols for interdiction of information flows, and another about privacy and techniques for differentiation and modulation of information flows. Each story illustrates the increasingly complicated ways that code mediates relationships between truth and power. The concluding subsection of this section draws out some of those themes, considering the different ways in which power is produced, expressed and reinforced through information practices and architectures.

Cultural property: authorization and interdiction in global circuits

Twenty years ago, the principal modality of copyright enforcement was the infringement lawsuit, supplemented in particularly egregious cases by the criminal infringement prosecution. The past two decades have witnessed a deep and seemingly permanent shift in the nature of copyright enforcement. Copyright enforcement efforts have become efforts to rearrange information flows within circuits of authorization, and to block or remove entirely unauthorized flows and channels. The enforcement game is played on multiple fronts simultaneously: in lawsuits, legislative hearings, rulemakings and treaty negotiations. Efforts to strengthen legal support for interdiction fail with some regularity, but often are followed by 'voluntary' private schemes of interdiction adopted in the hope of minimizing litigation exposure.

Initially, takedowns of individual postings were the primary interdiction strategy. The legislative model adopted in the United States, which relies on a streamlined process triggered by notice without prior judicial review, has been imitated around the world. Opponents of the takedown regime feared that the process would lead to abuse, and the data have borne out those fears: significant numbers of takedown notices are either meritless or legally questionable (Urban and Quilter 2005; Seltzer 2010). Widespread publicity given to abusive take-down practices has not had the deterrent effect that had been hoped. A significant counteracting factor appears to be the increased reliance on automated processes for detecting infringement and generating takedown notices. Some of the results are eyebrow-raising. Consider, for example, the publicity generated by a recent takedown notice to Twitter about a tweet that linked to a blog post that commented on the fact that the new album by a band called The National had leaked elsewhere on the internet, or the takedown notices that targeted authorized copies of a well-regarded documentary film about the Pirate Bay, an organization dedicated to facilitating peer-to-peer file-sharing.[2]

Notably, within the more privacy-protective European legal environment, there is ongoing tension between takedown regimes and regimes of privacy protection. While US courts have rejected privacy challenges to subpoenas for production of subscriber information, European courts have attempted to define a compromise path, refusing to reject out of hand the possibility that subscribers accused of online infringement might have meaningful privacy interests at stake. In 2012, the European Court of Justice invalidated a Belgian court order requiring an internet access provider to monitor its subscribers' peer-to-peer downloads and filter out works included in the catalogue of the plaintiff, a collective rights management organization. The court observed that:

> in the context of measures to protect copyright holders, national authorities and courts must strike a fair balance between the protection of copyright and the protection of the fundamental rights of individuals who are affected by such measures.[3]

The precise nature of that balance has become a hot-button issue in negotiations over data protection regulation, with right holder organizations pushing for exceptions to facilitate their enforcement efforts.

From the copyright industry perspective, however, the notice-and-takedown regime has always been a second-best strategy, worth pursuing only until more direct and effective interdiction measures could be implemented. The outcome of those efforts is still undetermined. On both sides of the Atlantic, efforts to impose proactive filtering obligations by legislation, regulation and litigation have failed repeatedly. Efforts to identify and penalize individual users have been more successful, but courts in both the United States and Europe have resisted procedural innovations designed to make litigation against users more cost-effective, such as joinder of large numbers of potential defendants or discovery of large numbers of names. The French HADOPI law,[4] which allowed copyright industry plaintiffs to pursue termination of individual internet accounts in an administrative proceeding, was amended to incorporate judicial supervision following a court judgment that it was constitutionally defective, and later was suspended entirely.

Yet this recounting of legislative and litigation failures overlooks the extent to which direct interdiction of infringing content has become a norm in the marketplace. Every major internet company that hosts user-provided content uses automated filtering technology to prevent the posting of infringing content. Legislated takedown regimes operate against background legal doctrines that establish indirect liability for contributing to infringement; such doctrines supply powerful incentives to engage in proactive screening. Other market initiatives are being brought to bear on users. Although HADOPI-like proposals have gained no legislative traction in the United States, the major internet access providers have agreed to adopt a 'six strikes' menu of graduated sanctions to be levied on customers who are thought to be trafficking in infringing content. Lastly, many commercially available systems for delivering and playing audio-visual content incorporate both technical protection against copying and some type of trusted-system functionality designed to prevent retransmissions to unauthorized platforms and devices.

More recently, formal interdiction initiatives have grown increasingly draconian, targeting not just individual files but also entire web domains and the search and payment infrastructures that support them. Law enforcement authorities that bring criminal piracy proceedings have access to a variety of strategies for achieving site takedowns, including both forfeiture provisions in domestic laws and co-operation by foreign authorities. The copyright industries have vigorously sought parallel civil interdiction capabilities. In the United States, efforts to legislate *ex parte* procedures for blocking access to domains and isolating them from their payment providers advanced rapidly in Congress, and were defeated only by a massive mobilization of the online community. Those celebrating the demise of these bills, known as SOPA and PIPA, may be taking too narrow a view. Google has announced that it will begin demoting or removing entirely from search results sites that generate repeated takedown notices. Notably, Google's widely publicized efforts to achieve transparency with regard to the takedown notices it receives do not extend to the details of this search manipulation. As Eric Goldman (2012) notes, to the extent this internal programme mimics the results that could have been achieved under the SOPA/PIPA regime, it accomplishes via private and wholly non-transparent measures what the combined lobbying might of the content industries could not.

Information privacy: surveillance and modulation in global circuits

Compared with flows of global culture, flows of information about network users appear to move in very different ways. The recent history of information privacy (in the United States) and data protection (in Europe) is not one of automatic interdiction or *ex parte* enforcement of draconian mandates. Instead, a burgeoning global information processing industry has drawn encouragement from a relatively relaxed privacy enforcement culture in the United States and from an increasingly ineffective data protection regime in Europe. When one pays attention to the question of control, however, the landscape begins to look more similar. Flows of personal information move in patterns controlled by the commercial entities that seek to convert them to flows of profit, and neither the channels of flow nor the uses to which the information is put are transparent to users. We are witnessing the emergence of a distinctly Western, democratic type of surveillance society, in which surveillance is conceptualized first and foremost as a matter of efficiency and convenience.

Within personal information-based business models, flows of personal information do not only travel in one direction. Increasingly, they are used to shape and personalize, or modulate, the information environments that individuals encounter. When networked, automated, persistent surveillance becomes modulation, 'the quality and content of surveillant attention is continually modified according to the subject's own behavior, sometimes in response to inputs from the subject but according to logics that ultimately are outside the subject's control' (Cohen 2013: 1915; see also Elmer 2004). The goal is not Orwellian political repression, but rather the much more prosaic objective of gaining competitive advantage in markets for goods, services and attention. For consumers, modulation enables seamless, convenient personalization, often accompanied by discount offers and other privileges; for information businesses, it promises more efficient identification of high-value consumers and more accurate projection and valuation of risk.

Unlike interdiction-based strategies, modulation thrives in an atmosphere of regulatory lenity. It has found a particularly congenial home in the United States, where information privacy regulation is sectoral and limited in scope, enabling virtually unfettered commercial information processing. With respect to most types of personal information, enforcement practices are designed to encourage notice and consent rather than transparency and minimization. Even when particular kinds of sensitive information (e.g. medical information) are subject to a prohibition against further processing in personally-identified form, there is no prohibition against the release of de-identified information. When combined with other publicly available datasets, such data often can be re-identified (Ohm 2010). The relatively unrestricted availability of information has fuelled the rise of a thriving and politically powerful data processing industry whose members have invested heavily in the development of cutting edge data mining capabilities and market their services to both businesses and governments (Hoofnagle 2004). In addition, many consumer-facing internet companies, such as Google, Facebook and Amazon, have developed business models that rely heavily on collection and use of personal information.

Although the United States is the epicentre of the modulated society, practices of modulation also are on the rise in the more privacy-protective regimes of the European Union. In Europe, the processing of personal information is currently regulated via the Data Protection Directive[5] and implementing legislation in EU member states. In the 17 years since its enactment, however, it has become evident that this framework does not effectively regulate information processing in the social media environment. Everyone is an information processor, information collection activities are dynamic, and the volume of information collection and processing is unthinkably large. Under such conditions, guarantees of transparency result in Kafka-esque moments, such as Facebook's delivery of a disc containing a 1,222-page file to an Austrian student who requested disclosure of his personally-identified information.[6] Efforts to re-establish more protective data processing norms via court proceedings, such as Sweden's criminal prosecution of church volunteer Bodil Lindqvist for posting information about congregants on her blog, seem both ridiculous and utterly ineffectual.[7] More generally, many of the regime's protections may be waived by consent, and the meaning of consent is unclear in ways that have enabled the concept to be strategically exploited by information businesses. The European commitment to dignity expressed in the Directive struggles with the desire of European consumers for access to mobile devices and social media.

The European data protection model is currently under revision, in part because of questions about its ability to respond effectively to social media, mobile platforms, and other contemporary data processing practices, and in part because of questions about the ability of a decentralized regime of nation-specific data protection regulations to maintain adequate levels of protection. European data protection regulators share a perception that decentralization has fuelled a 'race to the bottom' in which US-based information businesses lobby the more permissive regulators for increasingly lenient treatment. At the time of writing, the most recent draft of the proposed revision centralizes authority to define the scope and extent of data protection obligations in the Commission, and purports to establish more stringent standards for obtaining valid consumer consent. Much remains to be seen about the scope and success of that effort. In particular, it is unclear whether and how the proposed regulation will substantially change existing norms of widespread disclosure and sharing via social media.

Information flow and 'the idea of power itself'

Emerging patterns of interdiction and modulation within information networks challenge the prevailing understanding of power within legal thinking. For lawyers, the preeminent form of power is the power of state sovereigns to control their borders and discipline their populations, and the preeminent modality of power is the capacity for physical violence. From a purely taxonomic perspective, that understanding is out-dated. Foucault (1983, 2007) argued that the condition of modernity was characterized by the emergence of the capacity to discipline populations through organization and statistical normalization and by a shifting of pastoral power, or the power to define the individual as cultural subject, from the church to the state. Both of these conceptions of power attenuate the connection between power and violence and align power instead with knowledge practices that discipline though habituation. Deleuze (1995) thought that to speak at all about discipline was somewhat outdated, and the prevailing modality of power in the information age was no longer discipline, but rather control, as manifested through the ability to direct flows of capital, information and people.

The patterns of information flow emerging in the domains of copyright and information privacy/data protection illustrate these themes of discipline and control, and also reveal a dispersal of power over information from states to non-state actors and institutions. The purpose of interdiction-based copyright enforcement strategies is not to suppress (or censor) global flows of culture; without movement the culture industries would have no markets. Rather, it is to nurture markets for globalized forms of mass culture by channelling flows of cultural goods into authorized circuits, within which they can be experienced in the authorized ways. But because creation and cultural participation require borrowing, appropriation, and play (Cohen 2012a, 2012b), this shift has important consequences for both cultural development and subject-formation. It affects the everyday practices of individuals and communities, constraining interactions with and around cultural artefacts and channelling cultural development into preferred outlets. Marketing practices designed to extend the reach of global entertainment and information brands further reinforce authorized cultural and discursive practices and brand other practices as disobedient (Coombe 1998). Processes of gamification and crowd-sourcing of creative work broaden participation in cultural development but also reinforce capital's power to command labour; in such arrangements, consumers gain a measure of agency but also double as voluntary information workers (Terranova 2013). All of these practices exploit what Nygren and Gidlund (2012) call the pastoral power of technology, or the power of digital technologies to shape narratives of the self, under economic conditions in which ordinary people are alienated from the process of shaping.

Power over flows of personal information repeats the same patterns. Modulation is, first and foremost, a highly granular, feedback-driven approach to the study, organization and ongoing management of populations of consumers. But the entities that engage in modulation are not simply disciplining participation in the evolving global marketplace for goods and services. Like the purveyors of mass culture, they are also evoking our participation in our own construction as cultural subjects – and indeed self-surveillance has become an important form of mass culture (Ball 2009). Some practices of self-surveillance operate directly on the body, particularly those that exploit the growing popular fascination with the 'quantified self'; others seek to make visible and to instrumentalize (Steeves and Regan 2014) the networks of relationships within which consumers are located.

Modulation also represents a distinctive approach to knowledge production, one that appropriates for its practitioners a particular kind of power over knowledge. It expresses a highly fact-intensive mode of rationality that equates information with truth and pattern-identification with understanding. Practitioners of highly data-intensive forms of modulation argue strenuously that the resulting knowledge is neutral, and resist the idea that information processing designed simply to identify 'patterns' and 'preferences' might be systematically infused with a particular ideology. But the techniques of modulation are deployed in ways that align with a distinct, albeit deeply internalized, system of values: one that is calculative, instrumental, and unreflective. Participants in the personal information economy:

> rely on the flows of information to construct pricing and risk management templates that maximize the [. . .] ability to identify high-value consumers and to extract surplus from all consumers.
>
> (Cohen 2013: 1916)

Modulation identifies these uses of personal information as the highest and best uses.

Emerging patterns of interdiction and modulation frame a relationship between truth and power that is multiple, fractal and unprecedentedly intimate. The political becomes personal: as search and social networking become more seamlessly integrated, networked individuals move within personalized 'filter bubbles' (Pariser 2011) that both nudge them in profit-maximizing directions and conform the information environment to their political and ideological commitments. Modulation shapes and produces preferences for choices to be presented – choices not only among goods and services, but also among information sources, facts, theories and opinions. Meanwhile, interdiction takes other options off the table, foreclosing prohibited or undesirable interactions with cultural artefacts and forms. This twofold process aims to produce a particular kind of subject, the citizen-consumer, 'whose preferred modes of self-determination play out along predictable and profit-generating trajectories' (Cohen 2013: 1917). It also produces a different sort of relationship to reality. There has never been a single, Archimedean point from which to observe the world; truths about the world, and about power, have always been a function of perspective. Even so, the combination of modulation and interdiction represents something new: the continual production of multiple, finely differentiated truths carefully calibrated to their recipients, each subtly reinforced by protocols and norms that standardize interactions with cultural content. Under such circumstances, speaking truth to power becomes a much more complicated proposition.

This brief discussion of the power relationships emerging within information and communications networks suggests important questions to ask about the con-figuration of information architectures and the uses to which such architectures are put. In particular, if the most important kind of power is the power to choose between domination and human flourishing, then we should want to know whether emerging patterns of information flow are pre-empting pathways that people might have an interest in choosing. As we see next, however, asking those questions is becoming more difficult because information law and policy are evolving in ways that make private assertions of power less salient and less troubling.

The (re)conceptualization of information rights and harms

The rule of law is often conceptualized as a means for restraining the illegitimate exercise of power. Yet law is neither separate from nor conceptually independent of the larger social and economic systems within which it takes root. Law reproduces and reinforces the power relations that society accepts as natural and normal. This inevitable bias affects the legal system's ability to detect and restrain excessive power, and so it is a source of systemic risk. Specifically, in a capitalist political economy, law may fail to recognize and respond effectively to the forms of domination enabled by private economic power, and instead may characterize such results as the natural and normal outcomes of market processes. Within the US legal system in particular, this tendency is an old one. Both the legal realists' challenge to purportedly neutral regimes of property and contract and the critical legal theorists' challenge to the invocation of the public-private distinction to shield the behaviour of market actors from judicial scrutiny addressed the legal embedding of private economic domination. But the shift now underway within regimes of information law and policy on both sides of the Atlantic is deeper and more fundamental than a failure of recognition. As part of the ongoing definition and reconceptualization of rights, the public is becoming the handmaiden of the private. Private economic rights increasingly are understood as the highest and best way of pursuing even important public purposes.

This section of the chapter continues the stories of copyright and information privacy/data protection, but shifts the focus from the evolution of architectures and business models to the conceptualization of legal rights and obligations. The story of copyright becomes a tale of co-optation, in which rights of authors are redefined as incentives for information intermediaries. The story of information privacy/data protection becomes a tale of assimilation, in which the concept of privacy is redefined as waiver and in which more substantive visions of data protection are positioned as opposed to both free speech and innovation. Together, the two stories reveal the extent to which conceptions of private economic liberty have become potent drivers of doctrinal and theoretical neoliberalization within emerging regimes of information law and policy.

Co-optation: the case of copyright

Formally, questions about the optimal scope of copyright present a balancing problem. On one hand, copyright is understood on both sides of the Atlantic as effectuating fundamental values. The International Covenant on Economic, Social, and Cultural Rights (ICESCR) recognizes the right of an individual:

> [t]o benefit from the protection of the moral and material interests resulting from any scientific, literary or artistic production of which he is the author.[8]

Although the US Constitution frames the copyright power in utilitarian terms, legislators, courts and commentators also describe copyright protection as promoting deontological values relating both to the natural rights of authors and to the stability of ownership rights more generally. On the other hand, there is general agreement that overbroad copyright protection and overly aggressive copyright enforcement would destabilize other foundational commitments, including fundamental rights of speech and privacy, rule of law values such as notice and fair process, and the promotion of cultural and scientific progress. When both halves of the balance are articulated, the stage appears set for a careful process of boundary definition that would recognize the importance of considerations on both sides.

Increasingly, however, considerations of private economic interest masquerading as concern for authorship have been interpreted to trump other guarantees. Powerful global entertainment companies argue that aggressive enforcement of their 'property' rights does not contradict, but rather advances, speech values. Courts accepting this reasoning have tended to conclude that rights to freedom of speech, and also to privacy, end wherever another's copyright begins. So, for example, in *Eldred v Ashcroft*, the US Supreme Court reasoned that:

> [t]he First Amendment securely protects the freedom to make—or decline to make—one's own speech; it bears less heavily when speakers assert the right to make other people's speeches.[9]

The professed solicitude for authorship in these decisions masks the political and economic substance of what is really occurring. Copyright as it functions within contemporary legal systems is not operating as a human right; it is a commercial entitlement system that functions principally to promote the interests of the copyright assignees and other intermediaries. Within the US copyright system, the fig leaf of solicitude for authorship has become nearly transparent. Hearings on proposed legislation overwhelmingly concern the balance of power between established and would-be intermediaries. Incumbent copyright intermediaries regularly produce authors to testify about the importance of strong copyright protection. Often forgotten by all parties to this process is the fact that publishers, record companies and movie producers who style themselves as advancing the interests of authors are not themselves authors, but rather entrenched middlemen that have grown accustomed to claiming for themselves the status of authors-by-proxy. The courts as a rule have been more perceptive about the differences between authors and intermediaries, but seem to have decided that it does not matter because the interests of the two groups are presumptively aligned. They reason that incentives to intermediaries serve the purpose of stimulating creative work just as incentives to authors might do.

If one takes the European view of the dignity of authorship, whether copyright motivates creation might seem to be irrelevant; what is important, instead, is that protection of copyrights expresses respect for authorship after the fact. Yet this does not seem to be what European copyright is really about, either. Copyright developments in Europe also seem to proceed primarily at the behest of powerful corporate interests. The interdiction-based enforcement strategies pursued by European collective rights organizations have very little to do with the dignity of authorship. The three-step test for exceptions and limitations, which is mandated by European copyright directives and implemented in national laws, has evolved in a way that disserves the interests of authors as users who must explore, borrow and sample to create. It seems principally designed to ensure that established copyright intermediaries receive remuneration (Geiger 2006).

Assimilation: the case of information privacy/data protection

Formally, determining the optimal scope of information privacy protection also requires balancing, and here the doctrinal landscape reveals much less consensus on what is to be balanced. To begin with, European and US legal traditions differ on the importance of privacy. The European Convention on Human Rights[10] enshrines privacy as a fundamental right, while US legal culture is more grudging on this point, according constitutional protection to different types of privacy interests in more piecemeal fashion. European and US legal traditions also differ in important ways on the scope of freedom of speech and the press with respect to publication of private information about individuals. As a practical matter, however, there has been increasing convergence around the importance of consent as a standard for assessing compliance with legal obligations to protect personal information. This is so even though the two traditions do not understand the role of consent in the same way. The result is that, although baseline levels of protection in the United States and Europe differ starkly, consent-based practices surrounding privacy can work in a way that elides differences in first principles.[11]

The gravitational pull of consent-based reasoning is strongest in the United States. Privacy policymakers rely almost exclusively on what Daniel Solove (2013) calls the 'privacy self-management' paradigm, and both privacy sceptics and privacy advocates employ a vernacular that reveals the primacy of private choice. Information processing practices in the private sector have sought to capitalize on this orientation. Companies that process personal information tend to request broad, forward-looking consent based on vague, general descriptions of the sorts of uses that are contemplated. The European data protection framework envisions a much more limited role for consent as a basis for personal information process- ing. Most notably, consent stands in tension with the purpose limitation principle, which directs that personal information not be processed in ways incom- patible with the purpose for which it was collected. Formally, the interactions between consent and the purpose limitation principle are complex. On one hand, renewed consent can justify later processing for a new, incompatible purpose; on the other, consent is not supposed to become a mechanism for evading purpose limitations entirely.[12] In daily life, however, individuals wanting access to the social media services offered by global (often US-based) internet companies have elected to signal both initial and renewed consent by the means provided. Whether the reforms now underway will achieve a meaningful resolution of the divergence between law and practice remains to be seen.

The current draft of the proposed new data protection regulation attempts to minimize the potential for abuse of consent as a basis for personal information processing by requiring consent to be 'given explicitly by any appropriate method enabling a freely given specific and informed indication of the data subject's wishes', and to be solicited in a manner 'not unnecessarily disruptive to the use of the service for which it is provided' (European Commission 2012: Preamble 25). Faith in the possibility of meaningful indicia of consent, however, runs headlong into a growing body of research on the behavioural economics of privacy tending to suggest that providing meaningful notice is extremely difficult (Acquisti and Grossklags 2007), and that consumer-protective defaults are inevita- bly 'slippery' and amenable to manipulation (Willis 2013). This research raises hard questions about whether a consent-based standard for personal information processing can ever be meaningful. The proposed regulation attempts to counter the risk of slippery defaults by prohibiting reliance on consent in cases of 'a sig- nificant imbalance between the position of the data subject and the controller' (European Commission 2012: Article 7(4)). Examples of such an imbalance include data processing by employers and public authorities; it is unclear whether, and under what circumstances, data processing by commercial service providers would qualify. The answer to that question may determine whether the regula- tion's principal achievement will simply be greater disclosure about information processing practices, or whether it will result in more substantive protection for individuals.

Within US legal discourse about information privacy, an important minor theme relates to freedom of expression. Efforts have long been underway to position information processing as speech and to paint information privacy regulation as an abridgement of expressive freedom. In *Sorrell v IMS Health* (2011), the US Supreme Court appeared to endorse those efforts, ruling that constitutional protection for speech extended to an information-processing programme used to target pharmaceutical marketing to physicians.[13]

Properly understood, *Sorrell* was a market manipulation case rather than an information privacy case. The drug detailing programme in question used information about the past behaviours of prescribing physicians, not patient records, and the state of Vermont sought to regulate the programme principally because it had concluded that detailing activities increased health care costs by encouraging the prescription of brand name drugs. Because the Court found unpersuasive the state's *post hoc* attempts to rely on privacy interests as a justification for its actions, we still do not know how the Court might respond to a case that more directly implicated privacy interests. The analytical framework that the *Sorrell* majority devised, however, suggests that information privacy regulation would face an uphill battle. According to the majority, restrictions on information processing that target particular, disfavoured purposes must survive not only the heightened scrutiny applicable to commercial speech regulation generally, but also an additional layer of scrutiny necessitated by the fact that legislative articulations of disfavoured purposes will inevitably be content-based, or speaker-based, or both. The requirement of double scrutiny represents a departure for the Court's commercial speech jurisprudence. Three justices dissented, and depending on future changes in the Court's makeup, it is possible that the *Sorrell* approach will prove short-lived. If not, however, legislatures and agencies seeking to impose specific, targeted regulatory burdens on information-era commerce will be held to a very high standard indeed.

The European Union has a robust free speech tradition of its own, and that tradition does not purport to prohibit data processing regulation outright. Instead, conflicts between data protection and freedom of speech are resolved by application of the principle of proportionality, which subjects alleged infringements of fundamental rights to a balancing inquiry that also incorporates considerations of due process. At least so far, European data protection discourse has been more resistant to totalizing freedom of speech claims.

The neoliberalization of information law

One might attempt to discover internal, jurisprudential explanations for the state of contemporary legal discourse about information rights, but it bears repeating that law does not develop in a vacuum. Just as tort, contract and property law changed in response to industrialization and the emergence of national markets for goods and services, so the political economy of the emerging networked information society is shaping the evolution of the legal principles and policy discourses that define rights and obligations with respect to information.

The emerging patterns of information flow that the second section of this chapter described reflect (purported) economic imperatives. In the main, today's networked information technologies are developed in ways that serve the needs and priorities of the emergent regime of informational capitalism, and those of the Western, democratic governments that have enabled informational capitalism to thrive. Following Manuel Castells (1996), I use 'informational capitalism' to refer to the alignment of capitalism as a mode of production with informationalism as a mode of development: capitalism 'is oriented toward profit-maximizing, that is, toward increasing the amount of surplus appropriated by capital on the basis of the private control over the means of production and circulation' (Castells 1996: 16), while informationalism 'is oriented [. . .] toward the accumulation of knowledge and towards higher levels of complexity in information processing' (Castells 1996: 17). In a regime of informational capitalism, market actors use knowledge, culture and networked information technologies as means of extracting and appropriating surplus value, including consumer surplus.

The ability of powerful actors to engage in rent-seeking behaviour is well recognized, but within the emerging regime of informational capitalism, powerful actors do not simply deploy their considerable resources to garner advantages in markets and legislative hearing rooms. They also use their resources to shape underlying legal and policy narratives about right and obligation. In particular, they have sought to align these narratives with a political philosophy – neoliberalism – that most closely aligns with their goals. The political philosophy of neoliberalism 'propos[es] that human well-being can best be advanced by the maximization of entrepreneurial freedoms within an institutional framework characterized by private property rights, individual liberty, unencumbered markets, and free trade' (Harvey 2007: 22). Debates about the content of information law and policy reflect intertwined processes of doctrinal and theoretical neoliberalization at work.

The legal and policy discourses about copyright and information privacy/data protection described above reveal growing and ever more explicit reliance on the neoliberal tropes of property and economic liberty. Traditional accounts of copyright stressed the importance of a healthy balance between exclusive rights and limitations and exceptions, emphasizing that both rights and limitations had important roles to play in promoting artistic and cultural progress. Contemporary copyright discourse increasingly prefers a much more simplistic form of property-based reasoning, within which limitations are relegated to the margins. Traditional information privacy/data protection discourse, even in the United States, stressed the importance of a zone of protection against exposure to the world. Contemporary information privacy/data protection discourse, even in Europe, relies heavily on ideas of consent to mediate networked interactions. Debates about the criteria for overriding consent are heavily tinged with anxieties about the moral and welfarist implications of 'paternalism' (e.g. Solove 2013).

Two aspects of the ongoing neoliberalization of information law are worth noting especially carefully. One is the reframing of commercial speech jurisprudence undertaken in *Sorrell*, the case about the state of Vermont's attempt to regulate prescription detailing. Deven Desai (2013) thinks that *Sorrell* is a case about the unconstitutionality of attempts to regulate persuasion. The persuasion model does not quite fit, however. Although the ultimate goal of the detailing programme was to increase sales, it did not do this by persuasion; instead its point was to minimize the need to persuade by identifying and targeting the most likely prospective customers. Put differently, the detailing programme was an attempt to extract surplus more directly and efficiently by concentrating marketing efforts on those most likely to buy. Arguably, *Sorrell* stands for the proposition that operations directed at surplus extraction are to be privileged as speech. If so, then Sorrell is a powerful expression of the ideology of economic liberty. Within US First Amendment scholarship, the decision most often cited as evidence of neoliberalization is *Citizens United v Federal Election Commission* (2010), in which the Court ruled that fictional persons (such as corporations) are people for First Amendment purposes and that restrictions on political speech by corporations therefore must survive First Amendment scrutiny.[14] *Citizens United* and *Sorrell* are cut from the same cloth; together they stand for the proposition that flows of information and flows of money may be converted freely into one another with little fear of encountering regulatory obstacles.

The second aspect of contemporary discourse about information law and policy worth noting carefully is the increasing extent to which regulatory debates about personal information processing include claims about the enabling conditions for continued innovation. Particularly in the United States, but also to an extent in Europe, information businesses have worked hard to cast information privacy/data protection regulation as antiquated and anti-progressive. Sometimes the opposition between privacy and innovation is explicit; at other times it is implicit in rhetoric that aligns innovation with the absence of regulatory restraint. As noted in the second section of this chapter, the vision of innovation advanced by such rhetoric is not a neutral one; it is based on a highly instrumental view of knowledge production as pattern-identification directed toward specific, profit-motivated goals (see also Cohen 2013). As deployed in information policy discourse, it works in tandem with rhetoric about the expressive nature of information processing to foster a regulatory philosophy that shields the US information industries from legal interference.

Together, these discursive strands – property, consent, speech, and innovation – suggest at least the possibility that we are witnessing the emergence of a new and powerful jurisprudence of information rights, one organized comprehensively around neoliberal principles and values. That possibility is worth considering very carefully.

The evolution of governance institutions

The ongoing neoliberalization of information law sketched in the previous section is concerned with more than just the substance of legal restrictions. It also involves the restructuring of law-making processes and governance institutions. In some cases, governance of information processes is devolved to the private sector; in others, new types of governance institutions are evolving. Law-making affecting fundamental rights of communication, privacy and due process now proceeds in some unusual venues, such as trade negotiations and industry standards proceedings. Regulators and judges increasingly defer to the results of such processes and to the asserted needs of powerful corporate interests. When more traditional legal processes are invoked, they seem to be deployed after the fact to ratify results reached elsewhere. More traditional legal institutions – domestic courts, legislatures, and administrative authorities – seem mostly unprepared to engage in the sort of dialogue that is required to participate effectively in emerging processes of networked, transnational governance, and increasingly acquiesce in their own marginalization.

Intellectual property enforcement: governance by trade negotiation

In a time of global economic crisis, protection for domestic copyright industries has come to be seen as an increasingly powerful trade imperative. Officials from both the United States and Europe have eagerly sought opportunities to improve the global position of powerful domestic industries. Over the past two decades, the frequency of multilateral and bilateral treaty negotiations with provisions relating to intellectual property rights has risen dramatically (Valdes and Runyowa 2012). These processes, which now seem to be nearly continuous, have emerged as law-making institutions in their own right. Procedurally speaking, the new networked governance institutions tend to ignore important rule of law values such as transparency and reviewability. In substance, they represent opportunities for neoliberalized narratives of right and obligation to obtain additional leverage within domestic copyright laws.

Trade negotiations for expanded intellectual property protection and enforcement have important implications, first, for the process values that attach to copyright law-making. In stark contrast to domestic legislative processes conducted pursuant to open government mandates, such negotiations have been conducted by trade representatives in close consultation with the affected industries but with very little transparency and correspondingly little democratic accountability to other interested groups. Sometimes embargoes on access also flow the other way; in 2012, representatives of Knowledge Ecology International (KEI), an NGO that has played a prominent role as an advocate for the public interest in both treaty proceedings, recently discovered that the US Patent and Trademark Office had blocked access to the KEI website from its offices.[15]

Trade negotiators' cavalier attitude to open government values has drawn widespread public criticism, and the extent of the new multilateral model's reach is still uncertain. So far, the backlash has produced one notable failure: the Anti-Counterfeiting Trade Agreement (ACTA) negotiated between the United States and Europe failed when the European Parliament rejected the agreement, and the European Commission has withdrawn its referral of the treaty to the European Court of Justice. But here again a high-profile failure may be followed by more lasting success. Leaked drafts of the agreement now being negotiated within the Trans-Pacific Partnership (TPP) include provisions modelled on the specific provisions of US law that have supplied so much incentive for private 'self-regulation'. Some of the TPP counterparties lack strong open government traditions, and it is unclear whether any nations in the TPP group have both the bargaining power and the will to emulate Europe. Meanwhile, the United States and Europe have embarked on new negotiations towards a 'Transatlantic Trade and Investment Partnership' (TTIP).

Trade negotiations for expanded intellectual property protection and enforcement also have important implications for the substance of copyright law. So far, US negotiators appear to have devoted their energies to pressuring other countries to implement takedown and indirect liability regimes. It is still undetermined whether future treaty processes, or the TPP negotiation now underway, will seek to move beyond those requirements in a way that reverses recent domestic rejections of enhanced copyright enforcement measures (see the second section of this chapter). Yet there is very little safeguard against this.

No regularized mechanisms exist for requiring trade negotiators to consider, and systematically account for, effects on fundamental rights, and established procedures for recognizing and vindicating fundamental rights lack reliable purchase within the dispute resolution frameworks that attach to trade agreements. In domestic litigation challenging legislated expansions of copyright, US courts seem increasingly prone to accept asserted trade imperatives as arguments for deference. Thus, for example, in upholding legislation restoring copyright to works by nationals of Berne Convention[16] member states that had passed into the public domain due to failure to comply with formalities, the Supreme Court reasoned:

> Full compliance with Berne, Congress had reason to believe, would expand the foreign markets available to U. S. authors and invigorate protection against piracy of U. S. works abroad, [. . . .] thereby benefitting copyright-intensive industries stateside and inducing greater investment in the creative process.[17]

This pattern – gradual privatization of governance accompanied by unclear and possibly non-existent attention to public values – is repeated in other institutional experiments now underway. Systems for automatic, proactive filtering adopted by online service providers do not seem to be subject to judicial review at all; statutory provisions designed to deter bad faith takedowns target right holders, not service providers. Systems for extrajudicial enforcement of copyright, such as the French HADOPI and the nascent 'six strikes' regime, are ways of processing individuals through systems for mass resolution of disputes. Unlike the class action device for plaintiffs, however, systems for mass processing of defendants do not inevitably function as levelling devices and may have the opposite effect. The risks of abuse are heightened under privately agreed sanction regimes like the one now in place in the United States. In the civil litigation context, US courts have begun to resist what they perceive as overly broad and abusive discovery efforts in cases brought by so-called copyright trolls. It remains to be seen whether US courts will emulate the French solution of requiring judicial oversight if 'six strikes' cases involving more respectable right holders filter into the court system, and how meaningful that oversight might be.

Information privacy at a crossroads: the United States, the European Union and the new privacy governance

In the domain of information privacy/data protection, institutional innovation has been shaped by the tension between the American preference for self-regulation and the European preference for a stronger regulatory baseline. On both sides of the Atlantic, however, we are witnessing the gradual emergence of a constellation of new governance forms designed to smooth the way for cross-border operation by information businesses.

Information privacy policymaking in the United States increasingly conforms to a regulatory paradigm known as the 'new governance', which entails significant devolution of regulatory authority to private entities or public-private partnerships (Freeman 2000; Lobel 2004). Normatively speaking, the paradigm of new governance is rooted in a regulatory ideology that systematically downplays the need to hold market actors accountable for harms to the public interest. New governance initiatives and rhetoric express what Jodi Short (2012: 635) has called the 'paranoid style' in regulatory reform: an intense worry about the risks of state coercion and/ or bumbling, combined with relative insensitivity to the ramifications of private power, that produces 'a regulatory reform discourse that is antithetical to the very idea of government regulation'.

The new privacy governance reflects this ideology in action. Rather than pursuing command-and-control regulation, public entities lead by exhortation and norm entrepreneurship, extracting private-sector commitments to follow so-called 'best practices' that reflect significant private-sector input and using their enforcement powers principally to ensure that information businesses live up to their own stated commitments. This approach may seem appealing precisely because US privacy regulation is sectoral and grants of jurisdiction are correspondingly limited; privacy regulators operating within limited spheres of authority likely see the new governance as an effective way of leveraging their powers. In discussions with European data protection regulators, the US Department of Commerce has adopted the role of evangelist for the new privacy governance, advocating a minimalist approach to regulation so that information businesses will enjoy maximum leeway and positioning that approach as essential to continued technological innovation.

The European proposal to centralize data protection regulation within the Commission, meanwhile, might seem to be an exception to the proposition that governance is migrating outside government. Instead, the debate over the proposed regulation appears to present the usual choices about the pros and cons of centralization versus decentralization. For the US observer, it is tempting simply to approach the problem through the distinctively American lens of federalism as the 'laboratory of the states'. Thus, one might argue that centralization is suspect because it eliminates the ability of the European member states to discover more effective regulatory strategies, much as California did with its pioneering data breach legislation. Yet there is more going on than meets the eye.

The Data Protection Directive represented an exercise of the principle of subsidiarity, which requires decentralized governance by the European member states wherever feasible. The Commission has advanced two principal justifications for centralizing regulatory authority over data protection. One is the power and reach of global information businesses such as Google, Facebook and Apple; arguably, to regulate effectively and to offer a meaningful counterweight to American laxity, Europe must speak with a more unified voice than the framework of the Data Protection Directive permits. The other, tellingly, sounds in administrative convenience. The regime embodied in the Directive has encountered powerful resistance from global data processing firms that viewed the resulting patchwork of national compliance requirements as expensive and unwieldy. The effort to rewrite the Directive to provide for boilerplate clauses and binding corporate rules may be seen as an effort to smooth things over with global data processing companies while ratcheting them up to a higher level of compliance with the European data protection regime's substantive provisions.

And so the struggle over subsidiarity is also a struggle between demands of the traditional paradigm, which stresses political accountability, and the impetus of neoliberalization, which seeks to reduce barriers to global economic enterprise. At a fundamental level, the purpose of data protection regulation is contested; even its proponents seem unable to agree whether the point is to establish a single clear, transparent footing for data processing and exchange or to impose meaningful substantive limits on the uses of information (see discussion in Schwartz 2013). This incoherence is deeply embedded in the history of data protection law; the original fair information principles articulated by the Organisation for Economic Co-operation and Development (1980) stressed the importance of self-regulation and the economic potential of information flows. The process of centralization also exposes the fault lines between the centralized, technocratic Commission and the more democratically accountable Parliament (Tsoukala 2013) – the same Parliament that, as noted above, voted to reject the ACTA. The law reform process now proceeding in the Commission is not secret, as the ACTA process was. Even so, there is concern that centralization also benefits global information companies from a process standpoint, because their (considerable) powers of persuasion can be concentrated on a single set of recipients and because their resources may allow them greater access to government officials.

All of this tends to suggest that the vaunted European data protection framework is undergoing a (largely unacknowledged) moment of crisis, which concerns whether it will be assimilated into the ongoing neoliberalization of information law, and into the emerging framework of the new privacy governance. The story is an unfinished one; it may well be true that centralization and harmonization are needed to enable meaningful regulatory leverage over global data processing enterprises. Much will depend on the Commission's willingness to grant itself the enhanced enforcement powers described in the original proposal, and to wield those powers once granted, and that remains to be seen.

Conclusion: three challenges for the future

The line of inquiry pursued here has suggested that networked information technologies enabled a qualitative, cumulative change in how power is to be exercised in the twenty-first century. This is not due to any inevitable attribute or configuration of such technologies; rather, it is due to their plasticity, which offers multiple points of entry for the exercise of power, and to the tendency of legal systems within capitalist political economies to interpret the exercise of private economic power as enlightened self-interest. If the most important kind of power is the power to choose between domination and fostering human wellbeing, then speaking truth to power in the twenty-first century requires opening a dialogue about the structural conditions of information freedom, and about the law's capacity to guard against or minimize its own ideological and institutional capture.

Until very recently, human rights narratives have had very little to say about any of this beyond the purely hortatory. A United Nations Special Rapporteur's Report (2011) has now recommended attention to the effects of filtering, blocking and takedown obligations on fundamental freedoms of expression. Such concrete inquiries are certainly a good idea, but there is a more basic problem. Emerging networked legal institutions systematically marginalize the institutions and legal frameworks that traditionally have borne responsibility for defending and advancing fundamental rights and other legal rights of natural persons. When the premier modes of law-making are trade negotiations and private best practices agreements, pursuing such a dialogue requires more than mere philosophy; it requires a politics capable of penetrating the insular worlds of trade policy and technical expertise, and it requires a counter-agenda for institutional innovation.

Legal scholars are beginning to grapple more systematically with the implications of privatized governance of information flows within global circuits of economic power, and with the gradual capture of law-making processes by regimes of global informational capitalism. Responding to controversies such as the struggle to assert authority over WikiLeaks and the push for the internet kill switch, Derek Bambauer (2012) argues that what is needed is a 'due process of censorship' that would establish procedural and transparency requirements for state control of information flows. That is fine as far as it goes, but the proposal does not address the effects of private economic power, or attempt to unravel the interlocking processes of interdiction, authorization and modulation that are reconfiguring global information networks. Important works by scholars such as Annemarie Bridy (2012), Danielle Citron (2007), Paul Ohm (2010), Frank Pasquale (2013), and others tackle the problems of privatized governance more directly. Following in the footsteps of the legal realists and the critical legal theorists, these scholars are seeking strategies for speaking truth to private economic power, and for holding such power accountable for human wellbeing.

A more comprehensive account of the role of law in information governance must answer the following three sets of questions. First, how are networked information technologies used to produce and entrench power, and what effects do those processes have on human wellbeing? Second, how does the evolving content of information law and policy contribute to the production and entrenchment of power? Lastly, how are governance institutions changing in response to the production and assertion of power in networked information environment? With those answers in hand, we can begin to consider how legal institutions might evolve to serve all of the constituencies whose lives they touch.

Notes

1 Philip Elmer-Dewitt, 'First Nation in Cyberspace', *Time Magazine*, 6 December 1993.
2 Jacqui Cheng, 'DMCA Abuse Extends to Twitter Posts', *Ars Technica*, 26 April 2010, http://arstechnica.com/tech-policy/2010/04/dmca-abuse-extends-to-twitter-posts/ (accessed 19 January 2016); Mike Masnick, 'Major Hollywood Studios All Sent Bogus DMCA Takedowns Concerning The Pirate Bay Documentary', *TechDirt*, 20 May 2013, www.techdirt.com/articles/20130520/11552823150/major-hollywood-studios-all-sent-bogus-dmca-takedowns-concerning-pirate-bay-documentary.shtml (accessed 19 January 2016).
3 *Scarlet Extended SA v Société belge des auteurs, compositeurs et éditeurs SCRL (SABAM)*, [2012] ECDR 4, ¶45.
4 Haute Autorité pour la Diffusion des Œuvres et la Protection des droits d'auteur sur Internet 2009.
5 Directive 95/46/EC of the European Parliament and of the Council of 24 October 1995 on the protection of individuals with regard to the processing of personal data and on the free movement of such data, [1995] OJ L 281/31.
6 Cyrus Farivar, 'How One Law Student Is Making Facebook Get Serious About Privacy', *Ars Technica*, 15 November 2012, http://arstechnica.com/tech-policy/2012/11/how-one-law-student-is-making-facebook-get-serious-about-privacy/ (accessed 19 January 2016).
7 Judgment of the Court of 6 November 2003 in Case C-101/01 *(Reference for a preliminary ruling from the Göta hovrätt): Bodil Lindqvist*, [2004] OJ C7/3.
8 ICESCR, Art 15(1)(c).
9 *Eldred v Ashcroft*, 537 US 186, 221 (2003).
10 European Convention for the Protection of Human Rights and Fundamental Freedoms 1950.
11 European Convention on Human Rights, Art 8; US Const. amdts. I, IV, V, IX.
12 Opinion of the Article 29 data protection working party of 03/2013 on purpose limitation (WP 203).
13 *Sorrell v IMS Health, Inc.*, 131 S. Ct. 2653 (2011).
14 *Citizens United v Federal Election Commission*, 558 US 310 (2010).
15 James Love, 'USPTO blocks web access to "Political/Activist Groups" including KEI, ACLU, EFF, Public Citizen, Redstate, DailyKos', *KEIonline*, 18 September 2012.
16 Berne Convention for the Protection of Literary and Artistic Works 1886.
17 *Golan v Holder*, 132 S. Ct. 873, 889 (2012).

References

Acquisti, A. and Grossklags, J. (2007) 'What Can Behavioral Economics Teach Us About Privacy?' In A. Acquisti, S. Gritzalis, C. Lambrinoudakis and S. di Vimercati (eds) *Digital Privacy: Theory, Technologies and Practices*. Boca Raton, FL: Taylor & Francis: 363–378.

American Friends Service Committee (1955) *Speak Truth to Power: A Quaker Search for an Alternative to Violence*. Philadelphia, PA: American Friends Service Committee.

Ball, K.S. (2009) 'Exposure: Exploring the Subject of Surveillance'. *Information, Communication, and Society* 12(5): 639–657.

Bambauer, D.E. (2012) 'Orwell's Armchair'. *University of Chicago Law Review* 79(3): 863–944.

Bridy, A. (2012) 'Graduated Response American Style: "Six Strikes" Measured Against Five Norms'. *Fordham Intellectual Property, Media and Entertainment Law Journal* 23(1): 1–67.

Castells, M. (1996) *The Rise of the Network Society*. New York, NY: Wiley-Blackwell.

Citron, D.K. (2007) 'Reservoirs of Danger: The Evolution of Public and Private Law at the Dawn of the Information Age'. *Southern California Law Review* 80(2): 241–297.

Cohen, J.E. (2012a) *Configuring the Networked Self: Law, Code, and the Play of Everyday Practice*. New Haven, CT: Yale University Press.

——. (2012b) 'Configuring the Networked Citizen'. In A. Sarat, L. Dougals and M. Merrill Umphrey (eds) *Imagining New Legalities: Privacy and Its Possibilities in the 21st Century*. Stanford, CA: Stanford University Press: 129–153.

——. (2013) 'What Privacy Is For?' *Harvard Law Review* 126(7): 1904–1933.

Coombe, R. (1998) *The Cultural Life of Intellectual Properties: Authorship, Appropriation, and Law*. Durham, NC: Duke University Press.

de Sola Pool, I. (1984) *Technologies of Freedom*. Cambridge, MA: Harvard Belknap Press.

Deleuze, G. (1995) 'Postscript on Control Societies'. In *Negotiations 1972–1990*. Transl. by Martin Joughin. New York, NY: Columbia University Press.

Desai, D.R. (2013) 'Speech, Citizenry, and the Market'. *Minnesota Law Review* 98(2): 455–510.

Elmer, G. (2004) *Profiling Machines: Mapping the Personal Information Economy*. Cambridge, MA: MIT Press.

European Commission (2012) Proposal for a Regulation of the European Parliament and of the Council on the protection of individuals with regard to the processing of personal data and on the free movement of such data (General Data Protection Regulation). COM(2012) 11 final.

Foucault, M. (1983) 'Afterword: The Subject and Power'. In M. Foucault, *Beyond Structuralism and Hermeneutics*, 2nd edn. Chicago, IL: University of Chicago Press: 208–226.

——. (2007) *Security, Territory, Population: Lectures at the College de France 1977–1978*. Transl. by G. Burchell. New York, NY: Picador.

Freeman, J. (2000) 'The Private Role in Public Governance'. *New York University Law Review* 75(3): 543–675.

Geiger, C. (2006) 'The Three-Step Test: A Threat to a Balanced Copyright Law?' *International Review of Intellectual Property and Competition Law* 37(6): 683–699.

Goldman, E. (2012) 'Why Did Google Flip-Flop on Cracking Down on "Rogue" Websites? Some Troubling Possibilities'. *Forbes*, 25 August 2012.

Harvey, D. (2007) 'Neoliberalism as Creative Destruction'. *Annals of the American Academy of Political Science* 610: 22–44.

Hoofnagle, C.J. (2004) 'Big Brother's Little Helpers: How ChoicePoint and Other Commercial Data Brokers Collect and Package Your Data for Law Enforcement'. *North Carolina Journal of International Law and Commercial Regulation* 29(4): 595–637.

Lessig, L. (1998) *Code and Other Laws of Cyberspace*. New York, NY: Basic Books.

Lobel, O. (2004) 'The Renew Deal: The Fall of Regulation and the Rise of Governance in Contemporary Legal Thought'. *Minnesota Law Review* 89(2): 342–470.

MacKinnon, R. (2012) *Consent of the Networked: The Worldwide Struggle for Internet Freedom*. New York, NY: Basic Books.

Nygren, K.G. and Gidlund, K.L. (2012) 'The Pastoral Power of Technology: Rethinking Alienation in Digital Culture'. *TripleC* 10(2): 509–517.

Ohm, P. (2010) 'Broken Promises of Privacy: Responding to the Surprising Failure of Anonymization'. *UCLA Law Review* 57(6): 1701–1777.

Organisation for Economic Co-operation and Development (1980) Recommendation of the Council concerning Guidelines Governing the Protection of Privacy and Transborder Flows of Personal Data, available at www.oecd.org/sti/ieconomy/oecdguidelinesonthe protectionofprivacyandtransborderflowsofpersonaldata.htm (accessed 19 January 2016).

Pariser, E. (2011) *The Filter Bubble: What the Internet Is Hiding from You*. New York, NY: Penguin.

Pasquale, F. (2013) *The Black Box Society: Technologies of Reputation, Search, and Finance*. Cambridge, MA: Harvard University Press.

Schwartz, P. (2013) 'The E.U.-U.S. Privacy Collision'. *Harvard Law Review* 126(7): 1966–2009.

Seltzer, W. (2010) 'Free Speech Unmoored in Copyright's Safe Harbor: Chilling Effects of the DMCA on the First Amendment'. *Harvard Journal of Law and Technology* 24(1): 171–232.

Short, J.L. (2012) 'The Paranoid Style in Regulatory Reform'. *Hastings Law Journal* 63(3): 633–694.

Solove, D.J. (2013) 'Introduction: Privacy Self-Management and the Consent Dilemma'. *Harvard Law Review* 126(7): 1880–1903.

Steeves, V. and Regan, P. (2014) 'Young People Online and the Social Value of Privacy'. *Journal of Information, Communication and Ethics in Society* 12(4): 298–313.

Terranova, T. (2013) 'Free Labor'. In T. Scholz (ed.) *Digital Labor: The Internet as Playground and Factory*. New York, NY: Routledge: 33–57.

Tsoukala, P. (2013) 'Euro Zone Crisis Management and the New Social Europe'. *Columbia Journal of European Law* 20(1): 31–76.

United Nations (2011) Report of the Special Rapporteur on the promotion and protection of the right to freedom of opinion and expression. A/HRC/17/27 (16 May), available at www2.ohchr.org/english/bodies/hrcouncil/docs/17session/A.HRC.17.27_en.pdf (accessed 19 January 2016).

Urban, J. and Quilter, L. (2005) 'Efficient Process or "Chilling Effects"? Takedown Notices under Section 512 of the Digital Millennium Copyright Act'. *Santa Clara Computer and High Technology Law Journal* 22(4): 621–693.

Valdes, R. and Runyowa, T. (2012) 'Intellectual Property Provisions in Regional Trade Agreements', available at http://papers.ssrn.com/sol3/papers.cfm?abstract_id=2174333 (accessed 19 January 2016).

Willis, L.E. (2013) 'When Nudges Fail: Slippery Defaults'. *University of Chicago Law Review* 80(3): 1155–1229.

Chapter 4

Data subjects or data citizens?
Addressing the global regulatory challenge of big data

Linnet Taylor

When we share personal data with others, we usually have an expectation about the purposes for which the data will be used.

– Article 29 Working Party (2013: 4)[1]

Even if you are looking at purely anonymized data on the use of mobile phones, carriers could predict your age to within in some cases plus or minus one year with over 70 percent accuracy. They can predict your gender with between 70 and 80 percent accuracy. One carrier in Indonesia told us they can tell what your religion is by how you use your phone. You can see the population moving around.

– Robert Kirkpatrick, UN Global Pulse (2012)[2]

Introduction

There is an inevitable ethnocentrism currently at play in debates about the power of data and the power over data. 'Global' data problems and solutions are conceived as beginning and ending in regions with meaningful and enforceable data protection regulation, namely the United States, the European Union and a small group of other countries of the Organisation for Economic Co-operation and Development (OECD) tightly bound to these regions by trade, such as Canada. Thus the 'we' of the Article 29 Working Party's statement quoted above is clear and justifiable in those regional contexts, but becomes hugely problematic when it is applied to the majority of people in the world. For these 'other' six billion, who live and use technology outside high-income countries (HICs) with clear data protection provisions, even an effort towards purpose limitation such as that quoted above raises some serious questions. Julie Cohen's exploration of the ways in which code mediates between truth and power (this volume at Chapter 3) is not only pertinent in the United States and the European Union where regulation battles are primarily being fought, but becomes even more applicable in places where information flows have even higher stakes. As a Zimbabwean participant in the 2005 World Summit on the Information Society put it when discussing internet freedom, 'if we have no freedom of speech, we can't talk about who is stealing our food' (MacKinnon 2012: 205).

Taking the implications of Cohen's analysis into the context of lower-income countries demonstrates how flows of data mediate power in myriad of ways, even where most people are not yet internet users. Let us take as an example a data analysis competition involving data from Côte d'Ivoire. In 2012, mobile company Orange released a year's anonymized call records from all its Ivorian subscribers (the D4D project) (Blondel et al. 2012). This was the first major release to researchers of this type of 'big data' stemming from a low- or middle-income country (LMIC), and the first to be labelled a development project. As such, the release gained huge publicity after it was endorsed by the United Nations, the World Economic Forum and a host of high-profile academic institutions including MIT and Cambridge University. Since the data were anonymized and blurred, subscribers were not asked for their consent to the release of their data. Yet this was not European data: it was gathered in Côte d'Ivoire, at the end of a year of civil war in that country, and despite its anonymization researchers were still able to derive communication networks and mobility patterns which in turn identified potentially sensitive ethnic and spatial characteristics and ties. Nor were national authorities invited to outline development aims which might be relevant to this 'development research'. Only one of the 250 research teams who received the data visited Côte d'Ivoire, and the project was governed by no national or international regulations or ethical framework with regard to the privacy of the individuals involved, or the subsequent use or sharing of the data – because such regulations and frameworks do not exist.

For mobile phone users such as those in the Orange D4D project, living in a Sub-Saharan African country with no enforceable regulations dealing with digital data, and using a network provider whose parent company is based in the European Union, the debates currently taking place in the European Union and United States about data regulation may seem irrelevant at best. If a network provider wants to share users' data in their own country or beyond, for research, commercial or 'development' purposes, as is occurring increasingly often, it becomes necessary to revisit the Working Party's statement. Who are 'we'? How do 'we' find out that 'our' data is being shared, and with whom? Is local knowledge considered relevant in assessing how to prevent harm from such a data release? What happens when the 'others' with whom data is to be shared are located in a political and legal system that is not in dialogue with ours or at least incentivized to find elements of compatibility, as is the case with the European Union and United States? And, perhaps most importantly, how are technology users to develop an 'expectation about the purposes for which the data will be used' in contexts where they suffer from disproportionate information asymmetries?

This chapter focuses on the question of how big data's potential and risks can be reconciled with regard to the global data landscape. 'Big data' is defined here as any dataset or, especially, combination of datasets which make possible an unprecedented depth and breadth of analysis on a particular question (Schroeder 2014). It is also possible to define big data as more a process than a type of dataset or particular product, where it is characterized by merging, linking and analysing across databases and data types. These characteristics raise new challenges to privacy, which are often illustrated more clearly by the context of the 'other six billion', where rules and standards are still in flux and where ethical debates are still being defined. I argue that considering this context can lead researchers to some new questions with universal relevance for conceptualizing privacy, and to some practical approaches to what might be termed 'emerging harms' relating to the misuse of digital data.

It would not be too extreme to say that there are two distinct contexts in which data is emitted, used and shared today: one where regulation exists and has traction, even though issues of jurisdiction and the compatibility of standards may be under strenuous debate, and another where firms and governments are free to gather, process and share digital data under conditions of self-regulation. These contexts may overlap, for instance with regard to intelligence services in HICs, but in general can be taken as a proxy for the divide between HICs and LMICs. I analyse the implications of these contextual differences with reference to what Scott (1998) has termed 'legibility' – the way in which citizens become visible, or legible, to authorities through data collection and analysis. These authorities may be governmental, since one central role of a functioning state is to establish the legibility of its citizens through the collection and processing of statistical data. However, in the era of big data the actors involved are changing as the private sector takes a leading role in generating, processing and acting on big data. This shift is giving rise to another where the state's role in identifying, classifying and intervening merges with that of corporations,[3] a process in which we can distinguish the reproduction of power relations through information technology (or what Deleuze (1992) has termed 'modulation').

This merging of state and corporate interests is progressing particularly freely in LMICs,[4] where corporate-sponsored 'dataveillance' using big data is being posited as a way to supplement – or replace – underfunded or understaffed state statistical apparatuses (Taylor and Schroeder 2015). Here, private-sector dataveillance, and the flow of data between corporations and international institutions such as development donors is facilitated by claims that better data is indispensable if countries are to develop (Jerven 2013). Supporting this argument is a widespread notion that people in developing countries do not care about privacy, or have such different perceptions of it that general standards for privacy-related data protection become meaningless when applied outside HICs.[5] This leads to a situation where increasingly sophisticated surveillance apparatuses are becoming normal in a context of little or no data protection regulation. It also creates the potential for a perfect storm for privacy and data protection rights in LMICs.

The new challenge big data analytics presents to the fundamental right to privacy can be seen most clearly – and in its most ethically complex form – in lower-income countries. This is for two reasons: first, because the mythologization of the power of big data analytics (Puschmann and Burgess 2014) is leading to the belief among data controllers that access to unprecedented amounts of digital data can solve problems which are in fact rooted in structural and political realities. For instance, claiming that big data analytics can create 'commercially viable solutions to Africa's grand challenges in healthcare, education, water and sanitation, human mobility and agriculture'[6] sounds impressive. Yet these things have not been achieved anywhere else in the world without building stable governance and rule of law, a strong civil society and creating processes of resource management that address the needs of the majority rather than the elite. It is unlikely that such problems can be solved by giving unregulated organizations licence to collect and share data as freely as possible. Furthermore, this discourse arguably gives rise to a false dichotomy where the right to privacy must be weighed against such emotive concepts as fighting poverty and disease. This ethical minefield is situated in a regulatory context where states have yet to develop comprehensive standards for data protection that relate to today's digital data, along with the capacity to identify data misuse and to enforce those standards against international corporations. If, as Cohen writes (2012: 2), privacy 'is an indispensable structural feature of liberal democratic political systems', should this be allowed to imply (as many currently believe) that it is a less fundamental right in places with different structural characteristics or more urgent basic needs?

This chapter begins from Cohen's challenge (this volume at Chapter 3) to examine the types of power emerging in relation to the information age. Going beyond the problem of state power, I reframe the current privacy and data protection gap in LMICs as a lack of effective regulation of corporate and development actors, and ask how privacy theory needs to stretch to accommodate this scenario. The legibilities created by the new data empires are not designed by states, and thus do not aim at representing citizens or supporting legitimate state interests such as the rule of law or taxation. Instead, they are aimed at making citizens better data subjects and consumers or, at best, better subjects of development interventions. This gives rise to a modulation of the kind Cohen describes, but one which operates at a societal level rather than targeting particular groups or behaviours. The use of observed and inferred data (Hildebrandt 2013) in countries where official data collection has always been limited gives rise, I argue, to a condition of ever-increasing legibility without better political representation. This implies that the common argument offered with regard to privacy in developing countries – that it is a luxury the poor cannot afford – may only be a convenient way to reproduce existing power relations. It gives corporate and development entities the opportunity to bypass human development (including political expression, security, health and education) in favour of forms of economic expansion which chiefly benefit a core of richer countries rather than the local subjects of development.

One way to address this problem, I argue, is through a regulatory approach that assumes that privacy is a fundamental right even in situations where it is inconvenient to economic development priorities. In this context, I argue that data protection regulation is an important instrument for protecting privacy in its various dimensions, and that holding HIC-based corporations to account for their actions worldwide could begin a global dialogue about privacy focusing on more than just HICs. I posit that political and economic context are essential to understanding how to establish the right to privacy, since they define the tensions between corporations, states and regulators. The contribution of this chapter is to propose both a rationale and an analytical framework for conceptualizing and enacting a global right to privacy in the era of big data, and to do so without engaging in a cost-benefit analysis which privileges transactional interpretations of privacy (such as privacy self-management, the idea that the individual can manage and control flows of data about themselves and that they will trade certain aspects of privacy for other advantages) over fundamental rights. To do this, I frame big data approaches as a socio-technical system which will have different features in different locations but which can be approached with a unified ethical framework and which can be subject to regulation anywhere in the world. I use examples to illustrate the heightened stakes with regard to privacy and data protection in LMICs, where harms to individuals may potentially be much greater than in HICs, and the ways in which data regulation may take this imbalance into account to provide a system which can grow with the expansion of technology instead of needing to be reinvented for every new location.

Evolving privacy debates with regard to low- and middle-income countries

Cohen (this volume at Chapter 3) has pointed out that traditional legal institutions are increasingly being side-lined in terms of regulating and adjudicating data and information-related governance issues. Instead, she has noted, new networked and often private-sector systems of governance are evolving around information processes. Looking at the international instruments which might be expected to set the initial parameters for data governance in LMICs, this marginalization is evident. Although privacy with regard to personal data has been established as a fundamental right in international declarations, it has yet to be set out in national law or enforced in practice across large portions of the world. As a right privacy is clearly defined in Article 12 of the Universal Declaration of Human Rights (1948) and in Article 17 of the International Covenant on Civil and Political Rights (1966), but regional charters have taken longer to establish it and national laws even longer. For example, the Organisation of African Unity Charter on Human and Peoples' Rights (the Banjul charter, passed in 1981) makes no reference to privacy, nor does China's constitution (White & Case 2012). Although more recent articulations of rights are starting to take privacy into account, such as Article 30 of Hong Kong's Basic Law (1997) and Article 14 of its Bill of Rights (1991), and Article 7 of the East African Community's Draft Bill of Rights (2009), the most recent analysis of global data privacy laws (Greenleaf 2014: 11) shows that the overwhelming majority of states without such laws are low- or lower-middle-income countries. For example, in Sub-Saharan Africa only eight states out of 55 have data protection laws (ibid.). Furthermore, there is little agreement over how data which does not identify individuals but which nevertheless enables proxy forms of identification such as by location and activity should be regulated (Irion and Luchetta 2013), and even in the field of traditional 'personal data' there is disagreement about which data types are most sensitive and why, and therefore about how to protect them.

Even as data protection legislation spreads, practical problems unfold as to how privacy principles apply practically (in terms of rules, regulation and standards rather than international norms or national legislation) to people in lower-income countries in the era of big data. First, privacy has so far been conceptualized in ways which are most applicable under conditions of strong statehood and rule of law, mainly as protecting individuals from *too much* statehood and law, i.e. surveillance, persecution by the state, and oppressive laws (e.g. Solove 2006; Nissenbaum 2009), or, more broadly, protecting a 'socially constructed self' from interference with their self-determination (Cohen 2013), with the assumption that the individual is positioned as the most important unit in society. Although these are desirable preconditions for legislating privacy, they may not be realistic or broad enough to encompass how privacy may be conceptualized in LMICs. For instance, the Banjul Charter frames some rights from the perspective of the individual and some from that of the group, examples of the latter being 'protection of the family and vulnerable groups', the 'right to free disposal of wealth and natural resources', and the 'right to economic, social and cultural development' (Banjul Charter 1981).

There is thus interplay between conceptualizations of privacy and the reality of governance, both of data and more broadly. A related problem is that the distribution of power over digital data is evolving differently in lower-income countries, where the dynamics of economic development are making corporations (and in some places international organizations) more important than national governments. The landscape of data protection is therefore weighted towards remote, multinational actors rather than domestically controlled entities. States are further disadvantaged by the technical resources and capacity necessary to manage and regulate big data, and therefore tend to contract in digital communications expertise (oAfrica.com 2013). Thus corporations become the main actors providing connectivity infrastructure, gathering and managing data, rather than governments.

Although data protection standards in LMICs tend to be low, digital technology use is rising exponentially and providing a rich market for data with few controls. Everywhere in LMICs, multinational technology corporations can be found stepping in to play the kinds of roles that in HICs were initially played by national monopoly providers, which were easier to regulate. Telephony in Sub-Saharan Africa is a prime example: due to the lack of resources for states to invest in landline infrastructure, once mobile phones became available they took hold rapidly. The proportion of people in the region with a mobile subscription rose from 12.4 per cent to 63.5 per cent across the region between 2005 and 2012 (ITU 2013). This dynamic also increasingly governs financial activity: day-to-day financial transactions in LMICs such as microfinance payments and individual transfers are increasingly taking place over mobile phones through e-payment and instant money systems. The system with the most widely-publicized and exponential growth is Kenya's MPesa money transfer network, where usership has risen from 19,600 in 2007 to more than 15 million clients in 2014 (Safaricom 2014; Heinrich 2014). Just as mobile phones have leapfrogged landlines and mobile transfers traditional banking systems, digitally based biometric identification systems are similarly gaining traction as an alternative to state-issued identification documents: in India, for instance, the biometric Unique Identification scheme was set up by corporate experts under circumstances described by Greenleaf (2010) as a 'privacy vacuum', and with only a fraction of the population registered is already the world's largest biometric database with more than 415 million records (Johri and Srinivasan 2014).

Each of these examples of corporate leadership helps to illustrate both how fast technology adoption may move in lower-income countries, and how little opportunity there is for conceptualizations of privacy and data protection to keep up with it. In contrast to Sub-Saharan Africa's lack of privacy legislation, 48 out of 55 countries have adopted compulsory SIM card registration (Donovan and Martin 2014), often with connections to central identification databases, so that any activated SIM card is now linked to an individual through both corporate and governmental information systems. Smartphones, which are more likely to identify their user through apps and more frequent contact with the network, are becoming more accessible: the share of Sub-Saharan Africans with smartphones is the world's lowest at 10.9 per cent (ibid.), but has risen six-fold since figures became available in 2010.

These new networks of information and identification have already seen significant privacy risks and some breaches. The release of mobile phone call records by mobile provider Orange, described in the first section, although anonymized to established HIC standards, was noted by privacy researchers to offer broad opportunities to identify the movements, communication networks and activities of Ivorians during a fragile postwar context using standard methods which could easily be used to inappropriate ends (Sharad and Danezis 2013). As these researchers point out, the risks to data subjects in such a case of big data analysis may accrue on a more general, group level – such as through the identification of a village rather than an individual. Kenya's MPesa payments system has seen an actual breach of client data protection (TechMtaa 2012), where would-be political parties have 'bought' their way into the financial transactions database, harvesting the names of users both to register them as party members and thus gain official standing as parties, and to send political messages during elections (a particularly dangerous abuse of personal data in a country with a history of extreme election-related violence). Meanwhile, in India's biometric ID system, it has recently become public that multiple foreign contractors have been involved in building and running the database, and that these include firms from the United States which are obliged under the Patriot Act to make their data (in this case Indians' private information) available to US intelligence services (New India Express 2014). These examples highlight how corporate data practices and alliances are likely to be the main sources of privacy violations regarding digital data in LMICs, and that corporations must be a central focus of regulation and reasoning with regard to digital data. I frame them as privacy risks, although they also inevitably imply broader issues of data protection, because they illustrate Warren and Brandeis' early articulation of the right to privacy (Warren and Brandeis 1890) as 'the right to be let alone'. In a context of data analysis for policymaking and intervention (as in the Côte d'Ivoire case), or for sending unsolicited political messages in a climate of unrest and violence (as in Kenya), the right to be let alone becomes the overarching issue.

Another risk to privacy is the involvement of international development actors – non-governmental organizations (NGOs), the United Nations, and bilateral development partners – all of which desire more and better data to inform and evaluate development interventions. One high-profile example is the UN's Global Pulse initiative, whose mission is to encourage 'data philanthropy': the donation of corporate datasets by large firms operating in LMICs to inform development actors. Through big data analytical methods, Global Pulse aims to predict economic shocks and provide information to humanitarian responders in LMICs – but it has also voiced a need for new ways to think about privacy in this context (Robert Kirkpatrick, UN Global Pulse[7] 2013):

> We think big data here is the greatest opportunity to present itself to global development in many, many years. Unless you fail to protect privacy in the process, in which case this may be the greatest threat to human rights the world has ever known.

There is reason to worry: the work of Sharad and Danezis (2013) along with that of other researchers working on LMIC privacy issues (e.g. Taylor 2016) points out how various bedrock concepts of data protection may need to be reconceptualized as data flows become multi-layered and multidirectional. As Solove (2013: 1891) has pointed out, in the era of big data analytics, the 'identifiability of data depends upon context'. Anonymization may be an even less reliable approach to data protection in LMICs than it is in HICs, and purpose limitation is already becoming a flimsy concept as 'development' and 'the public good' are used to justify uses of data for research and prediction far beyond the knowledge of ordinary technology users. Furthermore, these bedrock concepts of data protection, along with the EU's standard that data processing must have a legal basis (European Union 1995) are rendered effectively meaningless by the near-impossibility of enforcing any legislation based on them where the data originates in LMICs. Although there have been attempts to protect HIC citizens' data when it is processed in third countries in the form of safe harbour provisions and adequacy agreements, conversely no provisions have been developed to guard the integrity of LMIC citizens' data when it is analysed by HIC organizations under the rubric of development or humanitarian action, as in the Côte d'Ivoire example above.

The challenges noted above add up to a scenario of serious power and information asymmetries affecting citizens of LMICs with regard to their digital data. To summarize the main sources of these imbalances:

1. *Data maximization.* Big data is seen as a way to engineer development to overcome otherwise intractable problems,[8] and as a solution for structural and political problems.[9] The public commentary so far on digital data in LMICs focuses mainly on access to data (Green 2014), open data (World Wide Web Foundation 2014) and development data (Global Pulse 2013), but not on restricting or awarding rights over data. This leads to widespread acceptance of data maximization (in contrast to the standard privacy principle of data minimization (Schermer 2011)), in the interest of more effective data mining. In turn, this normalization of seeking as much data as possible leads to a false dichotomy being drawn between 'privacy' and the interests of the poor (with neither clearly defined), and to the almost religious idea that if enough data is made available, 'solutions' to complex problems such as poverty and disadvantage will be found. Data maximization, however, also presents a greater risk to privacy over the long term as the big-data approach of aggregating different data sources raises the likelihood that apparently innocuous information about people will become sensitive in connection with other datasets (Solove 2013).

2. *Differing parameters for conceptualizing privacy.* As noted in the examples cited above, and particularly the Côte d'Ivoire case, the parameters for defining privacy may shift with regard to LMICs. For example, it may become more important to consider group welfare and harms alongside individual identifiability, something that challenges the current focus of privacy scholarship and legislation on personal information – and possibly also on the conflation of the concepts of privacy and data protection. For instance, being identified as part of a community that is prone to HIV infection or that is likely to be forced to migrate across international borders is potentially valuable in that it allows protective intervention, but also holds risks where those communities may be subjected to unwarranted or pre-emptive action by outsiders based on predictive analytics. Equally, the risks involved may start with individuals' right to be let alone, but also incorporate problems best articulated by the broader concepts of data protection that also regard the presumption of innocence. However, the main current articulation of data protection principles (European Union 1995) encapsulates exactly this conflict. The EU Data Protection Directive (Ibid.) states that data should not be used to profile where this can cause discriminatory action (Article 8.1), but also notes that this does not apply where 'data processing is necessary to protect the vital interests of the data subject or of another person' (Article 8.2(c)). In the context of extreme poverty, disease and the other challenges in LMICs which might prompt data analysis by outside organizations, it is fair to assume that an analyst trying to comply with available data protection rules will believe

herself to be acting to protect the vital interests of data subjects, and therefore to be exempt from restrictions.

3. *Distributed governance scenarios.* Information and power asymmetries with regard to digital data are created and reproduced where states lack the resources or capacity to effectively regulate data flows and to enforce rules and standards. Where this occurs there is a corresponding empowerment of corporations to connect people, gather and analyse their data, and a feedback loop where the state is not incentivized to rectify the asymmetries as long as corporate self-regulation appears not to be causing visible harms.[10] This imbalance in governance is supported by the almost universal promotion of the Public-Private Partnership as a mode of delivery for development interventions and decentralization initiatives in LMICs, seen as the best way to keep donors' costs down and increase efficiency in humanitarian and development activities (Miraftab 2004). In a context of strong corporate empowerment and limited state involvement in digital data flows, individuals are also less likely to be informed of their rights with regard to their data, to have experience of or capacity for actively managing their electronic privacy, or to know through the media if their data is being misused.

4. *Higher stakes.* The categories of harm set out in Solove's taxonomy (2006) are a useful starting point for any analysis of the stakes involved in privacy and data protection: he distinguishes between more ad-hoc 'reputational harms' and longer-term 'architectural issues' which are more relevant to today's uses of digital data. However, Solove's examples of possible future harms illustrate perfectly the different considerations that are appropriate for HIC and LMIC contexts. Solove refers to the risk of 'being victimized by identity theft or fraud' (Solve 2006: 487), and the way that 'People's behaviour might be chilled [by surveillance], making them less likely to attend political rallies or criticize popular views' (ibid.). These risks are real, but in an LMIC context it is easy to see how possible harms may go beyond those conceivable for citizens of HICs. For example, exposing ethnic, religious and political affiliations or identifying dissidents' social networks has been shown to constitute an actual risk of harm for individuals in authoritarian states (MacKinnon 2012). Similarly, researchers have shown that it is a relatively simple process to determine people's sexual orientation through the public information disseminated by social networking websites (Jernigan and Mistree 2009), something which is relatively innocuous in the academic context but highly sensitive in the many countries where harsh laws against homosexuality combine with low standards for evidence.

Zuiderveen Borgesius (2013: 11) points out that according to Article 8 of the Data Protection Directive, 'data protection law has a stricter regime for "sensitive data", such as data revealing racial or ethnic origin, religious beliefs, and data concerning health or sex life'. The examples offered above suggest that in relation to big-data-type analytical processes, not only is anonymization insufficient to protect what Floridi (2013) might refer to as people's 'ontologically constitutive' information, but for those living at risk of violence or persecution, apparently anonymous data such as social network structure may reveal highly sensitive and potentially harmful information about them which under the EU's rules should be protected. Again, this blurs the distinction between privacy and data protection more broadly, where the right to be let alone may be the primary issue, but the way in which that right can be claimed may involve issues more associated with data protection, such as non-discrimination and transparency.

The next section outlines how a global approach to data protection might be created by taking into account the factors explored above, suggesting that data protection needs to be treated primarily as a regulatory problem rather than a holistic one of conceptualizing, advocating and realizing global norms with regard to privacy.

Can privacy and data protection principles apply beyond high-income countries?

The main debate on privacy and data regulation is taking place within a core of HICs, mainly the EU states, the United States and Canada. Many other countries are included in these debates as legal satellites to which the US/EU approaches to data protection are radiating due to those countries' pragmatic adoption of similar codes and standards due to trading and colonial relationships (Greenleaf 2014). A broader view, as set out in the previous section, shows however that there are extensive regions of the world that may be conceiving of people's rights in relation to data, corporations and the state (if they do so at all) according to very different rules and precepts. Bradford (2012) argues that the European Union's effective monopsony power as a consumer bloc combined with its strong regulatory capacity mean that other countries effectively have to adopt EU regulations on data protection and privacy, even if they have their own differing systems in place. However, the uses of data described above (development-related research such as the Orange D4D project, or India's domestic biometric identification system) are effectively outside the realm of EU influence because they involve functions that are not directed towards engagement with the European Union.

There is thus a substantial category of 'other' comprising a majority of the world's technology users, and increasingly including a variety of hybrid uses of data involving multiple actors only some of whom may be subject to regulation or influence by existing data authorities. Given the governance factors set out above, these territories far from regulators' grasp also represent an increasingly viable place of refuge for firms or organizations which are interested in stretching the boundaries of permissible data use. It is in the context of this broader picture that the debate between US and EU data protection principles and laws should be framed analytically. If digital technologies are being used worldwide and data emitted from every country on earth, it is inevitably the global context that will determine whether data privacy provisions such as the forthcoming EU directive will play a role in creating just and fair uses of data.

The realist argument offered above is important to consider because it affects the way laws can be enforced with regard to the transnational collection and use of data, practices which are almost universal amongst large technology firms. If the actual global scenario with regard to data protection frameworks (United States, European Union and 'other') is not taken into account, both international co-ordination and the ability to understand the evolution of regional regulatory frameworks suffer. Privacy as a fundamental right (the dominant perspective in the European Union according to the Charter of Fundamental Rights) versus privacy as a transactional attribute which can be managed and weighed against other benefits (dominant in the United States due to its more piecemeal approach to data regulation) are only two of many ethical perspectives which may inform data protection regimes. Others include customary or common law frameworks which may be biased towards communal rather than individual rights (loosely, the African idea of Ubuntu, or collectivity, see for example Du Plessis 2011); the view that privacy has a chiefly instrumental value as a way of preserving social order (China's evolving articulation of the problem, see Yao-Huai 2005) or that groups have bounded and contingent rights to privacy depending on their socioeconomic status and country of citizenship (as applies to certain categories of migrants, resident foreigners and the poor worldwide, see Gilliom 2001).

Table 4.1 compares the central aspects of privacy with regard to data in HICs versus LMICs. The main elements covered are the principles for regulation; the governance conditions which determine the degree of traction any regulation may gain, and the types of risk associated with each regulatory environment.

Table 4.1 Privacy in HICs versus LMICs

	High-income countries	Low- and middle-income countries
Regulation	'information relating to an identified or identifiable natural person' (Data Protection Directive); 'personally identifiable information' (McCallister, Grance and Scarfone 2010)	Little regulation; status quo weighted in favour of surveillance and control, e.g. eight of 55 countries in Africa have data protection laws, mainly analogue (Greenleaf 2014), but 48 have SIM registration (Donovan and Martin 2014)
Governance	Centralized governance: rule of law, more accountable states, enforceable limits on corporations	Distributed governance: limited statehood, less accountable states, few enforceable limits on corporations
Analytical challenges	Anonymization/blurring of data; data aggregation level; access provisions; jurisdiction of data protection rules	HIC concerns *plus* a lack of supplemental country data may lead to inaccuracies in remotely-conducted data analysis
Risks	Individual harms: discrimination, tracking, identity theft, unwanted marketing	HIC risks *plus* displacement; blocked mobility; violence; political repression *plus* group harms

Table 4.1 helps to illustrate, as Greenleaf points out, that 'a law on the books is not to be confused with effective privacy protection' (Greenleaf 2014: postscript). Notwithstanding the presence in a country of a comprehensive data protection act, or privacy legislation more broadly, it may not be realistic to lean on state legislation and enforcement. For example, for a citizen of Côte d'Ivoire whose data was involved in the Orange D4D project of 2013, the ability to contest the reuse and sharing of their data for broad research purposes, or the way in which it had been anonymized, involved first gaining the knowledge that the data had been used; second, understanding how this use might impact them; third, having a local data protection authority to complain to; and fourth, for that authority to have the resources and influence to hold data processors accountable in an EU or US court. These factors are further problematized by the fact that the dataset was, according to European, US and industry standards (e.g. Data Protection Directive; GSMA 2011), 'properly anonymised', which would have rendered data protection law inapplicable if it applied to the Ivorians' data – which it did not.

This example suggests that the inclusion of a more global perspective in thinking about data regulation is not only wise, but pragmatically important. The problem of privacy is similar to that of pollution: if effectively regulated with industrialized countries in mind, the problem will simply move elsewhere to where laws become principles and thus unenforceable. This is already occurring with data self-regulation by corporations in the sphere of international development (Taylor and Schroeder 2015), where the public announcement of good intentions allows data sharing and access which would not be permissible under any other conditions. Carly Nyst of Privacy International has said that (Nyst 2013):

> it would be impossible for any European-based enterprise to collect location data on minorities, require SMS-reporting about drug adherence, or establish large databases of sensitive information without safeguards.

Yet this is currently the scenario for data use and reuse in most LMICs, either under the banner of standard corporate data processing practices, as Kirkpatrick's quote at the start of this chapter indicates, or in the course of devising interventions in the name of development.

Nissenbaum (2009) has written that one important function of privacy is to take control away from states. Solove has written that privacy guards self-determination (Solve 2006). Despite the evident usefulness of their perspectives, they contrast strongly with the way that big data analytics are evolving with regard to LMICs. In the global landscape, there are multiple actors already involved in analysing personal data, ranging from multinational technology giants to development organizations and the United Nations, for purposes ranging from economic empowerment to humanitarian and development interventions. This highly varied landscape is more like that described by Neil Richards (2013: 1940), when he notes that:

It might seem curious to think of information gathering by private entities as 'surveillance' . . . [yet in the era of big data] government and nongovernment surveillance support each other in a complex manner that is often impossible to disentangle.

A similar problem is outlined by Cohen (this volume at Chapter 3) where she notes that:

Debates about state censorship [. . .] represent only one piece of a larger puzzle, which concerns the extent to which global circuits of information flow are settling into patterns that serve larger constellations of economic and political power.

The range of actors involved in the power dynamics of dataveillance in LMICs is particularly broad, ranging from states interested in surveillance to NGOs working exclusively with the aim of public benefit. Any meaningful data protection established in LMICs therefore has to take this range of actors into account, and allow for some uses of data which are potentially invasive of privacy, particularly in the humanitarian sphere, while also strongly curtailing practices of data maximization and surveillance leading to social control and the suppression of dissent. Moreover, there is no guarantee that these two ends of the spectrum will not sometimes merge. Unregulated actors with privileged access to personal data, even those with infinite goodwill, will not always use it in ethically desirable ways or ensure that it never reaches those who may have worse motives: the development and humanitarian communities certainly have no history of being right all the time. Yet data privacy is entirely a matter of self-regulation among these groups, nor have ethical frameworks yet been developed to guide data use in these cases.

The following section looks at principles and practical ways to address this scenario of self-regulation, with particular attention to the tension between privacy self-management and workable solutions for the LMIC contexts analysed here.

Creating international checks and balances for data flows

The examples outlined here have illustrated the particular difficulties facing citizens of LMICs in resisting unwarranted uses of their digital data. First, the political and economic architectures within which big data is produced and analysed in lower-income countries – particularly the extra-national and transnational flows of data characteristic of multinational corporations and development organizations – tend to place citizens at even more of a disadvantage than people in HICs in terms of controlling what happens to the data they emit. Second, if an unwarranted use of data is identified, a lack of local legislation or rules may prevent citizens from seeking recourse. Such action has to be backed up by local authorities in the case of the transnational use of data – something which is both difficult where lower-income or smaller states are structurally disadvantaged in terms of international influence, but is also a challenge for those equipped with the full force of the law and acting from within the European Union (as can be seen from Max Schrems' attempt to use EU privacy regulations to sue Facebook in the European Union (Press Association 2014)).

These structural problems are what Solove (2013) refers to when he argues that privacy self-management is not an option for ordinary technology users. They also support Cohen's statement (this volume at Chapter 3) that the new pathways of data governance are frequently hidden within the auspices of the private sector, and that they are not even theoretically accessible to citizens in the way that national laws and regulations should be. The conditions of corporate self-regulation and little state intervention or power over data flows which currently prevail in most LMICs strongly support this argument. If US citizens (as argued by Solove, ibid.) and EU citizens (as argued by Zuiderveen Borgesius 2013) cannot be realistically expected to manage their own privacy with regard to digital data, what should be the solution in places with greater structural disadvantages and information asymmetries? A global perspective makes it clear that privacy self-management is an approach that inevitably favours certain economic and geographic groups over others, namely those who are continuously connected to the internet by smart devices and are technologically well informed, and are therefore more able to regulate their own data effectively or to seek legal redress in case of misuse. A large proportion of the 'other' 6 billion people currently emitting digital data, then, are not only unprotected but, under current assumptions, unprotectable.

Even where people can be effectively informed of their rights with regard to their data, a further problem arises: various solutions which have been proposed that weight the informed consent process in favour of the individual seem a bad fit for the context of development/humanitarian data uses described here. For instance the idea of privacy self-management via a 'personal data store' (Hardjono, Deegan and Clippinger 2014) or creating greater user awareness through 'visceral notification' tactics (Calo 2012) cannot be considered appropriate in a context where people have too-simple devices or intermittent connectivity. There is also a problem where the data is to be used for health or humanitarian purposes, where data processors will almost inevitably classify their analysis as important to the wellbeing of the data subject and therefore justifiable even without ethical checks or user permission.

Moreover, the framing of 'big data' as a solution for problems which have a structural and political origin makes it more possible that regulation will be de-prioritized in favour of a race to practise the most innovative methods of data analysis (as with Orange's D4D project, described above). This framing also distracts from the other facet of big data in LMICs, and everywhere else – as a form of economic activity relating strongly to growth and innovation. This facet, however, is also liable to misuse in LMICs if regulation is not established and made enforceable. There has been a tendency among development donors to attempt to replicate economic models that have worked in HICs as a way to alleviate problems of governance and production in LMICs. Perhaps the clearest example of this was the imposition of Structural Adjustment Programmes in the 1980s and 1990s, which attempted to impose a neoliberal market model on low-income countries, and which resulted in the forced marketization of public services, currency devaluations and, in consequence, political instability and elevated mortality rates amongst vulnerable groups. Programmes such as these, introduced without considering local and contextual factors or the limitations of local systems and resources, illustrate the possible long-term consequences of treating development as an engineering problem and data as the essential input.[11]

One classic example of data-driven sorting and categorizing with profoundly negative consequences was the passbook system which formed the bureaucratic underpinning for apartheid policy in South Africa (Kahn 1966: 91):

> Every African over sixteen must have on his person what is called a reference book, a bulky document measuring five by three and a half inches and containing ninety-five pages. As a rule, it is only Africans who are stopped by the police and asked to produce their passes. 'The African must be a collector of documents from the day of his birth to the day of his death', says a publication issued by the Black Sash. His passbook must contain particulars about every job he has had, every tax he has paid, and every X-ray he has taken. He would be well advised, the Black Sash has suggested, not to let himself get too far away from his birth certificate, baptismal certificate, school certificates, employment references, housing permits, hospital and clinic cards, prison discharge papers, rent receipts, and, the organization has added sarcastically, death and burial certificates.

In cases where people's data was mishandled or misreported, Horrell (1960) notes, the individual became liable for any mistakes in the dataset and was subject to a prison term for misidentifying themselves, even in cases where they were illiterate and had no idea what their passbook contained. A better example of information asymmetry is hard to find. In the context of development policy-making, people's digital traces may become the contemporary equivalent of the pass book – a complete record of movements, activities and social connections that may be subject to search by a myriad authorities in the name of care and protection.

Structural factors such as poverty and lack of political rights serve as confounders in an analysis that considers how privacy can be a fundamental right everywhere. Yet they should be seen as complications, not contra-indications. Activism occurs in relation to connected types of fundamental rights even in situations where they are strongly contested. For example, the right to self-determination is not lessened because certain groups believe women should be subject to men in many societies; similarly the right to equality before the law can coexist in places such as India with caste systems which restrict the ability of individuals to claim that right. Nevertheless, structural complications are real and meaningful, since in the case of privacy they have contributed to a lack of necessary civil society pressure towards digital privacy in most LMICs. The example of India, however, suggests that the evolution of public pressure in favour of digital privacy will evolve where a high-profile use of personal data, such as that country's biometric ID project, combines with highly visible and publicized risks to privacy and actual harms.[12]

Given that civil society will respond at a slower pace than the uses of digital data can evolve, and given that national legislation (where it exists) will only gain traction where structural factors support it, both nationally and internationally, what kinds of solutions are useful in the current landscape of big data analytics? Solove (2013), writing of the US and EU context, advocates keeping privacy self-management in play, both because it plays an important role in initially making people aware of their rights with regard to their own data at the point where they begin using a new technology product or service, and because in some cases it is sufficient to the privacy management task at hand. He suggests moving towards what he terms 'paternalistic' approaches, which are relevant to all data use contexts: structuring people's choices so that they lean towards choosing privacy over openness with the data they emit; limiting the role of self-management to what is clear and understandable rather than expecting people to micro-manage; moving privacy decisions 'downstream', i.e. coming back to people for consent when new uses of their data are going to occur; and establishing default rules for data processors according to 'basic privacy norms'. These are all useful, but are inevitably partial in the contexts described above, where consent decisions are easily rendered more complicated by the belief that certain uses of data may contribute to overall wellbeing, or by lack of access on the part of data processors to subscribers in remote areas or those who spend most of their time offline.

For more global solutions, it becomes necessary to move towards a more layered approach to data management, where checks and balances are established and applied at the point of the technology or service's origin, and again at the international level in the case of transnational data sharing and reuse. For example, some possible approaches to take into account the global nature of data flows might include:

1. *Trade restrictions*. Imposing export controls on data processing technologies developed in the European Union or the United States, as occurs with dual-use technologies with possible military ends under the 1994 Wassenaar Arrangement. This has already begun to take place with various surveillance technologies being placed on the Arrangement's 'control list' (Privacy International 2013). It is possible to posit that as well as the data-gathering surveillance technologies that have been the focus of Privacy International's advocacy, particular data analytic technologies may also be eligible for such treatment.

2. *Redefining checks and balances*. Moving from fixed definitions of personal information and potential harms to a more flexible, easily contextualized,

risk-based approach to privacy. This would involve corporations having to submit a form of Privacy Impact Assessment (PIA) to local data protection authorities in their headquarter countries for their work in LMICs, as if they were going to use personal data belonging to US or EU citizens, but in an adapted form. These reworked PIAs would include analysis of local factors in the data's country of origin, preferably involving natives of that country with local knowledge, and would provide information to weigh the immediate benefits 'of a particular use of data against the potential future risks of re-identification and harm. This approach, though contested (Cavoukian and Castro 2014) would provide an initial impulse for corporations to consider the potential impacts of their use of data outside the established regulatory constraints, and is currently the subject of discussions led by the Centre for Information Policy Leadership and the World Economic Forum, among others.

3.   *Creating institutional reference points.* Such a risk-based approach also suggests real-time, case-by-case institutional support for decision-making about data uses that is enforceable against corporations in their place of origin if they misuse data. Several models are available, and though all are far from perfect, a combination would provide greater protection to people outside the HICs than is currently available:

    a.   *Institutional review boards.* These have been used by humanitarian projects looking to perform big-data analytics in emergency situations (for example, the epidemiological analysis of NGO Flowminder during the Haiti cholera epidemic beginning in 2010, which used detailed mobile phone call data from Haitian providers, was reviewed by a Swedish ethics committee at the main researcher's home university);

    b.   *International ethics committees.* These sector- or field-specific committees can be found in areas ranging from medicine (the World Health Organization's Research Ethics Review Committee is one example) and livestock research (the Institutional Research Ethics Committee of the International Livestock Research Institute) to accountancy (the International Ethics Standards Board for Accountants). These ethical bodies gain traction for their decisions from a combination of factors: strong network incentives to be part of professional bodies and associations which can then become subject to the ethics committee's governance, and the ability to restrict funding or de-certify members who do not play according to the rules established. Both these conditions are problematic with regard to multinational technology firms, however. It has been demonstrated (most notably by the lack of growth in the Global Network Initiative's membership) that such firms are more likely to join associations when forced to by political pressure, while they have the financial and political autonomy to withdraw at will from any inconvenient international arrangements;

c.   *Add-ons to the functions of existing international organizations.* Although many international organizations with links to LMICs are already involved in the kind of big data analytics described above (including the United Nations and the OECD), there are many organizations with both technical capacity and extensive international networks which could take on a standard-setting or ethical role with regard to data processing in LMICs. Election monitoring provides a possible model: here, the organizations involved are primarily regional bodies (the Organization of American States, the African Union, the European Union and the Council of Europe) but there is also involvement from other types of grouping (the Organization for Security and Co-operation in Europe and the Commonwealth Secretariat) which could provide a model for the registration and monitoring of large-scale data processing projects, and call offenders to account in the international public sphere.

These more protective approaches may be termed paternalistic in the sense of Solove (2013) because they aim to limit harm in specific ways, in advance of data access or processing. They become appropriate, however, in cases where information asymmetries are not rectifiable by other means due to the kinds of structural constraints outlined above, involving both states and individuals. These approaches might address both of the problems of data governance set out by Cohen (this volume at Chapter 3) by integrating control over information flows in traditional legal and rights systems, and also by helping those systems evolve to deal with the challenges posed by new types of data generation and processing. Avoiding such protective strategies in the hope that individuals will become ready to self-manage their privacy through advances in technology and connectivity is unrealistic both because such an evolution is unlikely to occur in the short term, and because the increasingly complex ways in which data are shared and reused are leading to a scenario where it is impossible for anyone to be fully aware of and manage the data they emit, regardless of their level of technological access and sophistication.

Concluding remarks: expanding data protection from 'we' to 'everyone'

Empirical analysis shows that people in LMICs do not have the same access to data protection as those in HICs, and that this is both actually and potentially harmful in a variety of ways. The 'we' of data protection, ascribed as if it were universal, in fact denotes citizens of EU countries, the United States, and a few other HICs. As importantly, this 'we' also tends to denote the elites who can use the range of options currently available, from privacy-self-management tools to legal recourse if necessary. If 'informational capitalism' (Castells 1996) is a reality, as asserted by Cohen (this volume at Chapter 3), then those situated nearest to the global centres of the tech economy are likely to benefit from the economic returns created by the new flows of data. In contrast, citizens of LMICs have been largely excluded from the economic benefits of the new data economy, and, further, have less protection from its negative and exploitative effects. Moving beyond the convenient idea that people in lower-income regions are less capable of conceptualizing privacy clearly, of advocating for it, or of enforcing rules should they become available, it is clear that advances in big data availability and analytics are everywhere overtaking people's ability to resist the misuse of data about them – and that under certain political and economic conditions there are structural barriers to resisting this process effectively. In order to be able to assume that the right of privacy is indeed fundamental, i.e. applicable to everyone, everywhere, it is necessary to understand those structural barriers, and how to mitigate them with additional types of protection that will allow people to claim and enforce their rights regardless of location.

This chapter calls attention to the ways that existing systems may evolve to deal with new data problems, and the ways in which that evolution may be fostered in the immediate term. It addresses Cohen's point (this volume at Chapter 3) that the emerging systems for data governance are often based more in the private than the public sector, and that these tend to bypass traditional legal and rights instruments which have not yet evolved to deal with new technologies. The points made here address the practical question of how to create an international architecture for the responsible use of data about individuals. I have outlined the problems that stand in the way of such an architecture: first, that data from developing countries is being shared, reused and analysed in ways that are effectively far beyond the jurisdictional reach of current privacy and data protection regulations; second, that these uses are seen by data processors as justifiable on humanitarian grounds and therefore not subject to existing ethical frameworks; and third, that current assumptions about ethical data use may not fit with the way that rights are being conceptualized in developing countries. I have argued that the way to help such an architecture for the ethical use of data to evolve worldwide is to treat multinational corporations processing data as if they were liable for their actions in a similar way worldwide, and to provide clear and usable ways for them to do this.

The analysis above has highlighted how structural barriers to the establishment of a right to privacy and data protection are present in places with limited statehood and rule of law, where standards that are in force may in fact be unenforceable. Political and economic inequalities between states and regions also create information asymmetries that reinforce and exacerbate these structural barriers to protection. Thus even if the first set of barriers can be overcome, i.e. if LMICs behave like HICs in terms of passing and enforcing data protection standards, the results will not be comparable since they often do not have the same power to rule and enforce, notably with regard to the transnational use of data.

The establishment of clear rules for privacy and data protection worldwide is further complicated by the fact that assumptions about LMIC data are different in various dimensions: the cost-benefit analysis can be skewed by factors such as poverty or crises, making purpose limitation and anonymization less of a priority; big data is being mythologized as the answer to intractable problems, leading international institutions to advocate for data maximization; and corporations become more important actors in data flows where states are weak or have few resources, leading to a merging of public- and private-sector functions with regard to governance and the idea that regulating data flows will harm basic governance.

This powerful discourse about the potential benefits of big data analytical methods is a greater barrier to extending privacy as a fundamental right than it might at first seem. Nissenbaum (2009) argues that the fuzziness of the borders and the essential nature of privacy are its greatest strength, since they provide adaptability and demand ongoing debate. Yet that fuzziness will inevitably make it hard to set the right to privacy against simple statements about how data mining can 'solve' problems such as disease, lack of education, poor sanitation and food insecurity.[13]

Despite the extent of the problem and the multiplicity of ways by which it is configured, HICs with established data regulation regimes may have a particular (and time-limited) chance to affect the fairness of data protection practices worldwide. I have argued above that processes of establishing data protection regulation in LMICs are likely to be strongly influenced by the need for compatibility with trading partners rather than a strong domestic call for a fundamental right to privacy, as was the case in the United States and many EU states. Given the inevitable imbalance in power and influence between these regions and their LMIC trading partners, HIC regulatory standards and practices are likely to have disproportionate influence over LMICs in terms of setting the parameters for data use and sharing – but also in terms of offering protection to citizens in regions where HIC corporations are operating.

The most effective way to begin a global dialogue about privacy that is based on the idea of privacy as a fundamental right rather than as a transaction or a cost-benefit analysis, then, may be to reframe LMIC privacy from the international perspective as a regulatory problem that HICs can influence, rather than as a challenge that LMICs must overcome. If the question becomes one of limiting HIC-based corporations' ability to misuse data from LMIC technology users, rather than how LMICs should frame privacy for their own citizens, it becomes both more manageable and more easily related to existing models of regulation such as those set out in the fourth section. If such a debate can take place, it may drive the evolution of data governance towards, and one that does not rely solely on, country-level judicial apparatuses to resolve what are fundamentally international asymmetries.

The big data era may come to be seen as the starting point for digital privacy as a global debate. As power through data evolves and replicates itself across sectors and regions, the power to identify and categorize people and to modulate their behaviour is shifting from the auspices of states to those of international corporations and institutions, with far-reaching implications for individual citizens, and particularly those in countries without enforceable privacy or data protection provisions. On the other hand, however, this extension of the power to make people visible through data may be seen as so extreme that it could also constitute a moment where inequalities can be seen and mitigated. As those outside the HIC technology and regulatory bubble make themselves legible by joining the global technological commons, the next step is to extend to a global context the discussion about how big data analytics affects social existence. It is becoming possible to take into account a diverse range of discourses on data and privacy and to consider how the use of digital technologies makes *everyone* identifiable and legible, in various dimensions and to various authorities and institutions, and how the unrestricted processing and reuse of data reproduces power asymmetries. Paradoxically, however, the most effective way to respond to this imbalance may be at the local level in HICs, by reworking basic local tools as instruments for international influence.

Notes

1 Article 29 Data Protection Working Party, 'Opinion 03/2013 on purpose limitation', 2 April 2013, available at http://idpc.gov.mt/dbfile.aspx/Opinion3_2013.pdf (accessed 19 January 2016).
2 Robert Kirkpatrick, interview with *Global Observatory*, 5 November, 2012, available at http://theglobalobservatory.org/interviews/377-robert-kirkpatrick-director-of-un-global-pulse-on-the-value-of-big-data.html (accessed 19 January 2016).
3 For instance, the role of corporate data-processing strategies in the 2012 US presidential election, available at www.nytimes.com/2013/06/23/magazine/the-obama-campaigns-digital-masterminds-cash-in.html?pagewanted=all&_r=0 (accessed 19 January 2016).
4 I use the World Bank's definitions grouping countries, available at http://data.worldbank.org/about/country-classifications (accessed 19 January 2016), where LMICs have incomes of $1,036–$12,616 per capita and high-income countries (HICs) above that threshhold. My particular focus is the low- and lower-middle-income countries, with an upper threshhold of $4,085 per capita, which includes India and most of Africa.
5 For example, see www.bloombergview.com/articles/2013-06-10/snowden-is-in-hong-kong-chinese-don-t-care- (accessed 19 January 2016).
6 IBM research makes this claim for its 'Project Lucy', involving the Watson super-computer, available at www.research.ibm.com/labs/africa/project-lucy.shtml (accessed 19 January 2016).
7 Presentation, WS 203 'Big Data: Promoting Development and Safeguarding Privacy', 8th Internet Governance Forum, Bali, 22–25 October 2013.
8 For a clear example of this belief, see IBM's Watson project in Kenya, which aims to solve Africa's grand challenges using big data analytics, available at www.economist.com/blogs/baobab/2013/11/ibm-africa (accessed 19 January 2016).
9 Jack Walsh quote from IGF 2013.
10 One exception to this is the Indian government's move to regulate the Unique Identification Authority after the 2014 change in leading party (Business Standard 2014).
11 The discourse on development as a unitary issue lending itself to engineering solutions is common to many big data projects, for example the 'Big Data for Social Good' project at Harvard, available at www.hsph.harvard.edu/ess/ (accessed 19 January 2016).
12 This was the type of evolution posited by Sunil Abraham, Director of India's Centre for Internet and Society, in a speech at the 8th Internet Governance Forum, Bali, 22–25 October 2013.

13 See IBM's 'Lucy' project for example, available at www.research.ibm.com/labs/africa/ project-lucy.shtml (accessed 19 January 2016).

References

Banjul Charter (1981) 'African Charter on Human and Peoples' Rights', available at www. achpr.org/files/instruments/achpr/banjul_charter.pdf (accessed 19 January 2016).

Blondel, V.D., Esch, M., Chan, C., Clérot, F., Deville, P., Huens, E., Morlot, F., Smoreda, Z. and Ziemlicki, C. (2012) 'Data for Development: The D4D Challenge on Mobile Phone Data'. *arXiv preprint arXiv:1210.0137.*

Bradford, A. (2012) 'The Brussels Effect'. *Northwestern University Law Review* 107(1): 1–68.

Business Standard (2014) 'Modi Backs UIDAI, Seeks Accelerated DBT Rollout', available at www.business-standard.com/article/economy-policy/modi-backs-uidai-seeks-accelerated-dbt-rollout-114070500756_1.html (accessed 19 January 2016).

Calo, M.R. (2012) 'Against Notice Skepticism in Privacy (and Elsewhere)'. *Notre Dame Law Review* 87(3): 1027–1072.

Castells, M. (1996) *The Rise of the Network Society.* New York, NY: Wiley-Blackwell.

Cavoukian, A. and Castro, D. (2014) 'Big Data and Innovation, Setting the Record Straight: De-identification Does Work'. *The Information Technology and Innovation Foundation*, available at www.ipc.on.ca/images/Resources/pbd-de-identification_ITIF.pdf (accessed 19 January 2016).

Cohen, J.E. (2012) *Configuring the Networked Self: Law, Code, and the Play of Everyday Practice.* New Haven, CT: Yale University Press.

——. (2013) 'What Privacy is For'. *Harvard Law Review* 126(7): 1904–1933.

Deleuze, G. (1992) 'Postscript on the Societies of Control'. *October* 59(1): 3–7.

Donovan, K.P. and Martin, A.K. (2014) 'The Rise of African SIM Registration: The Emerging Dynamics of Regulatory Change'. *First Monday* 19(2–3), available at http:// firstmonday.org/ojs/index.php/fm/article/view/4351/3820 (accessed 19 January 2016).

Du Plessis, W.J. (2011) 'African Indigenous Land Rights in a Private Ownership Paradigm'. *PER: Potchefstroomse Elektroniese Regsblad* 14(7): 45–69.

European Union (1995) European Union Data Protection Directive. EU 95/46/EC, available at http://eur-lex.europa.eu/LexUriServ/LexUriServ.do?uri=CELEX:31995 L0046:en:HTML (accessed 19 January 2016).

Floridi, L. (2013) *The Ethics of Information.* Oxford: Oxford University Press.

Gilliom, J. (2001) *Overseers of the Poor: Surveillance, Resistance, and the Limits of Privacy.* Chicago, IL: University of Chicago Press.

Global Pulse (2013) 'United Nations Global Pulse Information Sheet', available at www. unglobalpulse.org (accessed 19 January 2016).

Green, D. (2014) 'Big Data and Development: Upsides, Downsides and a Lot of Questions', available at http://oxfamblogs.org/fp2p/what-is-the-future-impact-of-big-data/ (accessed 19 January 2016).

Greenleaf, G. (2010) 'India's National ID System: Danger Grows in a Privacy Vacuum'. *Computer Law & Security Review* 26(5): 479–491.

——. (2014) 'Sheherezade and the 101 Data Privacy Laws: Origins, Significance and Global Trajectories'. *Journal of Law, Information & Science* 23(1): 1–29.

GSMA (2011) 'Mobile privacy principles', available at www.gsma.com/publicpolicy/ wp-content/uploads/2012/03/gsmaprivacyprinciples2012.pdf (accessed 19 January 2016).

Hardjono, T., Deegan, P. and Clippinger, J.H. (2014) 'Social Use Cases for the ID3 Open Mustard Seed Platform'. *Technology and Society Magazine* (IEEE) 33(3): 48–54.

Heinrich, E. (2014) 'The Apparent MPesa Monopoly May Be Set to Crumble', available at http://fortune.com/2014/06/27/m-pesa-kenya-mobile-payments-competition/ (accessed 19 January 2016).

Hildebrandt, M. (2013) 'Slaves to Big Data. Or Are We?' *Idp. Revista De Internet, Derecho y Política* 16.

Horrell, M. (ed.) (1960) *The 'Pass Laws'. (Vol. 7).* Braamfontein: SA Institute of Race Relations.

Irion, K. and Luchetta, G. (2013) 'Online Personal Data Processing and EU Data Protection Reform'. CEPS Digital Forum.

ITU (2013) 'The World in 2013: International Telecommunications Union', available at www.unapcict.org/ecohub/the-world-in-2013-ict-facts-and-figures (accessed 19 January 2016).

Jernigan, C. and Mistree, B. (2009) 'Gaydar: Facebook Friendships Expose Sexual Orientation'. *First Monday* 14(10), available at http://firstmonday.org/article/view/2611/2302 (accessed 19 January 2016).

Jerven, M. (2013) *Poor Numbers: How We Are Misled by African Development Statistics and What to Do about It.* Ithaca, NY: Cornell University Press.

Johri, A. and Srinivasan, J. (2014) 'The Role of Data in Aligning the "Unique Identity" Infrastructure in India'. In *Proceedings of the 17th ACM conference on Computer Supported Cooperative Work & Social Computing* ACM: 697–709.

Kahn, E.J. (1966) *The Separated People: A Look at Contemporary South Africa.* New York, NY: WW Norton & Company.

MacKinnon, R. (2012) *Consent of the Networked: The Worldwide Struggle for Internet Freedom.* New York, NY: Basic Books.

McCallister, E., Grance, T. and Scarfone, K. (2010) 'Guide to Protecting the Confidentiality of Personally Identifiable Information (PII)'. *National Institute of Standards and Technology Special Publication* No. 800–122, Gaithersburg, MD: National Institute of Standards and Technology.

Miraftab, F. (2004) 'Public-Private Partnerships: The Trojan Horse of Neoliberal Development?' *Journal of Planning Education and Research* 24(1): 89–101.

New India Express (2014) 'Aadhaar Data Minefield Threatens to Blow Up in Government's Face', available at www.newindianexpress.com/thesundaystandard/Aadhaar-Data-Minefield-Threatens-to-Blow-Up-in-Government%E2%80%99s-Face/2014/06/08/article2268540.ece (accessed 19 January 2016).

Nissenbaum, H. (2009) *Privacy in Context: Technology, Policy, and the Integrity of Social Life.* Stanford, CA: Stanford University Press.

Nyst, C. (2013) 'The Road to Surveillance is Paved with Good Intentions – and Warning Signs. Poverty Matters Blog'. *The Guardian Online*, available at www.theguardian.com/global-development/poverty-matters/2013/nov/12/surveillance-aid-iris-scanning-gps-tracking (accessed 19 January 2016).

oAfrica.com (2013) 'Huawei Going Strong in Africa', available at www.oafrica.com/mobile/huawei-going-strong-in-africa/ (accessed 19 January 2016).

Press Association (2014) 'European Court to Rule on Allegations Facebook Passes Personal Data to NSA'. *The Guardian*, available at www.theguardian.com/world/2014/jun/18/facebook-personal-data-nsa (accessed 19 January 2016).

Privacy International (2013) 'International Agreement Reached Controlling Export of Mass and Intrusive Surveillance Technology. Press release', available at www.scoop. co.nz/stories/WO1312/S00123/international-agreement-controls-export-of-surveillance-tech.htm (accessed 19 January 2016).

Puschmann, C. and Burgess, J. (2014) 'Metaphors of Big Data'. *International Journal of Communication* 8: 1690–1709.

Richards, N.M. (2013) 'The Dangers of Surveillance'. *Harvard Law Review* 126(7): 1934–1965.

Safaricom (2014) 'MPesa timeline', available at www.safaricom.co.ke/mpesa_timeline/timeline.html (accessed 19 January 2016).

Schermer, B.W. (2011) 'The Limits of Privacy in Automated Profiling and Data Mining'. *Computer Law & Security Review* 27(1): 45–52.

Schroeder, R. (2014) 'Big Data: Towards a More Scientific Social Science and Humanities'. In M. Graham and W.H. Dutton (eds), *Society and the Internet: How Networks of Information are Changing our Lives.* Oxford: Oxford University Press: 164–176.

Scott, J.C. (1998) *Seeing Like a State: How Certain Schemes to Improve the Human Condition Have Failed.* New Haven, CT: Yale University Press.

Sharad, K. and Danezis, G. (2013) 'De-anonymizing D4D Datasets'. *The 13th Privacy Enhancing Technologies Symposium.* 10–12 July 2013, Bloomington, IN.

Solove, D.J. (2006) 'A Taxonomy of Privacy'. *University of Pennsylvania Law Review* 154(3): 477–560.

——. (2013) 'Privacy Self-Management and the Consent Dilemma'. *Harvard Law Review* 126(7): 1880–1903.

Taylor, L. (2015). No place to hide? The ethics and analytics of tracking mobility using mobile phone data. *Environment & Planning D: Society & Space.* 34(2) 319–336.

Taylor, L., & Schroeder, R. (2014). Is bigger better? The emergence of big data as a tool for international development policy. *GeoJournal,* 1–16. doi: 10.1007/s10708-014-9603-5

TechMtaa (2012) 'Outcry Over Claims That M-Pesa Details Are Used "To Register" Party Members', available at www.techmtaa.com/2012/01/16/outcry-over-claims-that-m-pesa-details-are-used-to-register-party-members/ (accessed 19 January 2016).

Warren, S.D. and Brandeis, L.D. (1890) 'The Right to Privacy'. *Harvard Law Review* 4(5): 193–220.

White & Case (2012) 'Data Protection and Privacy in China. Briefing', available at www.whitecase.com/publications/alert/data-protection-and-privacy-china (accessed 19 January 2016).

World Wide Web Foundation (2014) 'Open Data in Developing Countries: Different Models, New Approaches', available at http://webfoundation.org/2014/07/open-data-in-developing-countries-report-results/ (accessed 19 January 2016).

Yao-Huai, L. (2005) 'Privacy and Data Privacy Issues in Contemporary China'. *Ethics and Information Technology* 7(1): 7–15.

Zuiderveen Borgesius, F.J. (2013) 'Consent to Behavioural Targeting in European Law: What are the Policy Implications of Insights from Behavioural Economics?' *Amsterdam Law School Legal Studies Research Paper* No. 2013-43: 1–58, available at http://ssrn.com/abstract=2300969 or http://dx.doi.org/10.2139/ssrn.2300969 (both accessed 2 February 2016).

Part III

What freedom of which information?

Chapter 5

ICT's architecture of freedom

David Koepsell and Philip Serracino Inglott

Introduction

Beginning with information and communication technology (ICT), leading to genes and then nanotechnology, we have delved into how various technologies have required altering our views of the underlying objects, and questioned how our legal institutions deal with them.

In each case, it seems that our initial instincts and intuitions, as reflected in our legal regimes, commit some sort of error or pose potential impediments to the promise of emerging technologies. Below we argue that emerging technologies, from ICT to nanotechnology, embody larger-scale historical trends in the development of innovation, and reveal both a richer and simpler ontology of expressions than our legal institutions have reflected. ICT is the backbone of revolutions in material culture, including genomics and nanotechnology, and serves as the proper focal point for a critical evaluation of our ontological assumptions. Moreover, the values that 'hacker' culture has come to adopt are the values inherent in the tools themselves, which are counterposed to the tendency towards monopoly that invariably accompanies innovation. The most radical contribution of ICT to human development is not how much faster and more powerful it has made human capacity for communication and symbol manipulation, which is already an amazing fact, but rather that it is bringing to the fore the realization that the use of complex tools is inexorably linked to freedom. The very nature of ICT undermines the tendencies against which today's hackers and pirates consistently fight. Below, we argue that exploiting ICT's affordances necessarily promotes a certain ethos, one which requires openness and opposes monopolies of any kind.

From Jacquard loom to nanotech: a spectrum

All our technologies are always also forms of expressions; whether they be expressed through words in fixed media or through other types of artefacts. Our earliest artefacts expressed numerous ideas simultaneously, from our desires to survive, to pride in craftsmanship, and ownership of tokens. One of us has argued before (Koepsell 2003) that an expression is any form of making manifest in the world some idea. No expression can exist without an idea, for expressions are *of* something, and that something is an idea. But ideas are distinct from their expressions. Ideas belong to minds, whether we wish to believe our thoughts are material or not. Regardless, the material of an idea is distinct from the material of its expression. The idea of a spear or arrow cannot kill a bison, only its expression can. Once we make manifest some idea in the world, whether by words, actions, or artefacts, the ideas behind them become knowable to others. They are no longer bound to the mind of the expresser. Once an idea is manifest in the world as an expression it is possible for others to replicate the artefact that embodies the expression, and hence the idea. Because other minds can now 'hold' the same idea, others can relate it on to thirds, via similar, or even dissimilar, expressions. Expressions are tokens, ideas are types. The distinction is clear in that multiple minds can presumably share the same idea – given we use symbols such as words commonly as representations of some shared notion, thus enabling communication – again, presumably – for instance, the idea of justice, the idea of the colour red, etc., yet each instance exists in a different time and place from each other instance or expression of a single idea.

Since we began expressing ideas, constructing artefacts, performing songs, plays, etc., or writing poems, stories, and histories, we have largely done so with almost complete disregard of the fact that ideas could, with enough effort, be constrained by formal institutions, monopolized by a single individual. In that time, the *nature* of our artefacts and expressions – as material objects distinct from the ideas they express – has not changed in kind, although the *ease and speed* by which they may be duplicated, modified and transferred has dramatically increased. Even so, many believe we are experiencing some sort of revolution in the nature of expressions, brought on first by computers, and now being realized in other media as well. We have challenged this assumption, arguing that expressions in current ICT technologies do not differ in kind from those from eras past (Koepsell 2003).

Sometimes, we happen upon a technology that eases the drudgery of expressing our ideas to such an extent that everything done through that technology seems new. This kind of technologically enabled jump in performance is not very common but it has happened before, for example with the printing press. The amazing changes that the printing press brought about were not due to the 'kind' of expression – books will be books, hand copied or printed, letter pressed or Linotyped – but in the amount of sweat that went into spreading an idea in textual form. One cannot stress enough how dramatic the magnitude of the reduction of sweat is,[1] especially since it is enabling another swath of other advances of similar magnitude in the form of biotechnology and nanotechnology. While we might be momentarily blinded by the scale of what is going on around us, careful analysis shows that the *nature* of our artefacts-as-expressions is nonetheless the same. Let us, therefore, review this argument, and then reconsider what this means regarding ICT.

A spear, a song, a Jacquard loom and a computer are all expressions in and of themselves and also a means of expression. That is to say, each expresses the idea of itself plus something else – like, for instance, its uses, historical context, embellishments, etc. – as well as provides a means of further expression, even of potentially unrelated ideas. Each is likewise the making-manifest of some idea into the world outside of a mind. The spear is a tool, with both utilitarian and potentially aesthetic components, and acts as a medium of expressing the idea of defence, offence, sustenance – for who wields a hunting spear can feed a family – or welcome (when lowered symbolically). As with any tool, new and unanticipated uses might be found as well, such as displaying in a museum, decorating a wall, propping open a door, *ad infinitum* (namely, Feenberg 1998 on how technologies are always open to new interpretations and uses). A song similarly expresses ideas in both utilitarian and aesthetic dimensions, telling stories intended to be told by the songwriter, provoking emotions, serving as parts of ceremonies, or actively encouraging actions by groups or individuals. Likewise, the potential uses and ideas that may be interpreted to be expressed by the song far outnumber those anticipated and intended to be expressed by its creator. To turn our attention to computers we begin with the Jacquard loom. We use this example because it illustrates graphically the weakness of the assumption that a difference in degree is a difference in kind. The Jacquard loom is reprogrammable. It is a machine that can itself be made to make artefacts with differing designs. It expresses the idea of the Jacquard loom and serves as the medium for expression of an infinite number of new ideas in the form of new weavings never before created, or numerous copies of the same design. The *program* of the Jacquard loom is stored on the punch-card-like loops that can be fed into it (Essinger 2004; Goldstine 1977: 340–341; Fernaeus, Jonsson and Tholander 2012: 1595–1597). This invention helped inspire one of the first important mechanical computer designs, that of Charles Babbage's Analytical Engine, which also was to store its programs on punch-cards. The distinction between the Analytical Engine and the Jacquard loom, is, however, a matter of degree. The loom was a machine designed to fulfil only the purpose of weaving, it could not be reconfigured by its program to, say, calculate pi to 20 digits. A multipurpose computer of the type designed by Babbage, and eventually realized through electronic computing, can be reconfigured to perform numerous tasks (Randell 1982). There is no theoretical reason a multipurpose Turing-complete computer cannot be realized by gears and steam, as envisioned by Babbage. Indeed, there have been several successful mechanical and electro-mechanical calculating devices working contemporaneously with their fully electronic alternatives (Swade 2011). This historical accident is largely responsible for our misconception of the nature of ICT as something 'special' and for reinforcing our prejudices regarding the natures of expressions according to their media.

It is a spectrum that links tools such as spears, books and printing presses, Jacquard looms, and the first electronic computers to iPads. It is the same spectrum that will include converging technologies such as nanotechnology and synthetic biology. Each of these expressions instantiates more than just the idea of itself, but also numerous other possible ideas. Our modern tools just happen to be very good at allowing us to express new ideas more easily. Each new spear had to be created from scratch, its stone or metal tip carved, beaten or created by a mould then attached to its shaft. The Jacquard loom marks an important step forward in artefact production by allowing for a machine to be reconfigured without reconstructing it. The computer is another step on this spectrum, facilitating the easier recreation of a machine without reconstruction, introducing instructions in the form of software that reconfigure the machine to perform new functions. The architecture of our creative environment, from our earliest artefacts, to Jacquard looms and modern digital computers, has moved us to a place on the spectrum of expressive media that *looks very much* like a sea-change, a change in kind rather than degree.

First, to defend the claim that the change we are currently experiencing is not one of kind, we raise the challenge of identifying a materially-relevant feature of ICT that differs in kind from spears or manuscripts. Those who wish to rise to the challenge, thus claiming a difference in kind, must keep in mind that ICT could well have developed along the lines of any of the pre-electronic machines described by Swade or Randell; that its current silicon form is a matter of accident only. The parts of electronic digital computers that do the work of storing and conveying information, processing and calculating, happen to be just as physical as the mechanisms of looms, just as real as spear tips and manuscripts. Why should we treat them any differently? Yet this is exactly what happened. Next, we consider the strange consequences of the positive law in our current treatment of ICT, and ask whether and to what extent this has stifled it as a medium of expression; and, lastly, how this might in turn stifle emerging technologies.

Metaphysics and the positive law: what is the matter with ICT?

Lawyers are generally trained to be good positivists. Legal positivism asserts that the law can create and destroy categories at will, and that there is no need or sense in trying to determine whether some 'first principles' apply. So, with the emergence of categories pertaining to the classification of types of expressions, so followed the legal and public minds, with little to no apparent regard for metaphysical issues. We refer here mainly to intellectual property (IP) law, which has for the past roughly 200 years distinguished between aesthetic and utilitarian expressions, granting one kind of monopoly to new, non-obvious, and useful (utilitarian) expressions – patent, and another kind of monopoly to aesthetic expressions 'fixed' in some medium – copyright. Even while the first ever copyright law, the Statute of Anne, was quickly followed by the acrimonious 'Battle of the Booksellers', which revolved around the proper nature of IP (and that same problem still troubles jurists today), the distinction between purely useful and exclusively aesthetic expressions did not emerge as a significant problem until the beginnings of the twentieth century.

With the increased popularity of pianolas, the mechanical devices which could play a piano using a perforated roll (utilizing a mechanism not too different from the way the Jacquard loom works) came IP litigation. A major issue faced by jurists was whether the punched rolls were 'made to be addressed to the eye as sheet music' or 'form a part of a machine' (*White-Smith Music Publishing Co. v Apollo Co.*, 1908). In other words, were the rolls merely instrumental artefacts, or a means of expressing an artist's ideas? The development of modern ICT, built upon an electronic and silicon infrastructure afforded us a radically quicker and easier medium for creating and disseminating certain types of expressions than previous infrastructures. The same distinction is now a much bigger problem, simply because the means of reproduction and translation from one medium to another have exploded in quantity and variety.

Prior to widespread networked ICT, the most efficient means of expression, namely printing presses, television, radio, and other forms of media were also expensive, centralized, difficult and costly to maintain, and often require licensure from the state for access. Creating newspapers, books, television shows, radio programmes, re-coded music LPs, etc., took substantial amounts of capital investment in the tools and means of production and distribution, leaving entry into these media markets closed to most but the very wealthy. Because the tools of production were specialized and expensive, unwieldy to move about, reconfigure and use, few creators had access to them. A partial solution to this scarcity took the form of various 'studio' systems, facilitated in no small part by IP, and various licensing arrangements, such as in the case of radio (Coase 1959).

ICT law has developed more or less around the available categories of IP law, treating modes of expression that use an electronic medium (based on electromagnetic pulses) in very much the same way as similar modes of expression that use a more tangible medium (such as ink on paper). This approach runs up against a serious conundrum with regard to software; something that seemed particular and new to computers: namely, software is treated, still, as though it can be either patented or copyrighted without worry about the contradiction of allowing two previously mutually-exclusive categories to suddenly merge. We have spent some time now trying to explain that the merging of these categories is rational, given that the two categories are not themselves founded upon a clear distinction. Another aspect of our spectrum is that the continuum between spear and nanotech also describes a continuum between aesthetic and utilitarian. No clear lines distinguish these types, and the law of IP has only confused matters. It did so for understandable reasons, as books and looms appeared in many ways to be two very different sorts of creations, but ICT has revealed reasons to question whether this ever was really so. It is not just that discriminating which kinds of expression is exclusively, or predominantly, useful and which is aesthetic that cannot be objectively grounded; the dividing line between software and hardware is also intrinsically fuzzy.

When you pick up your smart phone are you handling hardware, software, both or a different kind of entity made of a combination? To put the question another way, is computer hardware not simply a lump of matter no different from unformed clay, if not as the medium for software? To highlight the deep level to which software is to be found in various artefacts we should peek into the black box of ICT devices. Somewhere between software and hardware, most modern electronic devices have firmware. Firmware is defined by the dictionary as 'computer programs contained permanently in a hardware device (as a read-only memory)' (Merriam-Webster 2013) or 'software programs and procedures that are permanently stored in a computer's memory using a read-only (ROM) technology are called firmware, or "hard software"' (Encyclopaedia Britannica 2013). Like any term of art, definitions do not do justice to the notion. It seems that firmware is exactly the kind of expression that confounds the distinction between something that is an essential part of a mechanism, as would be a set of cogs, and an idea fixed as symbols, as would be a poem. While the first instances of firmware where microcode for CPUs – machine code instructions for controlling the inner functions of a CPU to give the engineer a richer set of machine code – hardly a 'human readable' form of expression, modern firmware is developed just like any other software, using human readable programming languages. The difference between regular software and firmware is that without the correct firmware an electronic device is but a brick. This is not merely a play on words. The verb 'to brick' is another bit of jargon that refers exactly to the case when someone tries to replace the firmware of a device and fails, rendering the device into something no more useful than a brick (Wikipedia 2013). There is nothing in the physical matter of the device that has changed – or at least nothing above the molecular level, for admittedly, the charge states of individual bits in the permanent storage do differ – but a device can indeed be damaged beyond recovery by pushing into it bad firmware. It seems that to the masters of the art there is no question that what makes an ICT device is the coming together of the right bits of hardware, software and whatever lies in between.

Online forums frequented by hackers and tinkerers of computers, smart phones and digital cameras are littered with warnings of the kind 'this process can brick your device' and people grumbling or boasting about some device they have bricked. These same ICT enthusiasts refer to the process of replacing the firmware of an Android phone as 'updating the ROM'. Now ROM stands for Read Only Memory, so technically a ROM is a kind of memory that cannot be 'updated', and ought to be an integral part of the device. But because the core software of a smart phone is an inalienable feature that makes a smart phone what it is, this misnomer make sense to that crowd, and therefore is common terminology for those with 'skill and practice in the art'. What functions can one remove from a smart phone, and still be able to call it such?

It is worth keeping in mind that modern smart phones and Wi-Fi devices make use of so called 'software defined radios'. This is a radio where the transmission characteristics, including frequencies and power, are defined in its firmware. The implications of this include that regulatory authorities that oversee the market of radio devices, and regulate their trade and use on the bases of the transmission characteristics of the radio, must now face a similar conundrum. The physical device itself is no radio at all until its appropriate software is accounted for. But the problem is not simply solved by the regulatory authority dealing with limited – even if large – possible software varieties. As we have seen, the big idea behind ICT is that such devices are re-programmable. Using a publicly known set of commands, we can reconfigure the Wi-Fi transmitter in our home router to use a higher or lower power level or different set of frequencies. To be able to cater to different regulatory regimes, manufacturers build devices that are flexible and capable of operating within relative wide parameters and simply provide different firmware in different markets. There are three things that stop the user of such a device from re-programming it to operate as though it was in another jurisdiction, or with complete disregard of such radio frequency regulation. First, it is not very easy to program this kind of device. However, for more popular devices, there is enough skill available globally that via the internet it soon becomes public knowledge. Second, manufacturers can implement systems – voluntary or under pressure from the regulator – such that the device accepts only 'authorized' firmware. No such system is totally fool proof, so this often translates to making the required skills even rarer. But is that rare enough? No, so, third, the state can legislate to forbid people from sharing this knowledge publicly.

The end result is that if we take the distinction between expressions subject to patent and those subject to copyright seriously, then for a state to control productive acts – transmitting wireless signals – it has no other recourse than to regulate the expressive acts – sharing bits of text representing the sequence of instructions to make your Wi-Fi transmitter work in specific ways. As technologies become more modular, complex and distributed, and as the informational approach of ICT with its gargantuan capacity for storage and speed of processing spills over into the tangible, through today's cutting-edge 3D-printing, or tomorrow's nanotech, and touches life itself as does biotech, the overlap and intermingling of categories presumed in IP will get worse. Even limiting ourselves to the field of ICT, we have hardly scratched the surface of the tip of an iceberg.

It is a well-known trope that today's microelectronic components are so complex that they could never have been built if their designers did not make use of the ICT tools of yesterday. It is because computers are such powerful design aids for the next generation of computers that development in the field has been exponential. One method of prototyping new specialized chips, say music player system-on-chip, is to use another kind of integrated circuit called a Field Programmable Gate Array (FPGA) (Lysecky and Vahid 2005). FPGAs are not quite computers, but they are general purpose re-programmable electronic devices. The functions of an FPGA, that is, how its millions of logic gates and other components are to be interconnected, the output of one connecting to the input of another, etc., is done by means of a specialized programming language called Hardware Description Language (HDL). HDL was first used as a means of describing more traditional kinds (i.e. non-programmable) of chips (Melnikova, Hahanova and Mostovaya 2009).

But it is nonetheless a programming language, the kind you can print out on paper. In fact, to make the life of engineers easier, nowadays one can program an FPGA using a 'regular' programming language such as python, and have other software turn this into HDL. Moreover, there are available on the market and as Open Source programs called Soft Processors. These are in one sense an inverse of firmware, rather than 'Hard software' this is 'Soft hardware'. By programming an FPGA with a Soft Processor, the FPGA acquires the functionality of a regular general purpose CPU. I can develop some software and dedicate a computer to run that exclusively, essentially deploying the generic reprogrammable computer as a single purpose device (this is in fact the case with many of today's devices such as MP3 players, digital radios, digital cameras, GPS navigators, the list goes on). Alternatively, I can reduce my system to its minimal requirements, remove any generic components not used for my purpose and place that on an FPGA. Thus I have created single-purpose hardware. Or have I? Is it software, if the FPGA I chose can only be programmed once? Does it matter that the system in a learner version was entirely implemented in software on a generic PC and now is running on specialized dedicated hardware? This line of development has actually occurred in the highly specialized, sometimes bohemian, community of Bitcoin mining. Bitcoin is a virtual alternative currency that depends on 'mining operations' which are essentially software doing billions of complex mathematical calculations (cf. De la Porte 2012). This mining is needed to both 'find' new Bitcoins, and thus to ensure the integrity of the currency by requiring value to beget value. In order to speed up these operations, miners have developed their processes step-wise: first the algorithms were optimized for commodity hardware; then miners started running several machines in parallel; next they reprogrammed the same algorithms to run on Graphics Processing Units. Recently, miners started using dedicated FPGAs; and now dedicated microchips built specifically for the purpose are hitting the market. Clearly, the box containing the FPGA required only configuration, but no 'external' software is a piece of hardware (Monmasson and Cirstea 2007). Even more so with the emerging dedicated microprocessors built such that they are not reprogrammable at all. And yet, clearly all the steps mentioned somehow deploy the same algorithm, the same software, otherwise the different Bitcoins generated by each would not belong to the same virtual currency, whose value depends on the ascertainability of that first version of human readable code.

There is no need to restrict ourselves to the microscopic world of integrated circuits to see how ICT is undoing our preconceptions of how ideas, expressions and artefacts interrelate. A modern day sport hunter, let us call her Anna, uses a crossbow as her weapon, wants to put metal bodkin points on her arrows, but cannot find anywhere to buy them, so she resolves to make them herself. Anna considers two options: (1) get some metal, heat it up to a high temperature, and beat on it with a hammer on an anvil until the desired shape is obtained; or (2) mill the points out of solid metal using a computer-controlled milling machine. Anna is a geek, so she chooses option 2. She sits down at her computer and draws the point on CAD software. The software then generates a software program in a specialized programming language called G-Code. The hunter then sends this software – G-Code is not normally called software because it is not intended to run on general purpose computers, but is fundamentally equivalent, if not Turing-complete – to some company that owns a computer-controlled milling machine which makes the arrow points. A fellow hunter, call him Ben, likes the idea, but he is unskilled at using CAD. Ben can build the same bodkin points as Anna if he somehow obtained the G-Code. Ben also has two options: (1) get the G-Code, in textual format (this is to some extent human readable, in fact before it was widely deployed, advanced CAD engineers would hand-craft it) directly from Anna. He can copy it, buy it, or steal it; or (2) Ben can extract the software, the G-Code, out of one of Anna's points, by reverse-engineering. Anna does not like Ben, and makes sure he will not get the G-Code from her, so Ben must go for option 2. He manages to pick up a point Anna lost, as sometimes happens in their sport. He sends the point to a company that does 3D scanning, which sends him back a point-map. This is mechanically (on a PC) processed to generate G-Code. This G-Code is not the exact same one as Anna's, it is not bit-identical, but the bodkin points that it produces are indistinguishable from Anna's. Ben has clearly copied Anna's idea, even if he never had the opportunity to see it expressed in a 'readable' medium. He has extracted some software out of an artefact, even if the artefact is not a computer itself.

This story may sound a bit outlandish, but consider for a moment the level of precision already attainable by means of 3D scanning and printing. The level of precision required for such copies to be made is, perhaps, not yet available to the consumer, but in medical fields such techniques are already being deployed for hip replacement. 3D printing has already reached the level of precision required for hobbyists to be able to print their own gun parts. Reverse engineering also has a very long tradition, just now, with ICT, transcriptions of uncovered mechanisms can be shared in the form of code, rather than blueprints, tables of values, and descriptions in English. The software in the machine has always been there, even in arrow points and spears. The software of a single-purpose digital computer is simply part of the mechanism that makes it function just as it does. The pattern of switches and gates, the firing of electronic signals through a single-purpose digital computer is physically no different from the gears, cranks, levers, and switches of a steam-powered Jacquard loom with a programmed pattern feeding into it. The apparently static spear that lies there doing its job, or even a book, is what it is because of its software. The software of the book is the instructions built into it that make it function as a book, rather than a lump of dead organic material. Software has been all around us for as long as we have made artefacts, it just has not been very dynamic. Modern computers did not create something new in kind with the advent of digital software, they just made it clear that our prior distinctions among types of artefacts were built upon faulty dichotomies. The shame of it is that the positive law has not caught up.

The positive law continues to try to treat ICT erratically, sometimes as though it were like publishing companies, especially as concerns the application of laws of libel, defamation, as well as copyright, and sometimes as though it were machinery, as if its software component is another inventive physical object. This application of both IP schemes, as well as other torts and criminal law, reflects the preconceptions about the material nature of expressions through ICT as described above, and is founded upon a faulty ontology. Meanwhile, emergent social institutions are recognizing that they can treat ICT and its associated objects more rationally. This realization is driving the establishment of alternate institutional architectures better mapped to the material architecture of ICT.

The rapid and largely productive developments of ICT have ushered in numerous efficiencies, broken down many barriers to production and entry for creative expression, and underpin large parts of the global economy today. This encourages those with access to, and knowledge about, its tools to develop alternate conceptualizations of the technology-cum-medium markedly distinct from what the presuppositions of the positive law have allowed for. The emergence of open source as a development framework for code, and crowd-sourced methods for creative production, are clear examples of how creators are exploiting the material architecture of ICT for its inherently liberating potential. These new techno-social infrastructures engender creative activity beyond the restrictive bounds of the positive law's institutions. Society is free to build any institutional approach to artefacts it sees fit, constrained only by the laws of physics and, one would hope, rational coherence. Recognizing the proper metaphysical bounds of ICT mediated expression empowers us to reject the dichotomy embraced hitherto. We are thus free to develop fresh institutional approaches for handling the full spectrum of artefacts as expressions. The importance of this realization is now critical, given the trajectory towards which future modes of expression are trending, under the propulsive effects of ICT's exponential growth in reach and affordance.

The future of ICT and the future of expression

The major trends in the development of technology in general, and ICT technologies in particular are clear enough: smaller, cheaper, more flexible and more energy-efficient devices coupled with decentralization, delocalization and modularization of their constituent components. The same trends apply to the means of production, be it of hi-tech devices or of any other product, for the means of production are, bar their human component, also technological devices. Profitability, as well as ease of access and distribution are all aided by these trends. As these trends continue, it is becoming ever cheaper and more convenient to create ICT-centric products, as well as other products that have been facilitated by the rise of ICT. Independent film-making, sound recording, podcasts, and other forms of new or adapted media continue to become easier to produce and reproduce thanks to ever more powerful, cheaper tools of production. The ICT revolution is not yet complete, however. The forms of creativity and the types of artefacts enabled by ICT are still rather limited. But the lessons learned from the past few decades of software engineering practice are beginning to translate to new infrastructures, making the tools of production of new types of artefacts similarly available.

As mentioned above, until very recently most tools could only be programmed at the moment of manufacture. In any case, for most of history the re-programming of a tool, or form of expression, was very laborious and expensive, if possible at all. Indeed, it would have been the exception rather than the norm. In naval contexts, the practice of jury rigging is yet another example of the inherent re-programmability of technology, but the fact that it was an emergency practice attests to the impracticality of re-programming tools compared to building new ones. Software of a sort was already inherent in early, single-use tools, it was the 'type' that made it what it was, that was instantiated in its form, and that enabled others to reproduce the same tools, albeit with effort and time. The emergence of tools built to be re-programmable, of which the Jacquard loom and Movable Type printing are prototypical exemplars, reduced the effort to such an extent that re-programming made more economic sense than re-building the tool. The von Neumann architecture of a computer is a tool unlike earlier tools in that its very own output can be a program that is fed back into it. A Jacquard loom can make an infinite number of weaves, but it cannot output a new pattern. Computers can be used to produce even more computer software. This feedback mechanism, which distinguishes modern computers, accelerates development exponentially. But computers are just symbol manipulators. They have limited means of interaction with the world. They can become an unlimited number of new symbol manipulating machines, but they are still rather limited in how they can affect their external environments. Digitization is advancing rapidly, and sound, light and movement can all be converted to symbols that a computer manipulates (via cameras, microphones and accelerometers). Also, robotics (including computer controlled machinery) is similarly moving forward, allowing the symbols output by computers to affect the material environment. Nonetheless, in comparison to its capacity for symbol manipulation, the ability of a computer to affect the material world is rather crude and clumsy. A modern car is, for all intents and purposes, a computer-controlled machine. That computer can be re-programmed: different software can make the same engine perform in a 'sports mode' or an 'eco mode'. In this sense, we are already at the stage where a software choice determines to some extent the sub-type of a car – whether it is a sports car or a city car. But we are nowhere near the possibility of re-programming a car to make it into a yacht. Manipulating matter programmatically is still more expensive that building a new device, when it is possible at all.

Nonetheless, the re-programing of matter is not a pipe dream of science fiction. Rather, it is the declared aim of emerging (sometimes called 'converging') technologies such as synthetic biology and nanotechnology. These technologies, still in their infancy, show that it might indeed be possible to use the approach of software programming to reprogramme matter itself, to make machines that are as easily reconfigurable materially as computers are informationally. If the billions of dollars private investors, governments the world over, and scientific communities are investing in nanotechnology and biotechnology yield just a fraction of the possibilities being sought, incorporating current ICT's use of networks and programming into tangible objects, the dream will become reality sooner rather than later.

In synthetic biology, researchers are putting together a standard toolkit of biological instructions, derived from studying the working of genes in organisms, so that new forms of organisms can be built to make things we need and want such as fuels, super-strong materials, medicines, etc.. The methodology recognizes that organisms are computers of a sort, processing genetic information to perform tasks, to run biological machineries, and produce vital biological components for life. Reverse-engineering the code of life, assembling a standard toolkit, and utilizing those parts to make new code that nature did not yet devise will bring to bear the methods and tools of software to the biological world, producing organic artefacts.

In nanotechnology, much the same dream is thought to be possible with mechanisms at the nanoscale. This too is inspired in part by our understanding of the biological world in which nanoscale mechanisms abound. Through the combined science of engineering and programming, we ought to be able to construct very tiny mechanical computers that can accept programming, evolve their own, and reconfigure themselves as needed. In a world in which every artefact can be made or reconfigured at will, our previous mistaken approaches to the institutions we have devised around ICT will continue to be challenged.

The future we are imagining is one where the modular 'apps' familiar to millions of smart phone users, will be augmented by things that we more clearly recognize as artefactual: *artefapps*, if you will. Just as today one goes to the supermarket, picks a selection of items, and combines them in the kitchen following a recipe to produce a dinner, one could shop around for artefapps and combine them, following a recipe, to produce an on-demand device. And just as in the kitchen one might follow a recipe from a cook book, one he or she obtained from a friend, or be creative, and improvise a new dish on the spur of the moment; just as flour, sugar, potatoes, yeasts, ovens, pans and pots, can be combined in an infinite number of ways – most of which do not work, but some of which are surprisingly delicious; artefapps will allow the re-combination and programming of biological, symbolic and material elements to create either standardized or totally innovative custom devices, tools and consumables.

Until recently, expressing oneself in any number of available media was difficult. It was costly, relied upon a small number of gatekeepers, both private and public, and involved in many cases significant capital investment. The infrastructure for both production and dissemination of new expressions was difficult to access, and the barriers to entry too high for many creative people to manage. Luck, diligence, and talent might not have been enough. Mere physical access to the tools of production, much less the networks for dissemination, was necessarily limited.

Who knows how many brilliant artists, authors, filmmakers, or musicians came and went without ever having the chance to explore their talents, or share them with the world, simply because the systems necessary to do so were largely closed. ICTs have changed all that. As discussed above, to make a film today, or to record music, to write and publish a book, no longer presents the same technical barriers, and more or less the only remaining barrier is talent. While there is never a guarantee of success, and it remains difficult to find an audience, the production and dissemination part of creating has been significantly facilitated by modern ICT.

Expressing oneself will only become easier as the methods and tools of ICT spill into the space of the sort of things more typically referred to as artefacts.[2] Creators who lack talent in the arts, but who wish to bring new artefacts into the world that are valued for other reasons than primarily aesthetic, will be able to do so with ever decreasing costs using converging technologies, as described above; think of a new tool, or any item you need or want, then make one. Developers of mobile apps are aided by off-the-shelf app design software, by a healthy community or production sharing code, as members of a gardening club share seeds, and have access to a variety of ready-made libraries implementing common algorithms. Realizing new mobile apps occurs at a high level of abstraction, without requiring direct access to every model of and variant of hardware for which an app is designed. The developer needs only to be capable of programming in a very high level language, in a user-friendly software development environment. So too making any newly conceived widget is already becoming both easy and cheap, and even potentially profitable. On-demand 3D printing services (namely, Shapeways.com), with their networks for the sharing and selling of 'physical' goods – of which the stock consists in a blueprint and raw material – are appearing on the market. They are developing along the same social institutional arrangements their 'virtual' predecessors have done before. Think of making a loaf of bread, starting from a field of wheat and some hand tools compared to starting from a bag of bread-mix and a bread-making machine. We are still making the same 'bread' thing, but the opportunities for expressing oneself through bread-as-medium are radically increased in the latter case. This is the magnitude of sweat saved, and of opportunities added, by such technologies and services to the efforts of do-it-yourself enthusiasts, tinkerers and hobbyists today. They also make industrial prototyping in certain sectors an order of magnitude more efficient. Only law can hold this kind of innovation from benefiting a much wider swath of creative and productive endeavours in the future. Every innovation that brings us closer to programmable matter re-doubles that increase in opportunity, and stresses the given institutional framework that tries to keep the aesthetic and the useful distinct.

Current institutional constraints will no longer suffice, and will be worked around. Consider the jailbreaking and rooting of smart phones. In the world of online apps, for a while and to an arguable extent, Apple's iOS-based system was the dominant one. Apple brilliantly created a marketplace for all sorts of new creativity through its app store. Anyone with an idea, and some moderate skill or access to those with the skill, can create and market an app and release it all without significant capital expenditure. But Apple's market is constrained, and it does not let everyone in. Mindful and dependent upon the current system of IP and other concerns regarding its control over its products, Apple prevented certain apps from reaching its store. Additionally, developing iOS apps could only be done on Apple computers and using Apple software. Unfortunately for consumers, and those who had ideas they wanted to express and distribute for others to use – and maybe even sell and make some money from – Apple's policies were a barrier to entry for certain expressions. So programmers made their own markets, developed tools that enabled 'jailbreaking' iOS devices so that other app stores could be used, and began distributing their own apps, even making money in the process by charging users for some apps just as app-makers do on the Apple App Store. Apple's challenges to the legality of these new markets fell flat as the courts have held that they are legal, and people may jailbreak their devices as they see fit. The courts determined that the right to expression cannot be so limited. The market also seems to agree. Google's Android-based smart phone system is a major competitor to Apple. Google's system came to the market later, and imitated many aspects of Apple's approach, most importantly its app market. But Google's competitive value proposition to developers was that its market was much more open. Google is much less restrictive about which apps it chooses to 'censor'. Alternative markets do not require jailbreaking on Android. The Android app development environment is Open Source software and integrates into Eclipse, a pre-existing popular Open Source development environment. Android itself is largely Open Source, so that the entire system can be replaced with an independently developed alternative. In Android, rooting is merely a means of accessing the nuts and bolts of the system, which is not recommended, but neither is it forbidden. Google's own Play Store provides apps that require a rooted device.

It seems that in this cutting edge highly competitive market, the value proposition that allows a giant such as Google to break into the market is to forgo the protections of IP, and the power of control that come with it. Instead, an open market exploits the innovative potential of the architecture itself, and relies on the inherently free mechanism of technical development to direct the app market towards the most value-laden configuration. While the end result is that Android has overtaken iOS, and made Google and its partners a lot of money, the system is far from being as open as the technology actually allows.

The key to keep on evolving away from constraining the freedom of expressions in certain novel kinds of media, is to recognize that expressions are all of one kind: the making manifest of some idea into the world. Limits on expression in certain media must be justified by some overwhelming concern. Previously, when the tools and networks for creating and disseminating expressions were necessarily limited due to costs, scarce resources, etc., one's inability to express an idea could be better tolerated. The positive law that had been configured to purposely restrict expressions for the benefit of publishers and producers – and not so much artists or other creators – could be similarly tolerated. The number of individuals touched by such restrictions was, in any case, much smaller than it is now in real and relative terms. But when the tools became finally available to the artists themselves and to regular members of the public, and the means of production could no longer be monopolized by well-established networks, powerful lobbies worked to strengthen the old institutions, expand in time and scope the monopoly privileges over older expressions, and prevent new profitable resources from appearing by curtailing expressions from entering the public domain.

We claim that the curtailing of free expression is antithetical to the spirit of free markets. Where there is a free market and freedom of expression, there will also be a free market of expressions and of mediums of expression. Monopolies in the market of expressions will invariably damage the free market as well as freedom of expression. The same will be true with any new media, even when that new media will take the unfamiliar form of programmable matter. It is entirely predictable, even expected, that some early innovators in nanotech and synthetic biology will attempt to sew up the markets for themselves, and to prevent entry by later innovators. They will most likely try to do this by ensuring that the legal infrastructure leans in their favour. This happens in any new market. The question is: will the logic of jailbreaking's legality, alternative app markets, and others like it be applied consistently? Will the efficiency advantage of free innovation trump the incumbency provided by IP on the market? We argue that not only is it ontologically justified, it is also necessary if we want to retain freedom of both markets and expression.

Types, tokens and change in expression

The idea that one could monopolize *a type* is considerably new in the long history of expression. Ideas, once expressed, are nearly impossible to contain for long. There is no need to subscribe to the thesis that 'memes, once they exist, are independent of authors and critics alike' (Dennett 1990: 135) to appreciate that ideas are free, and remain under the dominion of their creator only until he or she thinks proper to emancipate them by fixing them in expressions. Artefact types dating from pre-history onward show a gradual evolution that reveals that ideas were, at times, widely distributed both within and among cultures. Both utility and aesthetics influenced changes over time in the types and nature of expressions. Cultures and what we know about them are contained in their artefacts and other expressions. So what are these expressions, how do they relate to types, and what are legitimate ways to control those types, if any?

As argued at length above and in our other works, there is no clear distinction between a 'utilitarian' artefact and any other. A song, for instance, has utility. Once fixed in some medium, it becomes an artefact. If I sing a song, and you hear it, you can reproduce it without depriving me of anything. This is the distinction between type and token. Tokens are limited in time and place, existing in alienable forms. Thus, a single instance of a recording of the song I sang is a token and is alienable. This, it seems, is a primary basis for the concept of property: alienability. If I own a token of anything, typically, I can do whatever I want with it. It is also part and parcel of my right to free expression to say, do, and perhaps make anything I wish, including copies of things I may have seen or heard elsewhere. The *natural right to express* means that whatever idea is in my head can be made manifest in any way I see fit, consistent and limited only by something like Mill's liberty or 'harm' principle. But the institutions we have developed to try to grant control over types do some rather fishy things with rights we generally take for granted over tokens.

Before the positive law created institutions that limit rights to free expression by limiting our abilities to reproduce tokens of certain types at will, other institutions, such as guilds, attempted to do so with secrecy and force. The difference in effect on free expression between the threatened violence of a guild and that of the state is a matter only of legal legitimacy. Is the use of force to limit free expression morally justified? Is it necessary? Can it co-exist with further technological innovation on the track laid by ICT? The answer to all of these is: no. The ontology of expressions reveals this, and the trajectory of the technology makes it inevitable. Let us revisit the continuum of expression, see how it is reflected in the development of technologies, and consider what this implies.

Ideas are types, they are distinct from tokens, which as mentioned above exist as instances of types, locatable in time and space, and exclusive. Each instance of a chair is nonetheless an expression of the type: chair. Each instance of a spear is an expression of the idea of a spear, as well as numerous other ideas. Some expressions are easily located in time and space, like a statue, or a bow-tie, or a gate, some are more difficult, like a radio broadcast, or a shout, or a dance. The right to expression means simply the right to be able to manifest an idea in the world, and does not depend at all upon the originality of the idea.[3] The right to conscience, which is closely related, is the right to hold any idea. There is no cognizable limiting principle to freedom of conscience, and the only good candidate for a limiting principle for free expression is the harm principle. In other words, we are free in every way to make manifest ideas into the world short of harming others. Except, perhaps, for certain deadly pathogens or materials, no token in itself violates the harm principle in its creation. Until recently, the creation of tokens expressing certain types was limited by material scarcity and natural monopolies. Those who possessed natural monopolies were likewise successful at gaining legal monopolies to support them and to maintain their privilege. Thus, while the rights to freedom of conscience and expression might have technically existed, other barriers prevented entry into the marketplace of ideas and expressions for many if not most. Those barriers to entry have eroded with the advent of new technologies, steadily reducing costs and capital needed, eliminating middlemen, and providing ever new and more flexible media for expression.

The distance between idea and expression has been shortened over time, though the ontological distinction between the two remains. The history of technological development has reduced the labour required for achieving so many human aspirations, but it has been most successful in lightening the burden of work involved in expressing ideas. This meant that the natural monopolies caused by exclusive access to resources or the use of violence began to erode. Monopolists obtained the state's help and procured legal monopolies over types, thus preventing certain expressions from being made without payment, or being enjoyed without a rent, and otherwise stifling free expression. This worked for a time as potential creators knew no better, and had no expectation of access to the tools of expression. Backed by law, the monopolists had the power to dictate the terms under which productive creativity was permissible. Those who wished to enter the marketplace of expressions under different terms always sought to subvert barriers, but it is the architecture of emerging technologies that empowers them to credibly threaten the incumbent power. First because of ICT, which has reduced the cost and difficulty of expression of certain sorts, and next with emerging technologies borrowing from ICT's methods and infrastructure, new markets will emerge regardless of states' and monopolists' attempts to prevent them. The critical question is whether the emergent markets where innovation flourishes will be black markets or not.

As the bridge between type and token grows smaller, the demand for quasi-unlimited freedom of expression continues to grow. There is a limit to how long creators will tolerate the barriers that have been erected, especially when long entrenched monopolies seek various states' recourse to build those barriers ever higher. Punishment for infringement of those barriers is becoming more severe, but technology is making infringement easier and cheaper every day. Attempted infringement, and disseminating infringement know-how, are also being punished in much more severe ways than the law allows damage to material property to be punished. Creators' allegiance to the rule of law is being pushed from both sides, the law, state and monopolists threats on the one hand, and new and emerging technologies and mediums tantalizing opportunities for expression on the other. So long as the friction keeps rising, the stability of the *status quo* is unsustainable.

Just as alternative approaches to the creation and dissemination of ICT expressions have undermined prior expectations and institutional prejudices, so too will emerging technologies undermine the remnants of the past 200 years. The fact of the error of the dichotomy between two allegedly different types of expression will come to be generally understood, and the inability due to the technology itself of maintaining meaningful monopolies over expressions of types will finally be complete. No one will be harmed in the process other than those whose fortunes are dependent on the extension of monopolies. Rather, full liberation of the tools of expression (and production) will mean that more potential creators will be able to enter markets, to realize their creations and offer them for sale. The scarcities that have so long protected monopolists will continue to dissolve, as they have in large part due to ICT itself, as the full panoply of material goods becomes more like ICT. Attempts to lock up expression through recourse to the state can only go so far. Underground movements (such as the Comex market, file sharing communities, independent artists whose reputations are built online) can assert a value proposition that is more attractive than what is on offer on the mainstream market. When one of the valuable assets that an underground movement offers is increased personal expression, that movement is likely to be judged as successful by society, as happened with Open Source. The result is that such a movement becomes attractive and grows exponentially. A counter-cultural movement can only remain hidden, underground and illegal so long as it is small and less powerful than the legal mainstream. Once its deviance is socially normalized it can quickly become legally legitimate. In other words, normal social behaviour cannot be illegal. The use of technology to express ideas outside of the institutional infrastructure of IP is still considered deviant today, but its added value is a guarantee that it will not be so for long. We suggest that future cultural analysts will consider the notion that the current legal regime does not abridge freedom of expression and conscience, as a powerful mythology, and that they, unlike many of us today, will have the good fortune to be aware of its falsity.

The future is writ in the technology that gravitates toward ease of creation, speed of dissemination, and non-scare reproduction. Undoing the natural and legal monopolies that have allowed a few to profit at the expense of the creativity of the many will open the floodgates for faster and easier innovation. The alternative is to arrest the development of ICT-driven innovation. Increasing demand for new products in a world of diminishing resources cannot last. Instead, innovation accommodates demand by reducing the necessity for scarce resources, and shifting to less scarce resources. In ICT, Moore's law defies Malthus's catastrophe, and there is no shortage of computing power or lack of space for storage and growth in ICT. Extending ICT's innovations to the world of more standardly-recognized goods may help solve scarcity problems in general given the distribution of knowledge to geographically remote locales with access to increasingly inexpensive means of assembly (nanofabrication, 3D printing, etc., will help overcome physical distribution impediments – assuming legal impediments to distributing IP are resolved). As matter can be reconfigured at will, at the molecular level, the costs of production will continue to decline, just as the costs of computing have. Distribution networks for physical goods will become less burdened and more easily lubricated, meaning local shortages will decline, and wealth will spread just as creativity does. All of this assumes a couple of things: we have rights to conscience and expression that are limited only by the harm principle, and current legal regimes limit expression by granting monopolies. We contend that these are two non-controversial claims. Those who seek to oppose them often do so from some utilitarian perspective, arguing that some expression must be limited to prevent not just harms, but also to encourage innovation – presumably because failing to do so will cause other harms. Moreover, utilitarian responses to the second claim, that IP is a monopoly privilege created by the state, often argue that this is again a necessary evil, causing in the long run more good than harm.

Markets and morals: our expressive future

ICT has paved the way for the total undoing of copyright, and both nanotech and synthetic biology will do likewise for patent. This is a trend to be embraced and prepared for, first, because short of turning vast numbers of citizens into criminals and punishing them accordingly, the trend is irreversible; and, second, even more importantly, because it is morally right. We must, therefore, consider the moral necessity to alter our institutions. This is not an incitement to civil disobedience on the basis of an unjust legal regime that is in conflict with the nature of reality present in modern technology. It is, rather, an invitation for all those implicated, which includes pretty much every human being where there is internet access, to collaboratively seek a mutually beneficial means for moving beyond the current IP regime before it implodes.

The right to freedom of expression has never required originality, nor is there any right to be compensated for expressing one's ideas. We take a chance, and see whether the market values our expressions. Valued expressions are often compensated, even when there is no legal institution enforcing it. Social institutions and custom that cause us to value and recompense valued services have enabled markets to thrive for fungible goods and services even where no monopolies exist either naturally or by fiat.

There are legitimate limits to our expressions, but these are very few and typically laws treat these via passive rather than active responsibility. Our positive moral duties include, always, to avoid causing harms. Depriving someone of a rightfully gained token causes harm. Injuring someone physically, or, in certain situations psychologically, causes harm. Expressions, whether manifest via the medium of words, actions, or artefacts should not be restrained, unless someone is harmed by their manifestation An expression which reduces the potential profitability of another expression does not cause harm – absent some dependence upon artificial market monopoly – to the expresser of the expression. If it were so, negative appraisal of a film by a film critic would be tantamount to a physical assault on the director. Restraining expression, on the other hand, causes harm, as it limits our most basic freedoms, it creates limits to possibilities of choosing who we want to be. In sum, it is a moral imperative, borne out by our technologies' natures as always, also, being mediums of expression, to better enable ourselves to express freely any idea in any medium, short of causing some harm.

Technology and morality are intertwined, but often our technology advances out of step with our laggard moral development. Before notions of free expression were recognized as natural rights, the tools that enabled certain expressions to be made more freely were developed. The natural reaction of societies that have become entrenched in privileged modes of behaviour and thought is to react defensively. Reactionary forces often seek to strengthen their hold on power by increasing the breadth and spans of monopolies. This is how churches reacted to the dissemination of printing presses, by attempting to maintain their monopoly on the printed word, and invoking laws to suppress competitors. The very same is going on with our current monopolists who are intent on curtailing the expressions of others while extending their own monopolies on expressions of all kinds.

In light of these trends, we have a duty to protect and encourage those who would liberate our media, and prevent monopolization. The technological inevitability of massively distributed means of production and dissemination of expressions in any media is not enough. As with any attempt to censor and stifle progress, we have a positive duty to conduct acts of civil disobedience as well as to try to change or subvert unjust laws. Three current and newsworthy phenomena that demand our attention include the actions of the group Anonymous, ongoing attempts by states to shut down sites such as the Pirate Bay, and the WikiLeaks case. In each of these cases, those who seek to subvert monopolies over expressions are being treated as criminals. These are test cases for the near future. If we have a right to jailbreak our devices, to use our tokens as we will, and to develop and express ideas, create artefacts for new networks and markets as we please, then we must recognize the need to defend the ethos that drives the Pirate Bay, Anonymous and WikiLeaks.

The 'hacker' ethos created the ICT age. The desire to liberate expression, to grow a body of communal knowledge, encourage individual entrepreneurship, and respect property rights even while ignoring the myth of rights over types, helped to develop the networks and machines that are undoing the past age of media monopolies. The hacker ethos is at work in the three phenomena noted above. The idea that one can distribute freely ideas in any medium, that states have no right to keep secret the mechanisms for their controls over us or the machinations of their power, and that attempts to curtail our free expression must be met with resistance, must be preserved if the full promise of the extension of the ICT revolution into the 'physical' world is to be completed. The hacker ethos contains an ethical kernel, one that must be nourished. The clash between technical possibility and reactionary attempts to control it is already playing out not just in expensive civil legal battles, but also in criminal proceedings. The hackers of the next age are threatened by the attempts by monopolists to prevent freedom from being achieved in the next media as it is becoming in ICT.

The ethos of ICT is an architecture of freedom, built into its networks and circuits, and demanding that we respond appropriately. The response must be to welcome it, to notice that each new advance in our expression has improved our lives and expanded our freedom. Attempts to curtail the freedoms built into the infrastructures we embrace result only in hypocrisy, and undermine both technical and social progress. These attempts are not founded upon any sound evidence of their necessity, and contradict our most basic values.

Concluding remarks

We have argued in this chapter that, although states have attempted to apply existing IP regimes to ICT and other related emerging media, these attempts will fail for the following reasons. The categories of IP have always been poorly drawn and entirely artificial, as well as inevitably inhibiting free expression which is a value we assume overrides any potential economic value of IP; ICT and related, emerging material technologies are inherently uncontrollable, and embody necessarily the ethos of 'openness' that IP law stifles; and, lastly, ICT is not necessary to produce the aims of incentivizing creation or promoting invention, and open legal regimes not depending upon artificial monopolies have proven to be attractive to innovators producing useful and desirable new products in an open marketplace. We do not argue so much that IP is morally unsuitable, but rather that it is materially necessary based upon its architecture that it will fail in ICT and emerging technologies. Its architecture is necessarily one that promotes and invites freedom that is, in many ways, antithetical to IP's structure and history.

Notes

1 According to Nordhaus (2006: 29):

> Performance in constant dollars has improved relative to manual calculations by a factor in the order of 2×10^{12} (that is, 2 trillion). Most of the increase has taken place since 1945, during which the average rate of improvement has been at a rate of 45 percent per year. The record shows virtually continuous extremely rapid productivity improvement over the last six decades. These increases in productivity are far larger than that for any other good or service in the historical record.

2 We hedge this because we still contend that software and all of its associated products in ICT are also artefacts, subsisting in a medium of expression that differs in degree but not kind from other expressive artefacts. We are just so used to calling these things 'virtual' objects, and treating them as though they are not in some real and relevant sense 'physical' that it is difficult for us to recognize their artefactuality.

3 If the right to express oneself depended on originality, no one would have the right to relay any idea using the same expression. But that sort of repetition is indispensable for the spread of knowledge, especially the knowledge of language itself!

References

Coase, R.H. (1959) 'The Federal Communications Commission'. *Journal of Law & Economics* 2: 1–40.

De la Porte, L.A. (2012) 'The Bitcoin Transaction System', available at www.computing science.nl/docs/vakken/b3sec/Proj12/Bitcoin.pdf (accessed 19 January 2015).

Dennett, D.C. (1990) 'Memes and the Exploitation of Imagination'. *The Journal of Aesthetics and Art Criticism* 48(2): 127–135.

Encyclopaedia Britannica (2013) 'Software (computing)'. In *Encyclopaedia Britannica*, available at www.britannica.com/EBchecked/topic/552496/software (accessed 19 January 2015).

Essinger, J. (2004) *Jacquard's Web: How A Hand-Loom Led to the Birth of the Information Age*. Oxford: Oxford University Press.

Feenberg, A. (1998) 'Escaping the Iron Cage, or, Subversive Rationalization and Democratic Theory'. *Democratizing Technology: Ethics, Risk, and Public Debate*. International Centre for Human and Public Affairs: Tilburg, available at www.sfu.ca/~andrewf/books/Escaping_Iron_Cage.pdf (accessed 19 January 2015).

Fernaeus, Y., Jonsson, M. and Tholander, J. (2012) 'Revisiting the Jacquard Loom: Threads of History and Current Patterns in HCI'. In *Proceedings of the 2012 ACM annual conference on Human Factors in Computing Systems*: 1593–1602, available at http://dl.acm.org/citation.cfm?id=2208280 (accessed 19 January 2015).

Goldstine, H.H. (1977) 'A Brief History of the Computer'. *Proceedings of the American Philosophical Society* 121(5): 339–345.

Koepsell, D. (2003) *The Ontology of Cyberspace*. Chicago, IL: Open Court Publishing.

Lysecky, R. and Vahid, F. (2005) 'A Study of the Speedups and Competitiveness of FPGA Soft Processor Cores Using Dynamic Hardware/Software Partitioning'. In *Design, Automation and Test in Europe, 2005. Proceedings*. IEEE: 18–23.

Melnikova, O., Hahanova, I. and Mostovaya, K. (2009) 'Using multi-FPGA Systems for ASIC Prototyping'. In *10th International Conference – The Experience of Designing and Application of CAD Systems in Microelectronics, 2009. CADSM 2009*. IEEE: 237–239.

Merriam-Webster (2013) 'Firmware'. In *Merriam-Webster Online Dictionary*, available at www.merriam-webster.com/dictionary/firmware (accessed 19 January 2015).

Monmasson, E. and Cirstea, M.N. (2007) 'FPGA Design Methodology for Industrial Control Systems. A Review'. In *IEEE Transactions on Industrial Electronics* 54(4): 1824–1842.

Nordhaus, W.D. (2006) 'An Economic History of Computing', available at www.econ.yale.edu/~nordhaus/homepage/computing_June2006.pdf (accessed 19 January 2015).

Randell, B. (1982) 'From Analytical Engine to Electronic Digital Computer: The Contributions of Ludgate, Torres, and Bush'. *Annals of the History of Computing* 4(4): 327–341.

Swade, D. (2011) 'Pre-electronic Computing'. In C.B. Jones and J.L. Lloyd (eds) *Dependable and Historic Computing*. Berlin/Heidelberg: Springer: 58–83, available at http://link.springer.com/chapter/10.1007/978-3-642-24541-1_7 (accessed 19 January 2015).

White-Smith Music Publishing Co. v Apollo Co., 209 US 1 (Supreme Court 1908).

Wikipedia (2013) 'Brick (electronics)'. In *Wikipedia, the free encyclopedia*, available at http://en.wikipedia.org/w/index.php?title=Brick_(electronics)&oldid=556064411 (accessed 19 January 2015).

Chapter 6

Freedom of expression, freedom of information and IP rights in the age of ICT

Alexandra Couto*

Introduction

This chapter has two main aims. One of these aims is to respond and address some of the issues discussed by Koepsell and Inglott (this volume, at Chapter 5). In order to do so, I sketch and critically examine the main claims I take Koepsell and Inglott to make in the first to third sections below. While doing so, I also expand on some of them to complement their arguments. The other aim is to present an alternative approach to this issue by considering and taking seriously the arguments on both sides of the debate (the fourth to sixth sections). I thus look at what interests can ground a right and what conditions need to be fulfilled to have a genuine conflict between the right to freedom of expression/freedom of information on the one hand, and intellectual property (IP) rights on the other hand. I also briefly examine, develop and criticize several arguments on the issue of whether we have a moral right to the economic benefits brought up by IP rights. The ultimate goal of the chapter is thus to show that the issue is more complex than what is implied by the argument put forward by Koepsell and Inglott.

Let me start by defining some of the terms I use in this chapter, beginning with information and communication technology (ICT). Although ICT has been used more broadly to refer to information technologies, this term refers more specifically to the technologies which allow the storage, manipulation and communication of information in a digital form. The term also emphasizes the use of a *unified network* to do so.

Second, the expression 'intellectual property' refers to all creations of the mind, whether they are designs, artistic works, ideas, inventions, or symbols. I sometimes refer to them as IP goods. IP rights include patents, trademarks and copyright, which protect the interests of the creators of IP goods (WIPO nd). They allow creators recognition and financial benefits from what they create. Too often, it is assumed that IP rights only protect financial interests but IP rights include both economic rights and author's rights (Couto 2008; Wilson 2009: 412). Economic rights associated with IP protect the financial interests that the author has in controlling who could access his or her work and at what price. Author's rights protect the non-economic interests that the author has in being credited with the authorship of the work in question and in not having one's work disfigured or falsely represented (WIPO 1971: Article 6bis). Economic IP rights are those that are at the centre of the debate when we consider freedom of expression and freedom of information, as author's rights conflict generally less with freedom of expression and freedom of information. In this chapter, I assume that some aspect of IP rights, namely, author's rights, are legitimate and I focus on discussing the more controversial aspect of IP rights, which are the economic rights associated with IP rights.

Third, the right to freedom of expression is a key liberal right, recognized as a human right by the Universal Declaration of Human Rights. According to Article 19 of the International Covenant on Civil and Political Rights, freedom of expression consists in the claim that '(e)veryone shall have the right to hold opinions without interference' and 'everyone shall have the right to freedom of expression; this right shall include freedom to seek, receive and impart information and ideas of all kinds, regardless of frontiers, either orally, in writing or in print, in the form of art, or through any other media of his choice' (United Nations 1966). Besides being institutionally recognized as a key liberal right, the right to freedom of speech is supported by strong arguments based on important informational, expressive and deliberative interests. One argument in its favour is based in the epistemic value of expression (Mill 2008). Another argument is based on its political function in a democratic society (Schauer 1982: 35–47). Another argument takes the value of the right to freedom of expression to be explained by its being constitutive of what it is to respect each individual equally (Dworkin 1977: 273).

Fourth, the right to information refers to the right to access information held by public bodies and is taken by international organizations, such as UNESCO, to be an integral part of the right to freedom of expression (UNESCO nd). Although the right to information has been much less discussed than the right to freedom of expression, there has been in the last 20 years a global trend to endorse various legislations defending the right to information, such as the Freedom of Information Act 2000 in the United Kingdom (HM Government 2000).

Koepsell and Inglott present the structure of their argument in the following way. They begin their chapter by rightly stating that emerging technologies, from ICT to nanotechnologies are in *continuity* with general historical trends: there is no fundamental difference in nature between books and software, which are merely different goods regulated by IP law. Although the ease and speed at which the expression of ideas is disseminated has changed, the nature of the expression of an idea remains the same. Whether it is the design of a specific spear or the code of a software, one can distinguish between a *token*, that is, a specific instantiation of a type (be it an actual spear or software) and the *type*, that is, the general design of the spear (that could be drawn or sculpted) or the code for the software in question. Every type, be it the design of a spear or a software code can have very many different instantiations. An idea behind an expression can be distinguished from its actual instantiation and reproduced elsewhere, as it is not protected by IP law. Lastly, they claim that there should be no IP regulation when it pertains to ICT. They end their chapter with a praise for the hacker ethos. I now examine in turn what I take to be the most problematic claims and arguments put forward by Koepsell and Inglott.

The inexorable liberation of ICT from IP regulation

According to Koepsell and Inglott:

> [t]he most radical contribution of ICT to human development is not how much faster and more powerful it has made human capacity for communication and symbol manipulation . . . but rather that it is bringing to the fore the realization that *the use of complex tools is inexorably linked to freedom.*
>
> (Koepsell and Inglott, this volume, at [109]
> of Chapter 5, emphasis added)

By freedom, they mean the abrogation of IP rights, so as to ensure that our freedom of expression and information is respected: 'ICT has paved the way for the total undoing of copyright, and both nanotech and synthetic biology will do likewise for patent' (ibid. at [126]). They formulate what amounts to a strong empirical prediction, as they hint that, given the technological development of ICT, there is no way to avoid the complete disappearance of IP rights. So Koepsell and Inglott claim that, *inexorably*, the use of ICT will lead us to freedom.[1] Given what Koepsell and Inglott say later on in their chapter, I take their argument for this claim to be that certain features of ICT make it difficult for the state to regulate it. In particular, I believe that they have in mind, in tension with the exact wording of their claim as quoted above, the speed and ease of creating and communicating various forms of information allowed by ICT *combined with* a facilitated process of creative production of films, songs and software. These features make it difficult to regulate IP goods, as they themselves claim. Making such an empirical prediction would require nevertheless much more data to justify it than is provided. But, more importantly, their argument is nevertheless fundamentally mistaken, as I explain below.

The main problem with the claim that, inexorably, the use of ICT will lead us to freedom is that it constitutes a move from a claim about how difficult it is to regulate IP goods to a normative claim that we ought not to regulate IP goods. This kind of argument commits the fallacy of moving from an *is* to an *ought* (Hume 2011).

I agree that the ease and speed by which information is circulated could be said to provide an obstacle to the effective regulation of the information and expression that is circulated. It is so easy to copy and disseminate content and have it made accessible to others via ICT, that this makes violations of IP rights relatively common. With so many violations occurring simultaneously, it is harder to sanction violations and enforce IP rights. But this difficulty in regulating IP rights should not lead us straight to conclude that we ought to abandon IP rights.

Let me illustrate this point with an example: the invention of guns might have increased the number of murders committed because murder is more easily committed with guns. And surely this increase in numbers might have made it slightly more difficult in practice to regulate and punish murder effectively. Yet that does not mean that because it is more difficult to regulate murder, this difficulty in itself speaks against its being wrong or against the need to outlaw it. Of course, this example uses murder and one might complain that, in my example, murder is obviously wrong, whereas we are presently debating whether or not the violation of IP rights is wrong, which is more controversial. But the point of this example is not to conclude that murder (or violation of IP rights) is wrong. The point of this example is merely to illustrate that the difficulty in regulating something does not entail anything about the normative status of what is being regulated. In other words, how hard it is to regulate x does not entail anything about whether x is truly wrong.

Of course, if we think it has become *impossible* to regulate at all IP rights, it might make a difference to the *relevance* of the discussion on the normative status of IP rights. But unless one makes the claim that ICT will render IP goods *impossible* to regulate, then the difficulties of regulation should not close the discussion on the topic.[2]

To sum up, we cannot deny the fact that ensuring that IP rights are respected and enforcing IP law has become more and more difficult given the development of ICT. However, this in itself does not resolve for us the question of whether we should at least *try* to ensure that IP rights are respected in their current or in an amended form, nor does it resolve the question of whether or not we should find an alternative system to reward inventors and innovators.

A radical claim: the rejection of any regulation of freedom of expression

The second major issue I find with Koepsell and Inglott's argument is that they are defending a radical claim, without considering well-known objections to it. Moreover, they concede that there will be exceptions to their claim that free speech should never be regulated (when it might cause physical harm). However, they completely overlook the extent to which granting these exceptions undermines the radicalness of their claim.

Koepsell and Inglott draw a parallel between the use of force and the use of law aiming to denunciate any attempt to regulate legally expressions as illegitimate:

> Before the positive law created institutions that limit rights to free expression by limiting our abilities to reproduce tokens of certain types at will, other institutions, such as guilds, attempted to do so with secrecy and force . . . Is the use of force to limit free expression morally justified? Is it necessary? Can it co-exist with further technological innovation on the track laid by ICT? . . . [N]o.
>
> (Koepsell and Inglott, this volume, at [124] of Chapter 5)

As it stands, this seems to reject the legitimacy of *any* regulation of expression. If free means entirely de-regulated, this is a radical claim to make. In one passage, however, Koepsell and Inglott recognize that harm could be a valid principle of restriction:

> . . . and the only good candidate for a limiting principle for free expression is the harm principle. In other words, we are free in every way to make manifest ideas into the world short of harming others.
>
> (ibid. at [124])

The implication of what Koepsell and Inglott are saying is that, sometimes, one ought to regulate the right to free speech and the right to free information, so as to ensure that others are not harmed. This stands in contradiction with the claim I just considered (as well as other claims to that effect) that there should be a *complete* deregulation of expressions and information. If harm is a valid principle of restriction of freedom of expression (and allegedly freedom of information), and given that Koepsell and Inglott recognize that there are some cases in which freedom of expression leads to physical harm, it entails that *some* regulation of expressions via ICT would be considered legitimate by Koepsell and Inglott. If the harm principle is relevant, then there is no such thing as a right to free speech or a right to freedom of information that could *never* be justifiably infringed. In other words, there is no absolute right to free speech, the right to free speech only functions as a presumption that any limitation to freedom of speech would require a stronger justification for it than in the absence of such a right (Schauer 1982: 8).

If we move beyond this inconsistency, one should note that Koepsell and Inglott claim (this volume, at [124] of Chapter 5) that '[e]xcept, perhaps, for certain deadly pathogens or materials, no token [expression] in itself violates the harm principle in its creation'. Not only do they take a very narrow definition of harm (lethal physical harm), but they seem to overlook the extent to which freedom of expression could cause harm even within their definition, as this statement assumes that the release of chemicals might be the only instance of free speech causing bodily harm. But there are quite a few cases of bodily harm caused by free speech (or communications of information). One of the most discussed cases in the literature is the case of hate speech, which might incite people to commit violent acts. These kinds of speech might incite hatred and can sometimes lead to aggressive actions that will injure and possibly kill others. Note that hate speech can also cause other kinds of harm, such as damages to the person's reputation, damages to the individual's capability to find work or to her capability to engage in public debate (Hildebrandt 2011: 383). Whether these expressions are relayed by ICT or not, the potential for harm remains.

Similarly, in the case of freedom of information, one of the weightiest considerations that has been invoked to curtail this right is possible harm to others. Take the case of the US ex-federal agent Robert Levinson, who disappeared during a trip to an Iranian island in March 2007. Although the official line of the White House was that he was not a government employee at the time, the Associated Press decided to spread the news in 2013 that Robert Levinson was actually in a rogue CIA operation (Ackerman 2013). However, this communication had been delayed for a number of years out of concern for Levinson's safety. The Associated Press justified the decision to spread the news by the enduring lack of confirmation that Robert Levinson was still alive.

These two examples point to the possibility of *physical* harm brought about by the exercise of the right to freedom of expression and the right to freedom of information. To think that possible bodily harm is only caused by expression of toxic chemicals released in the air, as Koepsell and Inglott seem to suggest, overlooks the diversity of cases in which free expression could bring about physical harm.

Moreover, given their definition of harm, Koepsell and Inglott are failing to consider the various *kinds* of harm (economic, psychological, reputational) beyond physical harm that can be caused by the exercise of a right to freedom of expression or freedom of information. Let me mention a few recently debated instances in which expressions relayed via ICT have caused different kinds of harm: online bullying and threats in social media, online libel and defamation in user-generated platforms and revenge porn. These are all instances in which freedom of expression and freedom of information could be invoked.[3] First, with respect to bullying and threats online, there have been recently many cases of teen suicides caused (at least partly) by bullying in social media (Alvarez 2013; O'Keeffe and Clarke-Pearson 2011: 800–804). Second, the potential for the harm caused by libel and defamation has taken a new turn since a platform for user-generated news link, reddit, had its users post pictures of individuals misidentified as terrorist suspects in the wake of the Boston bombings (BBC News 2013). Needless to say, beyond the harm caused by libel and defamation, this kind of intervention online could lead to vendetta actions, potentially causing physical harm. Third, revenge porn refers to the publication of sexually explicit material of men or women published by previous partners as an act of revenge.[4] Once again, in many of those cases, the contact details of the victims were given online, and led to the victims being harassed and threatened. If one takes these publications of pictures online to be protected by the right to free speech and if one believes, like Koepsell and Inglott, that speech ought not to be regulated, then explicit materials released (even without the individual's consent) ought not to be forbidden.

These are only three recently debated instances of expressions that have shown a greater potential to cause harm because they used ICT. In some of these instances, expressive acts led to the violation of individual rights (such as the right against defamation and the right to privacy). These instances should not lead us to condemn and reject the development of ICT as such, but rather should lead us to endorse a more sensitive approach to regulation. More fundamentally, even this brief overview of several instances where harm was caused by expressive acts should lead us to reject Koepsell and Inglott's claim that expressions are harmless.[5]

What is the alternative? No reward for creators

The third major issue I identify in the chapter by Koepsell and Inglott pertains to what they present as an alternative to IP rights. First, they fail to present a clear account of an alternative to IP rights. Second, in the brief description of the account they provide, they appear overconfident that creators will be adequately rewarded.

What do Koepsell and Inglott identify as an alternative to IP rights? It is slightly unclear. On one hand, Koepsell and Inglott seem to endorse a 'hacker ethos' and an Open Source model of creation. This praise for the hacker ethos and the Open Source model of creation suggests that they believe that it would be justified not to reward creators and inventors. On the other hand, in one passage, Koepsell and Inglott write (this volume, at [125] of Chapter 5) that creators will still be able to sell their creations: 'Rather, full liberation of the tools of expression (and production) will mean that more potential creators will be able to enter markets, to realize their creations, and offer them for sale'. This seems to assume that there will be a certain kind of rights attributed to creators. In order for creators to offer their creations for sale, Koepsell and Inglott must assume that: (1) authors are clearly identified; and (2) this identification gives them the right to sell their creation. Allegedly, if the market is to reward innovators, they need to know who the innovators are. Moreover, in order for creators to be able to sell their products, they must be legally entitled to do so and some legal regulation of the market needs to be done. This suggestion seems thus to rely on some kind of legal regulation.

In another passage, Koepsell and Inglott seem to assume that rewarding creators will occur anyway:

> Valued expressions are often compensated, even when there is no legal institution enforcing it. Social institutions and custom that cause us to value and recompense valued services have enabled markets to thrive for fungible goods and services even where no monopolies exist either naturally or by fiat.
>
> (Koepsell and Inglott, this volume, at [127] of Chapter 5)

This passage seems to indicate that Koepsell and Inglott would leave the rewards of creators and contributors to social and market forces. But this might mean two different things. It might mean, as discussed above, that creators would be free to sell their creations. Or it might mean that Koepsell and Inglott would let good ideas and contributions be rewarded by voluntary donations. This would then be in line with the other passages of the chapter in which Koepsell and Inglott suggest rather the endorsement of a hacker ethos and an Open Source model (in which the funding tends to be voluntary rather than market-based). I assume that these passages represent their views more accurately, as Koepsell and Inglott reserve a substantial amount of space to discuss Open Source models. If this analogy is taken seriously then, in Koepsell and Inglott's view, painters, writers and sculptors should not be legally entitled to any reward, but rely on voluntary donations such as Open Source software contributors.

Once again, this is quite a controversial claim to make. Koepsell and Inglott admit that there is an incentives-based objection to their view.[6] However, they do not address this objection. Let me thus discuss here some issues that need to be addressed if an alternative system without entrenched rewards for creators is put forward.[7]

First, there is a concern about failing incentives: fewer individuals might be wanting to create if financial incentives are not given. It might be true, as Koepsell and Inglott claim, that, psychologically, creators are mostly motivated by their own desire to create (whether it is a novel, a movie or anything else), and by the recognition of their peers rather than by the financial reward attached to their creation. But most creators would still need some financial reward to engage in their creative pursuits. Otherwise, only those who are independently wealthy would be able to create, and other creators would only be able to do so in their spare time. This would dissuade many to create and thus might have an impact on the quality and diversity of goods that end up being produced.[8] A decrease in the quality of IP goods might lead itself to a decrease in the total welfare over time.[9] This concern is often interpreted as only a consequentialist one, since it aims at ensuring that there are more good ideas than less, so as to optimize welfare.[10] And in some areas, this concern is more urgent than others (see my discussion below of treatments for tropical diseases). But a concern for incentives is not necessarily consequentialist: a maximum egalitarian is concerned with incentives to the extent that, in order to ensure that the worse-off are actually better off, she would need to take into account the effect of incentives (Gosseries 2008b: 17). Moreover, from a consequentialist perspective, it would be better if we could provide the same incentives without having to restrict access to IP goods, so there might certainly be a better alternative than the IP law currently in vigour (Waldron 1993).

Second, it just seems unfair not to reward at all creators and to assume that they should rely on voluntary contributions. After all, like any other purposeful work, creative endeavours require efforts towards the creation of a socially valuable good and to that extent, this work ought to be rewarded (I discuss different ways of defending this claim in the section on rights below).

Lastly, it is not enough to point to some creators who do contribute freely to Open Source models to assert either that others will continue to do so or that others ought to do so. A comparison to be made in this case is the case of doctors who volunteer to work pro bono to treat some patients. The fact that some doctors volunteer to help people without financial rewards has not led us to the conclusion that all doctors will do so or that they all should not be financially rewarded. Similarly, the fact that some innovators are generously inclined and contribute without the prospect of any reward should not lead us to the conclusion that innovators should not be legitimately entitled to some financial rewards.

In order to ensure that the interests of creators are protected and/or to ensure that important social goods are created, we need to consider alternatives to the current system of IP law. Rosenberg and Pogge consider a prizing system as an alternative to the current system (Rosenberg 2012; Pogge and De Campos 2012). The need for alternatives is due to the fact that IP rights protect legitimate interests: the interests of the creators and the interests of the general public to have certain goods produced. This does not amount to condoning the whole system of IP law as it currently exists, but rather encourages revising it so that it protects better the interests of all involved.[11]

Let me discuss briefly an area where the lack of incentives might have disastrous consequences; the development of treatment for tropical diseases. In the case of tropical diseases, the current system of IP rights fails to provide enough incentives for pharmaceutical companies to develop adequate treatment. But hoping that these treatments would be somehow funded by voluntary contributions seems a bit far-fetched, given that research and development in the creation of new treatments for diseases is generally very expensive. This is not to say that current IP law deals with this issue appropriately; as I said, it currently does not: not enough is invested into the development of tropical diseases that prevail in developing countries. But, realistically, some compensation needs to be given if we want research and development to be made towards curing tropical diseases. Otherwise, we would need to find a political commitment from better endowed nations to finance such research.[12]

I have so far discussed some of the major issues I found with Koepsell and Inglott's proposal. Next, I briefly present some fundamental considerations and arguments at the heart of any discussion of IP rights, so as to show some of its complexity.

Interests or rights?

The approach taken by Koepsell and Inglott seems to assume that there are only rights to freedom of expression and freedom of information but no genuine interest or right to IP. They suggest indeed that the deregulation of IP rights will be detrimental only to the powerful: '[no] one will be harmed in the process other than those whose fortunes are dependent on the extension of monopolies' (Koepsell and Inglott, this volume, at [125] of Chapter 5). This is an instance in which Koepsell and Inglott overlook seriously the diversity of individuals who could be harmed from deregulation. I disagree with the claim that only monopolies would be affected by such a deregulation, as there are cases in which the interests of individuals are protected by IP rights. One such instance is the case of an inventor who without IP rights would fail to secure enough financial profits to escape poverty.[13] As the reader might have guessed from what I have said so far, my approach would favour a careful consideration of all the interests at stake. I do not believe that one can so easily assume that only the interests of monopolies would be affected by giving up on IP rights, as Koepsell and Inglott assume – however, I agree that IP rights should be reformed when their current statuses protect asymmetrically the economically powerful.

To begin with, it should be noted that not every apparent conflict of *interests* turns out to be a genuine conflict of *rights*. There are certain conditions for having a *right* to freedom of expression and these conditions are not present every time an individual has a mere interest in freedom of expression (see my discussion in the next section). Moreover, having a right to free speech does not mean that no regulation of speech can take place. Lastly, there are certain provisions that are made by IP rights, which might restrict the number of cases in which there is a genuine conflict of rights between IP rights and the right to freedom of expression (Couto 2008).

Let me start by explaining why having a right to free speech does not mean that regulation cannot take place. An important distinction that is made in the literature is between regulations of *content* versus regulations of *form* of expression. Regulation of content is a regulation, which is based on the content of speech, that is, the meaning expressed by the speech in question. There is a legitimate concern that a speech regulated on the basis of content would amount to censorship and this is why regulations of content are usually excluded in a liberal state committed to protect freedom of expression. However, regulation of forms of speech is generally taken not to be in conflict with freedom of expression, as the regulation is not based on a desire to censure a particular message or discourse. Regulations of forms of speech occur for reasons that are not related to freedom of expression. A well-known example of what is taken to be a regulation of form: I might have a right to express my political views, but I do not have the right to do so at 2 am using a megaphone in a residential street. Forbidding discourses (whatsoever their content) at a certain level of decibels on a residential street is not violating freedom of expression, as it amounts to a regulation of form.[14] This amounts to say that both the right to free expression and the right to free information are not general rights to do whatsoever.

Moreover, conflict between the right to free expression and IP rights might also be prevented because IP law makes provision for the expression of ideas and information. First, it allows for the distribution of the content of ideas, as long as the form in which the ideas are expressed are not the same as the ones used by the creator/author. Second, the fair use policy allows for the exact reproduction in content and form of a *part* of the work in question.

All that I have said so far should not lead the reader to believe that I want to dismiss the view that there are strong interests in freedom of expression and freedom of information that might warrant a change in IP rights. I also believe that there are serious flaws in the way IP rights currently work. But I just do not think that the solution is to dismiss as obviously wrongheaded the idea that creators and innovators are entitled to some rewards for their work. I believe rather that we should recognize that there are some legitimate interests on both sides of the conflict. If this were not the case, the question of the legitimacy of IP rights would indeed be uncontroversial.

A key issue that needs to be determined in order to clarify what is going on when free speech and IP rights conflict is whether the interests in question ground a right to free speech. Why does it matter that the interest in question grounds a right if we all agree anyway that there are legitimate interests on both sides? What does it add to speak of rights instead of interests? Actually, it makes an important difference, because once an interest is taken to be weighty enough to ground a right, it gives a different normative status to the interest protected. In other words, having the status of a right flags the interest in question as a particularly important interest, which warrants particular protection.

Let me thus introduce briefly the theory of rights that I favour: the interest theory of rights, which is the predominant theory of rights. In the words of one of the main proponents of the interest theory of rights, Joseph Raz, an individual *x* has a right if and only if '*x* can have rights and other things being equal, an aspect of *x*'s well-being (his interest) is a sufficient reason for holding some other person(s) to be under a duty' (Raz 1988: 166). Only interests that are weighty enough to give such a sufficient reason will ground rights.[15]

To sum up, there is a huge importance given in legal and political philosophy to the recognition of a specific interest as grounding a right. If two strong interests conflict and, on one side of the conflict, there is a right to free expression, and on the other side, there is merely, say, an economic interest, the presumption is that one ought to give priority to the right.[16] This is why it is crucial, for our purposes, to establish whether there is a general right to IP in the first place. If there is no such right IP, then there would be a presumption towards giving a priority to the right to free speech when free speech conflicts with the creator's interest in getting some economic rewards from her creation.

However, figuring out whether there is a general right to IP does not immediately resolve the conflict. First, a right can be defeated if the interests on the other side are particularly weighty. Once a right conflicts with an interest, it does not thus automatically entail that the right should be given priority. Rights give weighty reasons that normally trump other interests but these reasons might be defeated by other weightier reasons (Hart 1955). If we have a right to free expression, it should not thus be taken to entail an absolute prohibition to regulate speech in all cases. It constitutes rather a presumption against state interference (Schauer 1982: 8).

Second, a situation in which the general right *seems* to be involved might turn out to involve no such right, as it might be difficult to establish whether a right is really at stake. It is not always clear whether or not a case truly involves a right to free speech/free information. For instance, Jeremy Waldron suggests that, for a right to be really involved, there needs to be an internal connection between the general justification of the right and the particular right which is held (Waldron 1989). Third, it might be the case that there are rights on both sides of the conflict, that is, a right to IP as well as a right to free speech/free information, in which case, it might be quite hard to know which one ought to be given priority to. We would then need to rely on a pre-existing hierarchical ranking of these rights.

Such a hierarchical ranking of rights could be based on the distinction between individually justified rights and non-individually justified rights (Cruft 2006). Fundamental moral rights, such as human rights, are individually justified.

Non-individually justified rights are rights each individual has in virtue of the interests a group of individuals has to a certain protection. Cultural rights can provide us a good example of a non-individually justified right (Raz 1988). I might not, on my own, have an interest strong enough in having my cultural involvement protected, but because the interests of all members of a particular culture might have a right to their cultural participation. Note the radical turn that rights take if this move is granted. This seems to allow for much more rights than one might first believe exist. When it pertains to their normative status, however, individually justified rights have normally normative priority over non-individually justified rights (Cruft 2006: 158). It is easy to see why: non-individually justified rights are by definition grounded on interests that are individually not strong enough to ground a right. When a cultural right competes with the right not to be tortured, it is fairly clear that one should give priority to the right not to be tortured.

This distinction might help us in determining what to do when a right to free speech conflicts with a right to IP. I cannot within the scope of this chapter engage in fully determining which right is individually justified and which right is collectively justified. But let us thus consider briefly how the right to free speech, the right to freedom of information and the right to IP are usually justified to see how this distinction applies to the rights we are examining. If the right to free speech were based on the informational argument, the epistemic argument and/ or the political argument mentioned at the beginning of this chapter, then free speech would be non-individually justified. But if the right to free speech is based on the individual expressive interest in being able to speak freely and/or on the individual interest in being treated equally and with respect, then it would be individually justified. Let us now look at IP rights. Although I examine below some of the individual arguments for grounding a right to the economic interests of IP, a common view is that we have a right to the economic rewards of IP because it provides the incentives necessary to bring about a higher average level of welfare. In this case, the right to IP would be non-individually justified. When it pertains to the right to free information, a common view is that its main justification is non-individual, as it relies on the importance of having an informed citizenry.

If it is the case that, as I briefly considered above, the right to free speech is the only one that can be successfully individually justified, then there should be a presumption in its favour. This section aimed to give a general depiction of some of the theoretical considerations about rights that should be carefully considered before any conflict between freedom of expression and IP can be resolved. But let me turn now to some of the actual arguments at stake in the conflict.

Type versus particular: developing the argument against a right to IP

In a previous publication, I looked at the conflict of rights between freedom of expression and IP rights (Couto 2008). There, I drew a sketch of how to proceed to evaluate which rights should be given priority, on the assumption that there was such a thing as a right to IP. Here, I sketch briefly the types of arguments that can be articulated in favour and against a right to IP. As I do not have the space to discuss in details each of these arguments, my main ambition is to show that this debate is more complex than what Koepsell and Inglott suggest.

Koepsell and Inglott claim that IP rights are not justifiable. They invoke the distinction between type and token and claim that IP rights are rights over types rather than rights over tokens. They further claim that IP rights are not justifiable because only ownership of tokens is justifiable. But since Koepsell and Inglott do not actually develop the argument required to explain why it is justifiable to own tokens but not types, I consider here the outline of such an argument.

Let me first clarify the distinction between type and token and say a bit more about how it is applied to property rights. The distinction between type and token is the following: whereas a type is a general good that can be reproduced, a token is a particular instantiation of that general good. A song is a type, whereas the mp3 of that song is a token. Property rights are thus rights over particular objects (particulars or tokens), whereas IP rights are rights over types. I might own this particular table (and hence have a property right over it), but this does not imply that I have a right over this table as a type. If I had such a right as the designer of this table, I would have a right over any table designed in this way.

What are the implications of this distinction for the legitimacy (or illegitimacy) of IP rights? Because IP rights are rights over types, IP goods can be enjoyed non-exclusively. Take the following example: if I listen to a Dylan song, my listening to it does not in itself undermine the enjoyment that Dylan gets from the song he created. He can listen to it too. Property rights over particulars are very different; they are exclusive: if I own a bike, your use of my bike for a certain period x will exclude me from using my bike for that period. In other words, unlike material objects, the objects of IP are not crowdable, that is their use by any one person does not preclude their use by any number of others (Waldron 2012).

It is generally recognized that the non-rival nature of IP renders it more difficult to justify the exclusive rights over IP goods (Gosseries 2008a; Posner 2005: 64; Barlow 1997). And in his paper 'Could there be a right to own intellectual property?', James Wilson (2009) goes as far as to claim that, if the creator is not excluded from the use of her product, as it is the case in IP goods, the creator should not have an intrinsic moral right to IP goods.[17] Wilson believes that if moral rights are to be justified, they need to protect the right-bearer from some wrongful harm that they would, in the absence of the right's protection, incur. And, the argument goes, there is no wrongful harm if the creator is not excluded from the use of her product. Wilson thus rejects the claim that authors are wronged by others benefiting unfairly from her creative effort because he assumes that 'benefiting from another's effort is unfair only where so benefiting imposes a cost on the person providing the benefit' (Wilson 2009: 414–415). Moreover, on his view, there is no other legitimate interest of the author that is weighty enough to recommend excluding others from accessing her work.[18]

Here I believe that Wilson's argument goes a bit fast, as this is exactly where the disagreement generally emerges. To begin with, one might argue that the argument assumes that it is an individual's right to gain access to goods protected by law. But Nozick has argued that there is no injustice committed in *denying* individuals access to goods created by others. This argument in support of a right to IP can be articulated in the following way: instead of assuming that I am entitled to benefit from everything currently created in the world, one might consider assuming that, as long as I am not harmed by another's action, none of my right is violated when I am denied access to a good created by someone else (Nozick 1974: 182). For instance, if I am sick and cannot use a treatment invented by you for my disease, I cannot be said to be deprived of anything. After all, had you not invented the treatment, I would not have had access to the treatment anyway. If you focus on the counterfactual claim that no treatment exists for my disease until the point at which you create it, I am not harmed by you if you choose not to provide me with the treatment, as I would be also without a treatment had you not created it in the first place. Even if this argument might not be very palatable, and even if I believe that it ultimately fails, it has some force.

Self-ownership and IP

Even if you reject this line of argument (as I do), it is controversial to claim, as Wilson seems to, that imposing a cost on the person providing you with a benefit exhausts what could be unfair in benefiting from another's effort. There are many possible grounds for believing that benefiting from another's effort is unfair (and that IP rights need to be preserved). Let me consider some of these possible grounds.

To begin with, let me mention one argument that I do not examine in further detail here. Axel Gosseries has suggested that the key issue is the question of whether or not someone financially capable of buying a good fails to do so or not. On this view, if, say, a pirate was financially able to buy a movie online but did not, she would be said to cause counter-factual losses to the director, producer and their staff, which makes free-riding in this case unfair (Gosseries 2008b: 12).

Another possible support for the claim that benefitting from another's effort is unfair is that it violates the right of self-ownership. This argument could take two possible forms: one grounded on labour-based Lockean claims, and the other grounded on a natural right to freedom. I am not defending here either version of this argument, but I believe that they need to be countered in order to claim that there is no justifiable right to IP. Let me thus just briefly sketch what these two versions of the argument are and the possible objections they could encounter.

According to the first version of the argument, what gives anyone property rights over goods is the investment of labour (Simmons 1992). If I put some effort into developing an unacquired plot of land (and if many other such plots of lands are available for others to use), then it seems plausible to hold the view that I ought to reap the rewards of my efforts. This general principle of property rights can and has been taken to apply to IP rights (Gordon 1993; Himma 2008). Moreover, some of the problems with this argument disappear when it is applied to IP rights instead of territorial rights. One of these problems is generated by the Lockean clause that there is left 'as much and as good for others' (Locke 2011; Sreenivasan 1995; Tully 1980). The scope of the principle is greatly restricted in a non-ideal world: land is often acquired and that makes it difficult for new generations to make first acquisitions. If newcomers do not have at all the opportunity to acquire property, then it undermines the legitimacy of a system grounded solely upon the labour-mixing argument. After all, as Proudhon argued, it seems incoherent to claim that only the labour of the first comers should matter (Proudhon 1994). However, what seems to be a damning problem in the case of property rights over territory does not cause any issue when we move to IP rights because innovation is not finite in a way that territory is. Of course, a specific innovation might have already been made but it does not exhaust the number of innovations that can be made. The labour-based argument might thus be more successful when dealing with IP rights than when dealing with property rights over territory.

But other problems generally raised against labour-mixing arguments might undermine the specific right to IP. Although they might justify the existence of some kind of reward for each good created, they fail to establish the legitimacy of IP rights (Cwik 2014; Gibbard 1976). They might establish that there ought to be some kind of reward attached to an individual's labour, which adds value to a good. But the reward does not need to take the specific form of an IP right.[19]

In order to argue more specifically in favour of IP rights, another kind of argument would be needed. For instance, it has been suggested that the role of IP rights is to help to protect individuals' ability to set the terms and conditions of the exercise of their productive capacities (Cwik 2014). The problem with this argument is that, currently, IP rights reward individuals according to popularity, and this is not something that creators can control.

Let us now consider the second type of argument. From a libertarian perspective, individual freedom is what is ultimately valuable. Any limitation of your freedom ought thus to be actually agreed upon by yourself in a contractual fashion. Since only an agreement between individuals that institutes property rights can legitimize such rights, the approach taken by those who resort to this line of argument is to consider what would be in the long-term interest of each to enter into such an agreement. On this view, the long-term interest of each individual to retain some of the benefits of any effort put into the cultivation of land (or say the development of a code) would lead individuals to get into a general agreement on property rights. I would be better off to agree to such property rights rather than exist in a world which did not include them. Take my effort to transform a piece of desert land into arable land. Without putting in the effort, nothing would grow out of such land. However, without property rights, anyone could benefit from my effort to transform this piece of land. If I know this in advance, I might become much less motivated to actually cultivate this land, as the benefits I would get in return are inversely correlated with the number of people who have access to the fruits of my labour. If you take the contractual approach, agreeing to property rights would thus ensure that each of us gets the reward from one's labour and that overall good incentives are present to generate enough socially valuable goods.

Let me raise here, nevertheless, one issue with the libertarian argument, which is to insist on an actual agreement taking place. It would not be possible for such an agreement to take place in our world, given the fact of overlapping generations.[20] In order to counter this objection, we might be inclined to consider property rights to be justifiable only to the extent that they *would be chosen* by individuals if they *were* to consider such a contract hypothetically. This would thus present the argument in a hypothetical form: it is not so much the existence of an actual argument that matters but the likelihood that one would have made the agreement if given the choice. Two problems might still be raised. First, it is not clear what the idea of the hypothetical contract brings as it ends up pointing to what would benefit individuals in the long term (and one could ground directly an argument on the long-term overall benefits of individuals). Second, we might be faced with the same issue that afflicted the labour-based argument: it ends up not being an argument in favour of property rights specifically but only in favour of some kind of rewards associated with creation. Alternative ways of rewarding efforts might be beneficial in the long term for everyone involved and could thus have been chosen by individuals considering a hypothetical contract.

I have tried here to sketch the main individually-based arguments for IP rights and I have outlined some of the issues they are faced with. I am personally not convinced by any of these arguments.[21] But even if both individually-based arguments presented above are rejected, there might still be a powerful case to that could be made in favour of (economic) IP rights based on collective interests. In this section, my motivation was just to point out that there are complex arguments that could be made in favour of IP rights and that these arguments cannot be dismissed without careful examination.

Conclusion

I have sketched here some possible arguments in favour of a moral right to IP, so as to complement the picture presented by Koepsell and Inglott, in which only freedom of expression and freedom of information are taken to be legitimate moral rights. Note that the arguments I have sketched stand in favour of taking the right to IP to go beyond author's rights and include economic rights. As mentioned earlier, there is however not much controversy in the literature as to the legitimacy of one component of IP rights, namely author's right. Finally, even if you, like Koepsell and Inglott, reject (economic) IP rights as such, I have tried to underline the importance of providing an alternative to IP law that would attribute appropriate rewards to creators.

Notes

* Work on this chapter was supported by funding from the Research Council of Norway and the European Research Council. I would like to thank Mireille Hildebrandt for her extremely helpful comments on this chapter.

1 Note that, although their argument targets also nanotechnology and synthetic biology, I focus in this chapter on ICT.

2 Alex Rosenberg argues indeed that, although he judges that patents are a good way to promote good ideas, piracy might be a threat to the extent of making IP *unenforceable*. He concludes from this that IP as they currently exist might be made irrelevant (Rosenberg 2012). Note that there is a considerable difference between Rosenberg's position and the claim made by Koepsell and Inglott, as Rosenberg still leaves open the possibility that the disappearance of IP is regrettable and that alternative models for rewarding creators need to be found.

3 However, if you believe, as I do, that not every kind of expression/information is worth protecting, then you might reject the very claim that, say, cases of revenge porn are cases of exercises of freedom of expression.

4 See www.theguardian.com/technology/2013/oct/08/evenge-porn-websites-new-york-state-ban; www.bbc.co.uk/news/magazine-25321301; www.theguardian.com/commentisfree/2013/nov/19/revenge-porn-victim-maryland-law-change (all accessed 19 January 2016).

5 In his 1993 article, Joshua Cohen has already rejected as wrong any minimalist strategy, which sees expressions as harmless (Cohen 1993: 218).

6 'Those who seek to oppose them [namely protect intellectual property regimes] often do so from some utilitarian perspective, arguing that some expression must be limited to prevent not just harms, but also to encourage innovation – presumably because failing to do so will cause other harms' (Koepsell and Inglott, this volume, at [126] of Chapter 5).

7 Note that I assume in what follows that relying on voluntary rewards might not ensure that enough incentives are provided for creators. However, to my knowledge, there is currently not enough empirical evidence on this issue. More empirical data would need to be gathered to back up either claim.

8 This is not to say, of course, that the present system only rewards the best creators. In fact, it only rewards the most popular ones. From a consequentialist perspective, you could argue that the most popular creations are the ones that increase overall welfare the most. However, even if we grant that the general audience is made better off by the current system, another issue with the current system is that it might fail to be collectively beneficial, because too many creators are not adequately rewarded. Demuijnck for instance describes a world of winner takes all, where there are a few big winners and many big losers. In his view, if the system is not collectively beneficial, it might not be worth protecting (Demuijnck 2012).

9 For a criticism of consequentialist arguments, see Moore (2003).

10 Koepsell and Inglott for instance identify this as a consequentialist concern.

11 Possible revision could be made for instance towards ensuring that IP goods that are really needed remain available and freely accessible for the most vulnerable population, and that the rewards to the creators are more proportionate to their efforts.

12 One of the most promising ideas along these lines is the Health Impact Fund proposal, which recommends the creation of an international fund that would compensate companies that allow their treatment to be produced at the generic cost and forgo the usual profits expected from the development of such a medication. The access to the medication would thus not be compromised by the need to compensate pharmaceutical companies for the investment made into research and development of the treatment. The Health Impact Fund would let the innovator ensure that the product is available for ten years (at the cheapest price necessary for its production) combined with

an additional payment by the institution to reward medications, the rewards being based on its health impact. The institution would be financed by governments and other donors. See Pogge and De Campos (2012). See also Belleflamme (2008).

13 Another such instance is the case of indigenous rights to the commercial rewards of their traditional herbal medications. It is generally not the case that indigenous groups obtain such rights as they tend not to take the procedural legal steps towards securing their IP rights, but without any IP right at all, they would not even have a ground to make a claim on such matters. Although a deregulation will prevent corporations to seize these rights, the indigenous populations themselves might remain vulnerable without a system that attributes rights to them. In the case of indigenous rights, it looks like a revision of IP rights would be more beneficial to them than giving up on them altogether. See, for instance, Munzer (2012).

14 Similarly, freedom of information does not allow me to require that I know everything about my neighbours' private lives, the marketing practices of my competitors or the writing up strategies of my colleagues.

15 In a competing theory of rights, predominantly defended by H.L.A. Hart and Hillel Steiner, based on the value of individual freedom, rights are also justified individualistically but they are grounded on the value of individual freedom.

16 Some even believe that this presumption is absolute and that rights are side-constraints restricting what we can do. As Dworkin has put it: rights are trumps (Dworkin 1977).

17 What Wilson describes as 'intrinsic moral rights' are rights that are justified by making reference to individuals' interests that are important enough to ground duties on the part of others. 'Intrinsic moral rights' are contrasted with instrumental rights, that is, rights that are justified on the grounds that they would secure a better state of affairs in the long run. Instrumental rights could be justified because they benefit the greatest number in the long term. Wilson uses thus a different terminology for the distinction I discussed earlier between individually and non-individually justified rights (following Cruft's terminology). Although Wilson believes that the interests of the author to have her work credited to her justifies her having intrinsic moral rights, they are restricted to her author's rights. He does not believe that the interests of the author in controlling access to her work justifies her having an intrinsic moral right to the economic profits from any use of the protected good (the economic rights associated with IP rights) (Wilson 2009).

18 Wilson's argument only concludes that there is no intrinsic moral right to the economic rights of IP but allows for the possibility that there are economic rights to IP justified by consequentialist considerations. This is a crucial qualification to make, as it allows for the possibility that economic rights are grounded on collective interests.

19 An alternative system of compensation might focus on compensating individuals for the purposeful use of their capacities irrespective of how popular their poems, designs or software are.

20 For a discussion of the objections that could be raised against this argument, see Gibbard (1976).

21 The main reason that I am not convinced by individually-based arguments is that, although they show that some rewards are owed to creators, they fail to show that these rewards should necessarily come in the form of IP rights.

References

Ackerman, S. (2013) 'Former FBI Agent Missing in Iran Was Working for the CIA-Report'. *The Guardian*. 13 December 2013, available at www.theguardian.com/world/2013/dec/12/robert-levinson-fbi-cia-iran-missing (accessed 19 January 2016).

Alvarez, L. (2013) 'Girl's Suicide Points to Rise in Apps Used by Cyberbullies'. *New York Times*. 13 September 2013, available at www.nytimes.com/2013/09/14/us/suicide-of-girl-after-bullying-raises-worries-on-web-sites.html?_r=0 (accessed 19 January 2016).

Barlow, J.P. (1997) 'The Economy of Ideas: Everything You Know about Intellectual Property is Wrong'. In A. Moore (ed.) *Intellectual Property: Moral, Legal, and International Dilemmas*. Lanham, MD: Rowman & Littlefield.

BBC News (2013) 'Reddit Apologises for Boston Bombings Witch Hunt'. *BBC News*. 23 April 2013, available at www.bbc.co.uk/news/technology-22263020 (accessed 19 January 2016).

Belleflamme, P. (2008) 'How Efficient is the Patent System? A General Appraisal and an Application to the Pharmaceutical Sector'. In A. Gosseries, A. Strowel and A. Marciano (eds) *Intellectual Property and Theories of Justice*. Basingstoke and New York, NY: Palgrave.

Cohen, J. (1993) 'Freedom of Expression'. *Philosophy and Public Affairs* 22(3): 207–263.

Couto, A. (2008) 'Copyright and Freedom of Expression: A Philosophical Map'. In A. Gosseries, A. Strowel and A. Marciano (eds) *Intellectual Property and Theories of Justice*. Basingstoke and New York, NY: Palgrave.

Cruft, R. (2006) 'Against Individualistic Justifications of Property Rights'. *Utilitas* 18(2): 154–172.

Cwik, B. (2014) 'Labor as the Basis for Intellectual Property Rights'. *Ethical Theory and Moral Practice* 17: 681–695.

Demuijnck, G. (2012) 'Illegal Downloading, Free Riding and Justice'. In A. Lever (ed.) *New Frontiers in the Philosophy of Intellectual Property*. Cambridge: Cambridge University Press.

Dworkin, R. (1977) *Taking Rights Seriously*. New Haven, CT: Harvard University Press.

Gibbard, A. (1976) 'Natural Property Rights'. *Noûs* 10(1): 77–86.

Gordon, W.J. (1993) 'A Property Right in Self-Expression: Equality and Individualism in the Natural Law of Intellectual Property'. *The Yale Law Journal* 102(7): 1540–1578.

Gosseries, A. (2008a) 'How (Un)Fair is Intellectual Property?' In A. Gosseries, A. Strowel and A. Marciano (eds) *Intellectual Property and Theories of Justice*. Basingstoke and New York, NY: Palgrave.

——. (2008b) 'Introduction'. In A. Gosseries, A. Strowel and A. Marciano (eds) *Intellectual Property and Theories of Justice*. Basingstoke and New York, NY: Palgrave.

Hart, H.L.A. (1955) 'Are There Any Natural Rights?' *The Philosophical Review* 64(2): 175–191.

Hildebrandt, M. (2011) 'Who Needs Stories if You Can Get the Data?' *Philosophy and Technology* 24(4): 371–390.

Himma, K. (2008) 'The Justification of Intellectual Property Rights: Contemporary Philosophical Disputes'. *Journal of the American Society for Information Science and Technology* 59(7): 2–30.

HM Government (2000) Freedom of Information Act 2000, available at www.legislation. gov.uk/ukpga/2000/36/contents (accessed 19 January 2016).

Hume, D. (2011) *A Treatise of Human Nature*. Oxford: Oxford University Press.

Locke, J. (2011) *Second Treatise of Government*. Seaside, OR: Watchmaker Publishing.

Mill, J.S. (2008) *On Liberty and Other Essays*. Oxford: Oxford University Press.

Moore, A. (2003) 'Intellectual Property, Innovation, and Social Progress: The Case against Incentives Based Arguments'. *The Hamline Law Review* 26(3): 602–630.

Munzer, S. (2012) 'Corrective Justice and Intellectual Property Rights in Traditional Knowledge'. In A. Lever (ed.) *New Frontiers in the Philosophy of Intellectual Property*. Cambridge: Cambridge University Press.

Nozick, R. (1974) *Anarchy, State and Utopia*. New York, NY: Basic Books.

O'Keeffe, G.S. and Clarke-Pearson, K. (2011) 'The Impact of Social Media on Children, Adolescents, and Families'. *Pediatrics* 127(4): 800–804.

Pogge, T. and De Campos, C.T. (2012) 'Introduction: Pharmaceutical Firms and the Right to Health'. *Journal of Law, Medicine and Ethics* 40(2): 183–187.

Posner, R.A. (2005) 'Intellectual Property: The Law and Economics Approach'. *Journal of Economic Perspectives* 19(2): 57–73.

Proudhon, P.J. (1994) *What is Property? An Inquiry into the Principles of Right and of Government*. Transl. by D. Kelly and B. Smith. New York, NY: Cambridge University Press.

Raz, J. (1988) *The Morality of Freedom*. Oxford: Oxford University Press.

Rosenberg, A. (2012) 'Designing a Successor to the Patent as Second Best Solution to the Problem of Optimum Provision of Good Ideas'. In A. Lever (ed.) *New Frontiers in the Philosophy of Intellectual Property*. Cambridge: Cambridge University Press.

Schauer, F. (1982) *Free Speech: A Philosophical Inquiry*. Cambridge: Cambridge University Press.

Simmons, A.J. (1992) *The Lockean Theory of Rights*. Princeton, NJ: Princeton University Press.

Sreenivasan, G. (1995) *The Limits of Lockean Rights in Property*. Oxford: Oxford University Press.

Tully, J. (1980) *A Discourse on Property: John Locke and His Adversaries*. Cambridge: Cambridge University Press.

United Nations (1966) 'International Covenant on Civil and Political Rights'. Article 19, available at www.ohchr.org/en/professionalinterest/pages/ccpr.aspx (accessed 19 January 2016).

United Nations Educational, Scientific and Cultural Organization (UNESCO) (nd) 'Freedom of Information', available at www.unesco.org/new/en/communication-and-information/freedom-of-expression/freedom-of-information/ (accessed 19 January 2016).

Waldron, J. (1989) 'Rights in Conflict'. *Ethics* 99(3): 503–519.

——. (1993) 'From Authors to Copiers: Individual Rights and Social Values in Intellectual Property'. *Chicago-Kent Law Review* 68(2): 841–888.

——. (2012) 'Property and Ownership'. *The Stanford Encyclopedia of Philosophy*, available at http://plato.stanford.edu/archives/spr2012/entries/property (accessed 19 January 2016).

Wilson, J. (2009) 'Could There be a Right to Own Intellectual Property?' *Law and Philosophy* 28(4): 393–427.

World Intellectual Property Organization (WIPO) (1971) Berne Convention for the protection of literary and artistic works. Revised Paris text of 24 July 1971, available at www.wipo.int/treaties/en/text.jsp?file_id=283698 (accessed 19 January 2016).

——. (nd) 'What is Intellectual Property?', available at www.wipo.int/about-ip/en/ (accessed 19 January 2016).

Part IV

An infraethics for an information society

Chapter 7

Hyperhistory, the emergence of the MASs, and the design of infraethics

Luciano Floridi*

Hyperhistory

More people are alive today than ever before in the evolution of humanity. And more of us live longer[1] and better[2] today than ever before. To a large measure, we owe this to our technologies, at least insofar as we develop and use them intelligently, peacefully, and sustainably.

Sometimes, we may forget how much we owe to flints and wheels, to sparks and ploughs, to engines and satellites. We are reminded of such deep technological debt when we divide human life into prehistory and history. That significant threshold is there to acknowledge that it was the invention and development of information and communication technologies (ICTs) that made all the difference between who we were and who we are. It is only when the lessons learnt by past generations began to evolve in a Lamarckian rather than a Darwinian way that humanity entered into history.

History has lasted 6,000 years, since it began with the invention of writing in the fourth millennium BC. During this relatively short time, ICTs have provided the *recording* and *transmitting* infrastructure that made the escalation of other technologies possible, with the direct consequence of furthering our dependence on more and more layers of technologies. ICTs became mature in the few centuries between Gutenberg and Turing. Today, we are experiencing a radical transformation in our ICTs that could prove equally significant, for we have started drawing a new threshold between history and a new age, which may be aptly called *hyperhistory* (Figure 7.1). Let me explain.

Prehistory (i.e. the period before written records) and history work like adverbs: they tell us *how* people live, not *when* or *where*. From this perspective, human societies currently stretch across three ages, as ways of living. According to reports about an unspecified number of uncontacted tribes in the Amazonian region, there are still some societies that live prehistorically, without ICTs or at least without recorded documents. If one day such tribes disappear, the end of the first chapter of our evolutionary book will have been written. The greatest majority of people today still live historically, in societies that rely on ICTs to *record* and *transmit* data of all kinds. In such historical societies, ICTs have not yet overtaken other

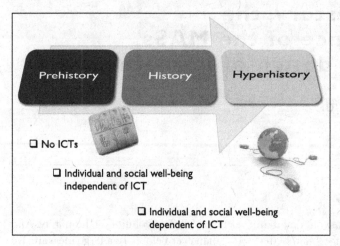

Figure 7.1 From prehistory to hyperhistory

technologies, especially energy-related ones, in terms of their vital importance. Then there are some people around the world who are already living hyperhistorically, in societies or environments where ICTs and their data *processing* capabilities are the necessary condition for the maintenance and further development of societal welfare, personal wellbeing, as well as intellectual flourishing. The nature of conflicts provides a sad test for the reliability of this tripartite interpretation of human evolution. Only a society that lives hyperhistorically can be vitally threatened informationally, by a cyber-attack. Only those who live by the digit may die by the digit.[3]

To summarize, human evolution may be visualized as a three-stage rocket: in prehistory, there are no ICTs; in history, there are ICTs, they *record* and *transmit* data, but human societies depend mainly on other kinds of technologies concerning primary resources and energy; in hyperhistory, there are ICTs, they record, transmit and, above all, *process* data, increasingly autonomously, and human societies become vitally dependent on them and on information as a fundamental resource. Added-value moves from being ICT-related to being ICT-dependent. We can no longer unplug our world from ICTs without turning it off.

If all this is even approximately correct, the emergence from its historical age represents one of the most significant steps ever taken by humanity. It certainly opens up a vast horizon of opportunities as well as challenges and difficulties, all essentially driven by the recording, transmitting, and processing powers of ICTs. From synthetic biochemistry to neuroscience, from the Internet of things to unmanned planetary explorations, from green technologies to new medical treatments, from social media to digital games, from agricultural to financial applications, from economic developments to the energy industry, our activities of discovery, invention, design, control, education, work, socialization, entertainment, care, security, business and so forth would be not only unfeasible but unthinkable in a purely mechanical, historical context. They have all become hyperhistorical in nature today. It follows that we are witnessing the defining of a macroscopic scenario in which hyperhistory, and the re-ontologization of the infosphere in which we live (Floridi 2003), are quickly detaching future generations from ours.

Of course, this is not to say that there is no continuity, both backwards and forwards. *Backwards*, because it is often the case that the deeper a transformation is, the longer and more widely rooted its causes may be. It is only because many different forces have been building the pressure for a very long time that radical changes may happen all of a sudden, perhaps unexpectedly. It is not the last snowflake that breaks the branch of the tree. In our case, it is certainly history that begets hyperhistory. There is no ASCII without the alphabet. *Forwards*, because it is most plausible that historical societies will survive for a long time in the future, not unlike those prehistorical Amazonian tribes mentioned before. Despite globalization, human societies do not parade uniformly forward, in synchronic steps.

Such a long-term perspective should help to explain the slow and gradual process of political *apoptosis* that we are undergoing, to borrow a concept from cell biology. Apoptosis (also known as programmed cell death) is a natural and normal form of self-destruction in which a programmed sequence of events leads to the self-elimination of cells. Apoptosis plays a crucial role in developing and maintaining the health of the body. One may see this as a dialectical process of renovation, and use it to describe the development of nation states into information societies in terms of political apoptosis (see Figure 7.2), in the following way.

Oversimplifying, a quick sketch of the last 400 years of political history may look like this. The Peace of Westphalia (1648) meant the end of World War Zero, namely the Thirty Years' War, the Eighty Years' War, and a long period of other conflicts during which European powers, and the parts of the world they dominated, massacred each other for economic, political and religious reasons.

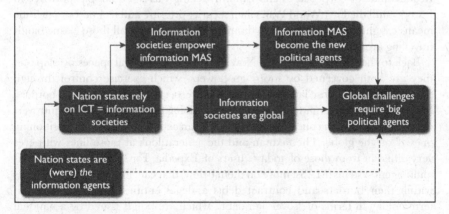

Figure 7.2 From the state to the multi-agent systems (MASs)

Christians brought hell to each other with staggering violence and unspeakable horrors. The new system that emerged in those years, the so-called *Westphalian order*, saw the coming of maturity of sovereign states and then nation states as we still know them today, France, for example. Think of the time between the last chapter of *The Three Musketeers* – when D'Artagnan, Aramis, Porthos and Athos take part in Cardinal Richelieu's siege of La Rochelle in 1628 – and the first chapter of *Twenty Years Later*, when they come together again, under the regency of Queen Anne of Austria (1601–1666) and the ruling of Cardinal Mazarin (1602–1661). The state became not a monolithic, single-minded, well-coordinated agent, the sort of beast (Hobbes' Leviathan) or rather robot that a later, mechanical age would incline us to imagine. It never was. Rather, it rose to the role of the binding power, the network able to keep together, influence, and coordinate all the different agents and behaviours falling within the scope of its geographical borders. Citizenship had been discussed in terms of biology (your parents, your gender, your age . . .) since the early city-states of ancient Greece. It became more flexible (degrees of citizenship) when it was conceptualized in terms of legal status as well, as under the Roman Empire, when acquiring a citizenship (a meaningless idea in purely biological contexts) meant becoming a rights holder. With the modern state, geography started playing an equally important role, mixing citizenship with nationality and locality. In this sense, the history of the passport is enlightening. As a means to prove one's own identity, it is acknowledged to be an invention of King Henry V of England (1386–1422), centuries before the Westphalian order took place. However, it is the Westphalian order that makes possible the passport as we understand it today: a document that entitles the holder not to travel (e.g. a visa may also be required) or be protected abroad, but to return to (or be sent back to) the country that issued the passport. It is, metaphorically, an elastic band that ties the holder to a geographical point, no matter how long in space and prolonged in time the journey in other lands is. Such a document became increasingly useful the better that geographical point was defined. Readers may be surprised to know that travelling was still quite passport-free in Europe until the First World War, when security pressure and techno-bureaucratic means caught up with the need to disentangle and manage all those elastic bands travelling around by train.

Back to the Westphalian order. Now the physical and legal spaces overlap and they are both governed by sovereign powers, which exercise control through physical force to impose laws and ensure their respect within the national borders. Mapping is not just a matter of travelling and doing business, but also an introvert question of controlling one's own territory, and an extrovert question of positioning oneself on the globe. The taxman and the general look at those lines with eyes very different from those of today's users of Expedia. For sovereign states act as multi-agent systems (MASs; more on them below) that can, for example, raise taxes within their borders and contract debts as legal entities (hence our current terminology in terms of 'sovereign debt', which are bonds issued by a national government in a foreign currency), and they can of course dispute borders. Part of the political struggle becomes not just a silent tension between different components of the state-MAS, say the clergy versus the aristocracy, but an explicitly codified balance between the different agents constituting it. In particular, Montesquieu suggests the classic division of the state's political powers that we take for granted today. The state-MAS organizes itself as a network of three 'small worlds' – a legislature, an executive and a judiciary – among which only some specific kinds of information channels are allowed. Today, we may call this Westphalian 2.0.

With the Westphalian order, modern history becomes the age of the state, and the state becomes *the* information agent, which legislates on and controls (or at least tries to control), insofar as it is possible, all technological means involved in the information life-cycle including education, census, taxes, police records, written laws and rules, press, and intelligence. Already most of the adventures in which D'Artagnan is involved are caused by some secret communication. The state thus ends by fostering the development of ICTs as a means to exercise and maintain political power, social control and legal force, but in so doing it also undermines its own future as the only, or even the main, information agent. As I explain in more detail below, ICTs, as one of the most influential forces that made the state possible and then predominant as a historical driving force in human politics, also contributed to make it less central, in the social, political and economic life across the world, putting pressure on centralized government in favour of distributed governance and international, global co-ordination. The state developed by becoming more and more an information society, thus progressively making itself less and less the main information agent. Through the centuries, it moved from being conceived as the ultimate guarantor and defender of a *laissez-faire* society to a Bismarckian welfare system that would take full care of its citizens. The two World Wars were also clashes of state nations resisting mutual coordination and inclusion as part of larger MASs. They led to the emergence of MASs such as the League of Nations, the World Bank, the International Monetary Fund (IMF), the United Nations, the European Union, the North Atlantic Treaty Organization (NATO), and so forth. Today, we know that global problems – from the environment to the financial crisis, from social justice to intolerant religious fundamentalism, from peace to health conditions – cannot rely on nation states as the only sources of a solution because they involve and require global agents. However, in a post-Westphalian world (Linklater 1998), there is much uncertainty about the new MASs involved in shaping humanity's present and future.

The previous remarks offer a philosophical way of interpreting the *Washington Consensus*, the last stage in the state's political apoptosis. John Williamson coined the expression 'Washington Consensus' in 1989, in order to refer to a set of ten specific policy recommendations that he found to constitute a standard strategy adopted and promoted by institutions based in Washington, DC – such as the US Treasury Department, the IMF, and the World Bank – when dealing with countries that needed to cope with economic crises. The policies concerned macroeconomic stabilization, economic opening with respect to both trade and investment, and the expansion of market forces within the domestic economy. In the past quarter of a century, the topic has been the subject of intense and lively debate, in terms of correct description and acceptable prescription: does the Washington Consensus capture a real historical phenomenon? Does the Washington Consensus ever achieve its goals? Is it to be re-interpreted, despite Williamson's quite clear definition, as the imposition of neoliberal policies by Washington-based international financial institutions on troubled countries? These are important questions, but the real point of interest here is not the hermeneutical, economic, or normative evaluation of the Washington Consensus. Rather, it is the fact that the very idea, even if it remains only an influential idea, captures a significant aspect of our hyperhistorical, post-Westphalian time. For the Washington Consensus may be seen as the coherent outcome of the United Nations Monetary and Financial Conference, also known as the *Bretton Woods conference* (Steil 2013). This gathering in 1944 of 730 delegates from all 44 Allied nations at the Mount Washington Hotel in Bretton Woods, New Hampshire, United States, regulated the international monetary and financial order after the conclusion of the Second World War. It saw the birth of the International Bank for Reconstruction and Development (IBRD, together with its concessional lending arm, the International Development Association, it is known as the World Bank), of the General Agreement on Tariffs and Trade (GATT, which would be replaced by the World Trade Organization in 1995), and the IMF. In short, Bretton Woods sealed the official emergence of a variety of MASs as supranational or intergovernmental forces involved with the world's political, social and economic problems. Thus, Bretton Woods and later on the Washington Consensus highlight the fact that, after the Second World War, organizations and institutions (not only those in Washington, DC) that are not states but rather non-governmental MASs, are openly acknowledged to act as major, influential forces on the political and economic scene internationally, dealing with global problems through global policies. The very fact – no matter whether correct or not – that the Washington Consensus has been accused of being widely mistaken in disregarding local specificities and global differences reinforces the point that a variety of powerful MASs are now the new sources of policies in the globalized information societies.

All this helps to explain why – in a post-Westphalian (emergence of the nation state as the modern, political information agent) and post-Bretton Woods (emergence of non-state MASs as hyperhistorical players in the global economy and politics) world – one of the main challenges we face is how to design the right sort of MASs that could take full advantage of the socio-political progress made in modern history, while dealing successfully with the new global challenges that are undermining the best legacy of that very progress in hyperhistory.

Among the many explanations for such a shift from a historical, Westphalian order to a post-Washington Consensus, hyperhistorical predicament in search of a new equilibrium, three are worth highlighting here.

First, *power*. ICTs 'democratize' data and the processing/controlling power over them, in the sense that both now tend to reside and multiply in a multitude of repositories and sources, thus creating, enabling and empowering a potentially boundless number of non-state agents, from the single individual to associations and groups, from macro-agents, such as multinationals, to international, inter-governmental as well as non-governmental, organizations and supranational insti-tutions. The state is no longer the only, and sometimes not even the main, agent in the political arena that can exercise informational power over other informational agents, in particular over (groups of) citizens. The phenomenon is generating a new tension between power and force, where power is informational, and exercised through the elaboration and dissemination of norms, whereas force is physical, and exercised when power fails to orient the behaviour of the relevant agents and norms need to be enforced. The more physical goods and even money become information-dependent, the more the informational power exercised by MASs acquires a significant financial aspect.

Second, *geography*. ICTs de-territorialize human experience. They have made regional borders porous or, in some cases, entirely irrelevant. They have also created, and are exponentially expanding, regions of the infosphere where an increasing number of agents (not only human, see Floridi 2013) operate and spend more and more time, the onlife experience. Such regions are intrinsically stateless. This is generating a new tension between geo-politics, which is global and non-territorial, and the nation state, which still defines its identity and political legitimacy in terms of a sovereign territorial unit, as a country.

Third, *organization*. ICTs fluidify the topology of politics. They do not merely enable but actually promote (through management and empowerment) the agile, temporary and timely aggregation, disaggregation and re-aggregation of dis-tributed groups 'on demand', around shared interests, across old, rigid boundaries, represented by social classes, political parties, ethnicity, language barriers, physical barriers, and so forth. This is generating new tensions between the nation state, still understood as a major organizational institution, yet no longer rigid but increas-ingly morphing into a very flexible MAS itself (I return to this point below), and a variety of equally powerful, indeed sometimes even more powerful and politically influential (with respect to the old nation state), non-state organizations, the other MASs on the block. Terrorism, for example, is no longer a problem concerning internal affairs – as some forms of terrorism in the Basque Country, Germany, Italy, or Northern Ireland were – but an international confrontation with a MAS such as Al-Qaeda, the notorious, global, militant Islamist organization.

The debate on direct democracy is thus reshaped. We used to think that it was about how the nation state could re-organize itself internally, by designing rules and managing the means to promote forms of democracy, in which citizens could propose and vote on policy initiatives directly and almost in real time. We thought of forms of direct democracy as complementary options for forms of representative democracy. It was going to be a world of 'politics always-on'. The reality is that direct democracy has turned into a mass media-led democracy in the ICT sense of new social media. In such digital democracies, MASs (understood as distributed groups, temporary and timely, and aggregated around shared interests) have multiplied and become sources of influence external to the nation state. Citizens vote for their representatives but influence them via opinion polls almost in real time. Consensus-building has become a constant concern based on synchronic information.

Because of the previous three reasons – power, geography and organization – the unique position of the historical state as *the* information agent is being undermined from below and overridden from above by the emergence of MASs that have the data, the power (and sometimes even the force, as in the very different cases of the United Nations, of groups' cyber threats, or of terrorist attacks), the space, and the organizational flexibility to erode the modern state's political clout, to appropriate (some of) its authority and, in the long run, make it redundant in contexts where it was once the only or the predominant informational agent. The Greek crisis, which began in late 2009, and the agents involved in its management, offer a good template: the Greek government and the Greek state had to interact 'above' with the European Union, the European Central Bank, the IMF, the rating agencies, and so forth, and 'below' with the Greek mass media and the people in Syntagma square, the financial markets and international investors, German public opinion, and so forth.

Of course, the historical nation state is not giving up its role without a fight. In many contexts, it is trying to reclaim its primacy as the information super-agent governing the political life of the society that it organizes. In some cases, the attempt is blatant. In the United Kingdom, the Labour Government introduced the first Identity Cards Bill in November 2004. After several intermediary stages, the Identity Cards Act 2006 was finally repealed by the Identity Documents Act 2010, on 21 December 2010. The failed plan to introduce compulsory ID in the United Kingdom should be read from a modern, Westphalian perspective. In many cases, it is 'historical resistance' by stealth, as when an information society – which is characterized by the essential role played by intellectual, intangible assets (knowledge-based economy), information-intensive services (business and property services, finance and insurance), and public sectors (especially education, public administration and healthcare) – is largely run by the state, which simply maintains its role of major informational agent no longer just legally, on the basis of its power over legislation and its implementation, but now also economically, on the basis of its power over the majority of information-based jobs. The intrusive presence of so-called state capitalism with its SOE (State Owned Enterprises) all over the world, from Brazil, to France, to China, is an obvious symptom of hyperhistorical anachronism.

Similar forms of resistance seem only able to delay the inevitable rise of political MASs. Unfortunately, they may involve huge risks, not only locally, but above all globally. Recall that the two World Wars may be seen as the end of the Westphalian system. Paradoxically, while humanity is moving into a hyperhistorical age, the world is witnessing the rise of China, currently a most 'historical' sovereign state, and the decline of the United States, a sovereign state that more than any other superpower in the past already had a hyperhistorical and multi-agent vocation in its federal organization. We might be moving from a Washington Consensus to a *Beijing Consensus*, described by Williamson as consisting of incremental reform, innovation and experimentation, export-led growth, state capitalism and authoritarianism. All this is risky, because the anachronistic historicism of some of China's policies and humanity's growing hyperhistoricism are heading towards a confrontation. It may not be a conflict, but hyperhistory is a force whose time has come, and while it seems very likely that it will be the Chinese state that will emerge deeply transformed, one can only hope that the inevitable friction will be as painless and peaceful as possible. The financial and social crises that the most advanced information societies are currently undergoing may actually be the very painful but still peaceful price we need to pay to adapt to a future post-Washington Consensus order.

The previous conclusion holds true for the historical state in general: in the future, we shall see the political MASs acquire increasing prominence, with the state progressively abandoning its resistance to hyperhistorical changes and evolving into a MAS itself. Good examples are provided by devolution, or the growing trend in making central banks, such as the Bank of England or the European Central Bank, independent, public organizations.

The time has come to consider the nature of the political MAS more closely and some of the questions that its emergence is already posing.

The political MASs

The political MAS is a system constituted by other systems,[4] which, as a single agent, is:

1. *teleological*: the MAS has a purpose, or goal, which it pursues through its actions;
2. *interactive*: the MAS and its environment can act upon each other;
3. *autonomous*: the MAS can change its configurations without direct response to interaction, by performing internal transitions to change its states. This imbues the MAS with some degree of complexity and independence from its environment; and finally
4. *adaptable*: the MAS' interactions can change the rules by which the MAS changes its states. Adaptability ensures that the MAS learns its own mode of operation in a way that depends critically on its experience.

The political MAS becomes *intelligent* (in the sense of being smart) when it implements features (1) to (4) above efficiently and effectively, minimizing resources, wastefulness and errors, while maximizing the returns of its actions. The emergence of intelligent, political MASs poses many serious questions, five of which are worth reviewing here, even if only quickly: identity and cohesion, consent, social versus political space, legitimacy, and transparency (the transparent MAS).

1. *Identity and Cohesion*. Throughout modernity, the state has dealt with the problem of establishing and maintaining its own *identity* by working on the equation between state = nation, often through the legal means of citizenship and the narrative rhetoric of space (the mother/father land) and time (story in the sense of traditions, recurrent celebrations of past nation-building events, etc.). Consider, for example, the invention of mandatory military service during the French Revolution, its increasing popularity in modern history, but then the decreasing number of sovereign states that still impose it nowadays. Conscription transformed the right to wage war from an eminently economic problem – Florentine bankers financed the English kings during the Hundred Years' War (1337–1453), for example – into also a legal problem: the right of the state to send its citizens to die on its behalf, thus making human life the penultimate value, available for the ultimate sacrifice, in the name of patriotism. 'For King and Country': it is a sign of modern anachronism that, in moments of crisis, sovereign states still give in to the temptation of fuelling nationalism about meaningless, *geographical* spots, often some small islands unworthy of any human loss, from the Falkland Islands or Islas Malvinas to the Senkaku or Diaoyu Islands.

The equation between state, nation, citizenship and land/story had the further advantage of providing an answer to a second problem, that of *cohesion*, for it answered not just the question of who or what the state is, but also the question of who or what belongs to the state and hence may be subject to its norms, policies, and actions. New political MASs cannot rely on the same solution. Indeed, they face the further problem of having to deal with the decoupling of their political identity and cohesion. The political identity of a MAS may be very strong and yet unrelated to its temporary and rather loose cohesion, as is the case with the Tea Party movement in the United States. Both identity and cohesion of a political MAS may be rather weak, as in the international Occupy movement. Or one may recognize a strong cohesion and yet an unclear or weak political identity, as with the population of tweeting individuals and their role during the Arab Spring. Both identity and cohesion of a political MAS are established and maintained through information sharing. The land is virtualized into the region of the infosphere in which the MAS operates. So memory (retrievable recordings) and coherence (reliable updates) of the information flow enable a political MAS to claim some identity and some cohesion, and therefore offer a sense of belonging. But it is, above all, the fact that the boundaries between the online and offline are disappearing, the appearance of the onlife experience, and hence the fact that the virtual infosphere can affect politically the physical space, that reinforces the sense of the political MAS as a real agent. If Anonymous had only a virtual existence, its identity and cohesion would be much less strong. Deeds provide a vital counterpart to the virtual information flow to guarantee cohesion. An ontology of interactions replaces an ontology of entities, or, with a word play, *ings* (as in interact-*ing*, process-*ing*, network-*ing*, do-*ing*, be-*ing*, etc.) replace things.

2. *Consent.* A significant consequence of the breaking up of the equation 'political MAS = nation state = citizenship = land = story' and of the decoupling of identity and cohesion in a political MAS is that the age-old theoretical problem of how consent to be governed by a political authority arises, is being turned on its head. In the historical framework of social contract theory, the presumed default position is that of a legal opt-out: there is some kind of (to be specified) *a priori*, original consent, allegedly given (for a variety of reasons) by any individual subject to the political state, to be governed by the latter and its laws. The problem is to understand how such consent is given and what happens when an agent, especially a citizen, opts out of it (the out-law). In the hyperhistorical framework, the expected default position is that of a social opt-in, which is exercised whenever the agent subjects itself to the political MAS conditionally, for a specific purpose. Oversimplifying, we are moving from being part of the political consensus to taking part in it, and such part-taking is increasingly 'just in time', 'on demand', 'goal-oriented', and anything but permanent or long-term, and stable. If doing politics looks increasingly like doing business it is because, in both cases, the inter-locutor, the citizen-customer needs to be convinced every time anew. Loyal membership is not the default position, and needs to be built and renewed around political and commercial products alike. Gathering consent around specific political issues becomes a continuous process of (re)engagement. It is not a question of political attention span – the generic complaint that 'new generations' cannot pay sustained attention to political problems is ill-founded. They are, after all, the generations that binge-watch TV. It is a matter of motivating interest again and again, without running into semantic inflation (one more crisis, one more emergency, one more revolution, one more . . .) and political fatigue (how many times do we need to intervene urgently?). The problem is therefore to understand what may motivate repeatedly or indeed force agents (again, not just individual human beings, but all kinds of agents) to give such consent and become engaged, and what happens when such agents, unengaged by default (note, not disengaged, for disengagement presupposes a previous state of engagement), prefer to stay away from the activities of the political MAS, inhabiting a social sphere of civil but apolitical 'nonimity' (lack of anonymity).

Failing to grasp the previous transformation from historical opt-out to hyperhistorical opt-in means being less likely to understand the apparent inconsistency between the disenchantment of individuals with politics and the popularity of global movements, international mobilizations, activism, voluntarism and other social forces with huge political implications. What is moribund is not politics *tout court*, but historical politics, that based on parties, classes, fixed social roles, and the nation state, which sought political legitimacy only once and spent it until revoked. The inching towards the so-called centre by parties in liberal democracies around the world, as well as the 'Get out the vote' strategies (GOTV is a term used to describe the mobilization of *voters as supporters* to ensure that those who can do vote) are evidence that engagement needs to be constantly renewed and expanded in order to win an election. Party (as well as union) membership is a modern feature that is likely to become increasingly less common.

3. *Social versus political space*. Understanding the previous inversion of default positions means being faced by a further problem. Oversimplifying once more, in prehistory, the social and the political spaces overlap because, in a stateless society, there is no real difference between social and political relations and hence interactions. In history, the state seeks to maintain such co-extensiveness by occupying, as an informational MAS, all the social space politically, thus establishing the primacy of the political over the social. This trend, if unchecked and unbalanced, risks leading to totalitarianisms (e.g. the Italy of Mussolini), or at least broken democracies (e.g. the Italy of Berlusconi). We saw above that such a co-extensiveness and its control may be based on normative or economic strategies, through the exercise of power, force and rule-making. In hyperhistory, the social space is the original, default space from which agents may move to (consent to) join the political space. It is not accidental that concepts such as *civil society* (in the post-Hegelian sense of non-political society), *public sphere* (also in a non-Habermasian sense), and *community* become increasingly important the more we move into a hyper-historical context. The problem is to understand such social space where agents of various kinds are supposed to be interacting and which gives rise to the political MAS.

Each agent, as described above, has some degrees of freedom. By this I do not mean liberty, autonomy or self-determination, but rather, in the robotic, more humble sense, some capacities or abilities, supported by the relevant resources, to engage in specific actions for a specific purpose. To use an elementary example, a coffee machine has only one degree of freedom: it can make coffee, once the right ingredients and energy are supplied. The sum of an agent's degrees of freedom is its 'agency'. When the agent is alone, there is of course only agency, but no social let alone political space. Imagine Robinson Crusoe on his 'Island of Despair'. However, as soon as there is another agent (Friday on the 'Island of Despair'), or indeed a group of agents (the native cannibals, the shipwrecked Spaniards, the English mutineers), agency acquires the further value of multi-agent (i.e. social) interaction: practices and then rules for co-ordination and constraint of the agents' degrees of freedom become essential, initially for the wellbeing of the agents constituting the MAS, and then for the wellbeing of the MAS itself. Note the shift in the level of analysis: once the social space arises, we begin to consider the group as a group – for example, as a family, or a community, or as a society

– and the actions of the individual agents constituting it become elements that lead to the MAS' newly established degrees of freedom, or agency. The previous simple example may still help. Consider now a coffee machine and a timer: separately, they are two agents with different agency, but if they are properly joined and co-ordinated into a MAS, then the issuing agent has the new agency to make coffee at a set time. It is now the MAS that has a more complex capacity, and that may or may not work properly.

A social space is thus the totality of degrees of freedom of the inhabiting agents one wishes to take into consideration. In history, such consideration – which is really just another level of analysis – was largely determined physically and geographically, in terms of presence in a territory, and hence by a variety of forms of neighbourhood. In the previous example, all the agents interacting with Robinson Crusoe are taken into consideration because of their relations (interactive presence in terms of their degree of freedom) to the same 'Island of Despair'. We saw that ICTs have changed all this. In hyperhistory, where to draw the line to include, or indeed exclude, the relevant agents whose degrees of freedom constitute the social space has become increasingly a matter of at least implicit choice, when not of explicit decision. The result is that the phenomenon of distributed morality, encompassing that of distributed responsibility, is becoming more and more common. In either case, history or hyperhistory, what counts as a social space may be a political move. Globalization is a de-territorialization in this political sense.

If we now turn to the political space in which the new MASs operate, it would be a mistake to consider it a separate space, over and above the social one: both are determined by the same totality of the agents' degrees of freedom. The political space emerges when the complexity of the social space – understood in terms of number and kinds of interactions and of agents involved, and of degree of dynamic reconfiguring of both agents and interactions – requires the prevention or resolution of potential *divergences* and the co-ordination or collaboration about potential *convergences*. *Both* are crucial. And in each case more information is required, in terms of representation and deliberation about a complex multitude of degrees of freedom. The result is that the social space becomes politicized through its informatization.

4. *Legitimacy*. It is when the agents in the social space agree to agree on how to deal with their divergences (conflicts) and convergences that the social space acquires the political dimension to which we are so used. Yet two potential mistakes await us here.

The first, call it Hobbesian, is to consider politics merely as the prevention of war by other means, to invert the famous phrase by Carl von Clausewitz, according to which 'war is the continuation of politics by other means'. This is not the case, because even a complex society of angels (*homo hominis angelus*) would still require rules in order to further its harmony. Convergences too need politics. Out of metaphor, politics is not just about conflicts due to the agents' exercises of their degree of freedom when pursuing their goals. It is also, or at least it should be, above all, the furthering of coordination and collaboration of degrees of freedom by means other than coercion and violence.

The second, and one may call this potential mistake Rousseauian, is that it may seem that the political space is then just that part of the social space organized by law. In this case, the mistake is subtler. We usually associate the political space with the rules or laws that regulate it but the latter are not constitutive, by themselves, of the political space. Compare two cases in which rules determine a game. In chess, the rules do not merely constrain the game, they are the game because they do not supervene on a previous activity: rather, they are the *necessary and sufficient conditions* that determine all and only the moves that can be legally made. In football, however, the rules are supervening *constraints* because the agents enjoy a previous and basic degree of freedom, consisting in their capacity to kick a ball with the foot in order to score a goal, which the rules are supposed to regulate. Whereas it is physically possible, but makes no sense, to place two pawns on the same square of a chessboard, nothing impeded Maradona from scoring an infamous goal by using his hand in the Argentina v England football match (1986 FIFA World Cup), and that to be allowed by a referee who did not see the infringement.

Once we avoid the two previous mistakes, it is easier to see that the political space is that area of the social space constrained by the agreement to agree on resolution of divergences and coordination of convergences. This leads to a further consideration, concerning the transparent MAS, especially when, in this transition time, the MAS in question is still the state.

5.   *The transparent MAS.* There are two senses in which the MAS can be transparent. Unsurprisingly, both come from ICTs and computer science (Turilli and Floridi 2009), one more case in which the information revolution is changing our mental frameworks.

On the one hand, the MAS (think of the national state, and also corporate agents, multinationals, or supranational institutions, etc.) can be transparent in the sense that it moves from being a black box to being a white box. Other agents (citizens, when the MAS is the state) not only can see inputs and outputs – for example, levels of tax revenue and public expenditure – they can also monitor how (in our running example, the state as) a MAS works internally. This is not a novelty at all. It was a principle already popularized in the nineteenth century. However, it has become a renewed feature of contemporary politics due to the possibilities opened up by ICTs. This kind of transparency is also known as *open government*.

On the other hand, and this is the more innovative sense that I wish to stress here, the MAS can be transparent in the same sense in which a technology (e.g. an interface) is: invisible, not because it is not there, but because it delivers its services so efficiently, effectively, and reliably that its presence is imperceptible. When something works at its best, behind the scenes as it were, to make sure that we can operate as efficiently and as smoothly as possible, then we have a transparent system. When the MAS in question is the state, this second sense of transparency should not be seen as a surreptitious way of introducing, with a different terminology, the concept of 'small state' or 'small governance'. On the contrary, in this second sense, the MAS (the state) is as transparent and as vital as the oxygen that we breathe. It strives to be the ideal butler.[5] There is no standard terminology for this kind of transparent MAS that becomes perceivable only when it is absent. Perhaps one may speak of *gentle government*. It seems that MASs can increasingly support the right sort of ethical infrastructure (more on this below) the more transparently, that is, openly and gently, they play the negotiating game through which they take care of the *res publica*. When this negotiating game fails, the possible outcome is an increasingly violent conflict among the parties involved. It is a tragic possibility that ICTs have seriously reconfigured.

All this is not to say that *opacity* does not have its virtues. Care should be exercised, lest the socio-political discourse is reduced to the nuances of higher quantity, quality, intelligibility, and usability of information and ICTs. The more the better is not the only, nor always the best, rule of thumb. For the withdrawal of information can often make a positive and significant difference. We already encountered Montesquieu's division of the state's political powers. Each of them may be carefully opaque in the right way to the other two. For one may need to lack (or intentionally preclude oneself from accessing) some information in order to achieve desirable goals, such as protecting anonymity, enhancing fair treatment, or implementing unbiased evaluation. Famously, in Rawls (1999), the 'veil of ignorance' exploits precisely this aspect of information, in order to develop an impartial approach to justice. Being informed is not always a blessing and might even be dangerous or wrong, distracting or crippling. The point is that opacity cannot be assumed to be a good feature in a political system unless it is adopted explicitly and consciously, by showing that it is not a mere bug.

Infraethics

Part of the ethical efforts engendered by our hyperhistorical condition concerns the design of environments that can facilitate MASs' ethical choices, actions, or process. This is not the same as *ethics by design*. It is rather *pro-ethical design*, as I hope becomes clearer in the following pages. Both are liberal, but the former may be mildly paternalistic, insofar as it privileges the facilitation of the *right* kind of choices, actions, process or interactions on behalf of the agents involved, whereas the latter does not have to be, insofar as it privileges the facilitation of *reflection* by the agents involved on their choices, actions, or process.[6] For example, the former may let people opt-out of the default preference according to which, by obtaining a driving licence, one is also willing to be an organ donor. The latter may not allow one to obtain a driving licence unless one has decided whether one wishes to be an organ donor. In this section, I call environments that can facilitate ethical choices, actions, or process, the ethical infrastructure, or *infraethics*. I call the reader's attention to the problem of how to design the right sort of infraethics for the emerging MASs. In different contexts or cases, the design of a liberal infraethics may be more or less paternalistic. My argument is that it should be as little paternalistic as the circumstances permit, although no less.

It is a sign of the times that, when politicians speak of infrastructure nowadays, they often have in mind ICTs. They are not wrong. From business fortunes to conflicts, what makes contemporary societies work depends increasingly on bits rather than atoms. We have already seen all this. What is less obvious, and philosophically more interesting, is that ICTs seem to have unveiled a new sort of equation.

Consider the unprecedented emphasis that ICTs have placed on crucial phenomena such as trust, privacy, transparency, freedom of expression, openness, intellectual property rights (IPR), loyalty, respect, reliability, reputation, rule of law, and so forth. These are probably better understood in terms of an infra-structure that is there to facilitate or hinder (reflection upon) the im/moral behaviour of the agents involved.

Thus, by placing our informational interactions at the centre of our lives, ICTs seem to have uncovered something that, of course, has always been there, but less visibly so: the fact that the moral behaviour of a society of agents is also a matter of 'ethical infrastructure' or simply *infraethics*. An important aspect of our moral lives has escaped much of our attention and, indeed, many concepts and related phenomena have been mistakenly treated as if they were only ethical, when in fact they are probably mostly infraethical. To use a term from the philosophy of technology, they have a dual-use nature: they can be morally good, but also morally evil (more on this presently). The new equation indicates that, in the same way that business and administration systems, in an economically mature society, increasingly require infrastructures (transport, communication, services, etc.), so too, moral interactions increasingly require an infraethics in an informationally mature society.

The idea of an infraethics is simple, but can be misleading. The previous equa-tion helps to clarify it. When economists and political scientists speak of a 'failed state', they may refer to the failure of a *state-as-a-structure* to fulfil its basic roles, such as exercising control over its borders, collecting taxes, enforcing laws, administer-ing justice, providing schooling, and so forth. In other words, the state fails to provide *public* (e.g. defence and police) and *merit* (e.g. healthcare) *goods*. Or (too often an inclusive and intertwined or) they may refer to the collapse of a *state-as-an-infrastructure* or environment, which makes possible and fosters the right sort of social interactions. This means that they may be referring to the collapse of a substratum of default expectations about economic, political and social conditions, such as the rule of law, respect for civil rights, a sense of political community, civilized dialogue among differently-minded people, ways to reach peaceful resolutions of ethnic, religious, or cultural tensions, and so forth.

All these expectations, attitudes, practices, in short such an implicit 'socio-political infrastructure', which one may take for granted, provides a vital ingredient for the success of any complex society. It plays a crucial role in human interactions, comparable to the one that we are now accustomed to attributing to physical infrastructures in economics.

Thus, infraethics should not be understood in terms of Marxist theory, as if it were a mere update of the old 'base and superstructure' idea, because the elements in question are entirely different: we are dealing with moral actions and not-yet-moral facilitators of such moral actions. Nor should it be understood in terms of a kind of second-order normative discourse on ethics, because it is the not-yet-ethical framework of implicit expectations, attitudes, and practices that *can* facilitate and promote moral decisions and actions. At the same time, it would also be wrong to think that an infraethics is morally neutral. Rather, it has a dual-use nature, as I anticipated above: it can both facilitate and hinder morally good as well as evil actions, and do this in different degrees. At its best, it is the grease that lubricates the moral mechanism. This is more likely to happen whenever having a 'dual-use' nature does not mean that each use is equally likely, that is, that the infraethics in question is still not neutral, nor merely positive, but does have a bias to deliver more good than evil. If this is confusing, think of the dual-use nature not in terms of an equilibrium, like an ideal coin that can deliver both heads and tails, but in terms of a co-presence of two alternative outcomes, one of which is more likely than the other, like in a biased coin more likely to turn heads than tails. When an infraethics has a 'biased dual-use' nature, it is easy to mistake the infraethical for the ethical, since whatever helps goodness to flourish or evil to take root partakes of their nature.

Any successful complex society, be this the city of man or the city of God, relies on an implicit infraethics. This is dangerous, because the increasing importance of an infraethics may lead to the following risk: that the legitimization of the ethical ground is based on the 'value' of the infraethics that is supposed to support it. *Supporting* is mistaken for *grounding*, and may even aspire to the role of *legitimizing*, leading to what Lyotard (1984) criticized as mere 'performativity' of the system, independently of the actual values cherished and pursued. Infraethics is the vital syntax of a society, but it is not its semantics, to use a distinction popular in artificial intelligence. It is about the structural form, not the meaningful contents.

We saw above that even a society in which the entire population consisted of angels, that is, perfect moral agents, still needs norms for collaboration. Theoretically, that is, when one assumes that morally good values and the infraethics that promotes them may be kept separate (an abstraction that never occurs in reality but that facilitates our analysis), a society may exist in which the entire population consisted of Nazi fanatics who could rely on high levels of trust, respect, reliability, loyalty, privacy, transparency, and even freedom of expression, openness and fair competition. Clearly, what we want is not just the successful mechanism provided by the right infraethics, but also the coherent combination between it and morally good values, such as civil rights. This is why a balance between security and privacy, for example, is so difficult to achieve, unless we clarify first whether we are dealing with a tension within ethics (security and privacy as a moral right), within infraethics (both are understood as not-yet-ethical facilitators), or between infraethics (security) and ethics (privacy), as I suspect. To rely on another analogy: the best pipes (infraethics) may improve the flow but do not improve the quality of the water (ethics), and water of the highest quality is wasted if the pipes are rusty or leaky. So creating the right sort of infraethics and maintaining it is one of the crucial challenges of our time, because an infraethics is not morally good in itself, but it is what is most likely to yield moral goodness if properly designed and combined with the right moral values. The right sort of infraethics should be there to support the right sort of axiology (theory of value). It is certainly a constitutive part of the problem concerning the design of the right MASs.

The more complex a society becomes, the more important and hence salient the role of a well-designed infraethics is, and yet this is exactly what we seem to be missing. Consider the recent Anti-Counterfeiting Trade Agreement (ACTA), a multinational treaty concerning the international standards for IPR. By focusing on the enforcement of IPR, supporters of ACTA completely failed to perceive that it would have undermined the very infraethics that they hoped to foster, namely one promoting some of the best and most successful aspects of our information society. It would have promoted the structural inhibition of some of the most important individuals' positive liberties and their ability to participate in the information society, thus fulfilling their own potential as informational organisms. For lack of a better word, ACTA would have promoted a form of *informism*, comparable to other forms of social agency's inhibition such as classism, racism, and sexism. Sometimes a defence of liberalism may be inadvertently illiberal. If we want to do better, we need to grasp that issues such as IPR are part of the new infraethics for the information society, that their protection needs to find its carefully balanced place within a complex legal and ethical infrastructure that is already in place and constantly evolving, and that such a system must be put at the service of the right values and moral behaviours. This means finding a compromise, at the level of a liberal infraethics, between those who see new legislation (such as ACTA) as a simple fulfilment of existing ethical and legal obligations (in this case from trade agreements), and those who see it as a fundamental erosion of existing ethical and legal civil liberties.

In hyperhistorical societies, any regulation affecting how people deal with information is now bound to influence the whole infosphere and onlife habitat within which they live. So enforcing rights (such as IPR) becomes an environmental problem. This does not mean that any legislation is necessarily negative. The lesson here is one about complexity: since rights such as IPR are part of our infraethics and affect our whole environment understood as the infosphere, the intended and unintended consequences of their enforcement are widespread, interrelated, and far-reaching. These consequences need to be carefully considered, because mistakes will generate huge problems that will have cascading costs for future generations, both ethically and economically. The best way to deal with 'known unknowns' or unintended consequences is to be careful, stay alert, monitor the development of the actions undertaken, and be ready to revise one's decision and strategy quickly, as soon as the wrong sort of effects start appearing. *Festina lente*, 'more haste, less speed' as the classic adage suggests. There is no perfect legislation but only legislation that can be perfected more or less easily. Good agreements about how to shape our infraethics should include clauses about their timely update.

Lastly, it is a mistake to think that we are like outsiders ruling over an environment different from the one we inhabit. Legal documents (such as ACTA) emerge from within the infosphere that they affect. We are building, restoring and refurbishing the house from inside, or one may say that we are repairing the raft while navigating on it. Precisely because the whole problem of respect, infringement, and enforcement of rights (such as IPR) is an infraethical and environmental problem for advanced information societies, the best thing we could do, in order to devise the right solution, is to apply to the process itself the very infraethical framework and ethical values that we would like to see promoted by it. This means that the infosphere should regulate itself from within, not from an impossible without.

Conclusion: the last of the historical generations?

Six thousand years ago, a generation of humans witnessed the invention of writing and the emergence of the conditions of possibility of cities, kingdoms, empires and nation states. This is not accidental. Prehistoric societies are both ICT-less and stateless. The state is a typical historical phenomenon. It emerges when human groups stop living a hand-to-mouth existence in small communities and begin to live a mouth-to-hand one, in which large communities become political societies, with division of labour and specialized roles, organized under some form of government, which manages resources through the control of ICTs, including that very special kind of information called 'money'. From taxes to legislation, from the administration of justice to military force, from census to social infrastructure, the state was for a long time the ultimate information agent and so I suggested that history, and especially modernity, is the age of the state.

Almost halfway between the beginning of history and now, Plato was still trying to make sense of both radical changes: the encoding of memories through written symbols and the symbiotic interactions between individuals and *polis*–state. In 50 years, our grandchildren may look at us as the last of the historical, state-organized generations, not so differently from the way we look at the Amazonian tribes mentioned at the beginning of this chapter, as the last of the prehistorical, stateless societies. It may take a long while before we come to understand in full such transformations. And this is a problem, because we do not have another six millennia in front of us. We cannot wait for another Plato in a few millennia. We are playing an environmental gambit with ICTs, and we have only a short time to win the game, for the future of our planet is at stake. We had better act now.

Notes

* This text is a revised and expanded version of Floridi (2012).
1 According to data about life expectancy at birth for the world and major development groups, 1950–2050. Source: Population Division of the Department of Economic and Social Affairs of the United Nations Secretariat (2005). *World Population Prospects: The 2004 Revision Highlights*. New York: United Nations, available at www.un.org/esa/population/publications/WPP2004/2004Highlights_finalrevised.pdf (accessed 19 January 2016).
2 According to data about poverty in the world, defined as the number and share of people living below $1.25 a day (at 2005 prices) in 2005–08. Source: World Bank, and *The Economist*, 29 February 2012, available online.
3 Floridi and Taddeo (2014). Clarke and Knake (2010) approach the problems of cyberwar and cybersecurity from a political perspective that would still qualify as 'historical' within this chapter, but it is very helpful.
4 For a more detailed analysis, see Floridi (2011).
5 On good governance and the rules of the political, global game, see Brown and Marsden (2013).
6 I have sought to develop an information ethics in Floridi (2013). For a more introductory text, see Floridi (2010).

References

Brown, I. and Marsden, C.T. (2013) *Regulating Code: Good Governance and Better Regulation in the Information Age*. Cambridge, MA: MIT Press.

Clarke, R.A. and Knake, R.K. (2010) *Cyber War: The Next Threat to National Security and What to Do About It*. New York, NY: Ecco.

Floridi, L. (2003) 'Informational Realism'. In J. Weckert and Y. Al-Saggaf (eds) *Selected Papers from Conference on Computers and Philosophy – Volume 37, Australian Computer Society*, available at http://philsci-archive.pitt.edu/2538/1/ir.pdf (accessed 19 January 2016).

——. (ed.) (2010) *The Cambridge Handbook of Information and Computer Ethics*. Cambridge: Cambridge University Press.

——. (2011) *The Philosophy of Information*. Oxford: Oxford University Press.

——. (2012) 'Hyperhistory and the Philosophy of Information Policies'. *Philosophy & Technology* 25(2): 129–131.

——. (2013) *The Ethics of Information*. Oxford: Oxford University Press.

Floridi, L. and Taddeo, M. (eds) (2014) *The Ethics of Information Warfare*. New York, NY: Springer.

Linklater, A. (1998) *The Transformation of Political Community: Ethical Foundations of the Post-Westphalian Era*. Oxford: Polity.

Lyotard, J.-F. (1984) *The Postmodern Condition: A Report on Knowledge*. Minneapolis, MN: University of Minnesota Press.

Rawls, J. (1999) *A Theory of Justice*. Cambridge, MA: Harvard University Press.

Steil, B. (2013) *The Battle of Bretton Woods: John Maynard Keynes, Harry Dexter White, and the Making of a New World Order*. Princeton, NJ: Princeton University Press.

Turilli, M. and Floridi, L. (2009) 'The Ethics of Information Transparency'. *Ethics & Information Technology* 11(2): 105–112.

Chapter 8

Coping with information underload

Hemming in freedom of information through decision support

Bibi van den Berg

> I have long had a favorite example to show how computational complexity can be greatly reduced if we are willing to accept approximations: it has to do with finding needles in haystacks. If needles are distributed randomly in a haystack of size, H, with an average density of distribution, d, then to find the sharpest needle in the stack, we have to search the entire stack, and the search time will vary with H. Search time will be linear with size, which does not seem too bad until we remember that the haystack of life is essentially infinite.
>
> – Herbert Simon (1978: 502)

Introduction

Never before in the history of mankind have we had so much information at our disposal. Information and communication technologies enable us to search for, find, access and share information in a host of different forms, ranging from text and images, to movie clips, books, blogs, wikis, and so on and so forth (Howe 2008; Leadbeater 2008; O'Reilly 2007; Scholz 2008). Since end users can not only find information that is shared through the internet by others, but can also individually or collectively share their own information, this entails that the volume of information that is available to all expands rapidly, even exponentially. Exact and recent numbers are hard to come by, but this quote from an article in the *Columbia Journalism Review* gives an indication of the volume of information that was available via the internet in 2008:

> There are more than 70 million blogs and 150 million Web sites today – a number that is expanding at a rate of approximately ten thousand an *hour*. Two hundred and ten billion e-mails are sent each day. Say goodbye to the gigabyte and hello to the exabyte, five of which are worth 37,000 Libraries of Congress. In 2006 alone, the world produced 161 exabytes of digital data, the equivalent of three million times the information contained in all the books ever written.
>
> (Nordenson 2008: 30, original emphasis)

When it comes to the internet, of course, 2008 is ancient history, so we can safely assume that a manifold of these numbers is applicable to the internet in 2016.

Of course, the availability of so much information has numerous benefits. We can get access to knowledge that was formerly unavailable to us, and enrich our lives through accessing sources from other cultures or historical ages, or sources that represent viewpoints that are (far) removed from our own. We can find social connections with individuals across the globe, based on shared interests, ideals, politics, norms, language, culture, and so on and so forth. The internet has empowered groups and individuals that lacked power before – by giving them a voice, a stage and an audience (cf. Chandler 2007). One could argue that the level of freedom we have in choosing and finding information has never been as widespread as it is today.

At the same time, however, as Shakespeare already noted in 1600, too much of a good thing can be bad as well (Shakespeare 1993). With so much information available to us, how do we choose what to read, see, access, which sources to look to first or trust the most? How do we find our way in the dense informational rainforests of the internet, especially since these are growing denser and more wildly populated every day? How do we know the difference between knowledge and opinion[1] in the barrage of information that is available to us on the internet? And, on a more mundane level, how do we know what or whom to like, what to believe, whom to follow, and what to buy? We have more information available to us than ever before, but with so much of it coming at us every day, how should we choose?

Luckily, some would say, help is under way from two different directions. First, over the past decades, internet companies have developed a number of technological solutions to help us grapple with the avalanche of information that is available to us on the internet. This is done, for example, through the sorting of search results in search engines (using algorithms to optimize the presentation of search results and, to a degree, even order them in accordance with individual users' (guesstimated) preferences), or through the use of behavioural data analytics, including data mining and profiling, which can be employed to provide end users with personalized services or targeted advertisements. Using such techniques end users no longer have to search actively to find the right (types of) information to answer their specific, personal needs. Instead, these technologies help them sort, categorize and organize information for them. The burden of hacking a way through the internet's informational rainforest, thus, is alleviated by the optimized, personalized inroads that such technological sorting mechanisms offer, or so their designers claim.

Second, in recent years policy-makers have discovered a set of behavioural influencing tools to help individuals make choices that will lead to 'better' long-term outcomes, for instance with respect to their health or wellbeing, thus contributing not only to an improvement of these individuals' own living situation, but also to a reduction of collective issues such as high costs for healthcare or state aid. Policy-makers and governments around the globe have embraced a policy tool that has come to be known as 'nudging': the use of 'techniques that deliberately seek to elicit a particular behavioral response from [citizens], whilst formally preserving [their] freedom of choice' (Yeung 2012: 122). 'Nudging' also explicitly aims at supporting individuals in making ('good') choices. Here, too, the burden of having to make choices is (partially) removed from the hands of end users and placed in the hands of technologies, in this case so-called 'choice architects', as we will see below.

In this chapter, I argue that there are significant similarities between the technological solutions that have been developed to help us sort through – and find a meaningful order in – the mass of information on the internet on the one hand, and the use of behavioural influencing in the realm of public policy (both offline and online) on the other hand. I show that both strategies build on insights relating to the nature of human cognition, or to be more precise, they build on the assumption that individuals have difficulties making (rational) decisions. Research in social psychology and behavioural economics on the ways in which human beings make choices has revealed that all sorts of biases and heuristics are at play whenever people make decisions, and that the traditional idea of the *homo economicus*, who rationally calculates the best possible outcome, has needed serious revision (cf. Cartwright 2011; Jolls, Sunstein and Thaler 1997). More importantly, research has also consistently revealed that when individuals are faced with the abundance of choices that is available to them in their modern everyday lives, this may easily lead to 'choice overload' (Botti and Iyengar 2006; Hanoch and Rice 2006; Iyengar and Kamenica 2010; Iyengar and Lepper 2000; Reed et al. 2011; Schwartz and Kliban 2005; Schwartz 2000). In the next section, I sketch the recent changes in our understanding of humans' capacities to make decisions and their tendencies to use biases and stereotyping to help reduce choice overload, and I explain how this has influenced both technology developers and public policy-makers in their attempts to develop mechanisms to support and influence individuals' decisions processes.

Next, I show that the proponents using these two different branches of decision support, which we will label as 'decision support' for short, use remarkably similar arguments to plead the usefulness, the relevance and the applicability of their solution (third section). The lines of criticism that have been launched against both forms of decision support also align neatly (fourth section). Lastly, and most importantly, I argue that while the use of behavioural data analytics and nudging is presented as a way of helping us deal with the risk of choice and information overload in a world of ubiquitous information technology, by the same token both of these solutions run the risk of hemming in our freedom of information, each from a different direction (fifth section). Profiling and personalization on the internet may hem in freedom of information by making a preselection of what information will be presented to end users. Since this is done in a way that is opaque and remains implicit for end users, this may have a negative impact on their ability to find and access information. Similarly, nudging builds on the idea that citizens can be influenced subtly, implicitly through the offering of certain 'choices architectures' with 'benign' defaults (Thaler and Sunstein 2008), thus seducing them to behave 'better'. This, too, happens largely outside citizens' awareness and hems in their free and unconstrained ability to choose for themselves. Each mechanism thus contributes to a decrease in our freedom to choose. It is in this light that I understand Luciano Floridi's contribution to this volume (Chapter 7) and his proposal for the creation of what he calls 'infraethics'. This article, then, ends with an appraisal and one potential legitimation of Floridi's chapter: I argue that the ways in which freedom of information is hemmed in by the dual forces of behavioural data analytics and nudging provide extra force to the urgency of the project that Floridi is undertaking (sixth section).

Overwhelmed by choice

A large portion of citizens and consumers in Western countries live in a world of abundance: an abundance of wealth, an abundance of opportunities and, as we have seen, an abundance of choice. They are capable, to a considerable degree, to shape their lives the way they see fit, to follow the careers they wish to pursue, to make life-choices in terms of relationships and family according to their own preferences, to buy the products and services they desire, and to live according to self-chosen values, norms and ideals. Choosing to follow one's own path towards wellbeing is valued as one of the highest ideals in our individualistic Western society and is considered to be fundamental in people's sense of autonomy and self-determination (Botti and Iyengar 2006; Schwartz 2000). As Botti and Iyengar point out 'both politicians and the lay public have presumed the superlative social benefits of choice' (Botti and Iyengar 2006: 24). The idea that more choice is better, then, has become a deeply rooted element of our way of thinking about what constitutes a good life and how it ought to be lived:

> It is a common supposition in modern society that the more choices, the better – that the human ability to manage, and the human desire for, choice is infinite. From classic economic theories of free enterprise, to mundane marketing practices that provide customers with entire aisles devoted to potato chips or soft drinks, to important life decisions in which people contemplate alternative career options or multiple investment opportunities, this belief pervades our institutions, norms, and customs.
>
> (Iyengar and Lepper 2000: 995)

However, since the middle of the twentieth century, this fundamental belief in the preferably unbounded degree of choice has come under attack (Simon 1955). In the past decades, research into the limitations of people's ability *and* desire to choose has proliferated in different scientific disciplines. For one, using core concepts from classical psychoanalysis Renata Salecl (2011) has argued that our emphasis on having the *freedom* to choose has overextended into a *burden* to choose. Not only are we constantly forced to make choices in our everyday lives, both

relatively minor ones and very fundamental decisions with far-reaching consequences, but we ,are also made ultimately responsible for these choices and
their outcomes. This leads to all sorts of forms of anxiety over what to choose
and how to cope when the result of a choice turns out to be different from what
was expected. It is unsurprising, according to Salecl, that many people postpone
making choices, or are left feeling anxious when they do. What makes things worse
is the fact that the choices that individuals have tend to be presented as though they
are all straightforward, simple consumer choices, when in fact, many choices,
especially the more important 'life choices' are not. Salecl writes:

> In today's society, [. . .] the problem is not just the scale of choice available but
> the manner in which choice is represented. Life choices are described in the
> same terms as consumer choices: we set out to find the 'right' life as we would
> to find the right kind of wallpaper or hair conditioner.
>
> (Salecl 2011: 8)

From a psychoanalytical perspective the overwhelming amount of choices
available to us, and the force of having to make decisions each and every day, lead
to classical Freudian anxieties, regret and stress symptoms. Hence, Salecl pleads
for a more nuanced picture of the all-out importance of maximizing freedom
of choice.

Meanwhile, a great number of empirical studies from social psychology and
behavioural economics have consistently shown that people are, in fact, rather
bad at making choices – or at least, at making choices *on rational grounds*.[2] This is so
when choices are complex and it is difficult to predict the potential outcomes
(Hanoch and Rice 2006; Iyengar and Lepper 2000), but it even applies to very
simple and mundane choices, such as which type of cereal or jam to choose in a
supermarket, since there is an abundance of choices for even these most ordinary
products (Iyengar and Kamenica 2010; Schwartz and Kliban 2005; Schwartz
2000). Confirming Salecl's psychoanalytical interpretation, these empirical studies
consistently reveal that too much choice is simply overwhelming and may lead to
insecurity, anxiety and regret (Hanoch and Rice 2006; Reed et al. 2011; Schwartz
2000). More broadly, the obligation to choose constantly in modern life may lead
to what has been termed *choice overload*[3] (Botti and Iyengar 2006; Hanoch and Rice
2006; Iyengar and Kamenica 2010; Reed et al. 2011; Schwartz and Kliban 2005),
which is the idea that when individuals have '*too many* options [this] results in
adverse experiences, including a depletion of cognitive resources and postdecision
feelings of regret' (Reed et al. 2011: 547, original emphasis).

Choosers can easily feel burdened by having too many options. And to make
matters worse, when they *do* decide from a large set of possibilities, 'people [may]
be more dissatisfied with the choices they make' (Iyengar and Lepper 2000: 1004).[4]
Different contributing factors have been established with respect to these findings
in relation to humans' capacity to make decisions. Combined, these point towards
the key flaws in the paradigm of rational choice and the *homo economicus*, which

is one of the most widespread paradigms in Western culture. For one, while rational choice theories assume that people will tend to use their rational minds to think through the many different potential outcomes of each choice in order to maximize the outcome for themselves, in the real world this is simply practically impossible, let alone desirable. The more complex choices are, the more cognitive resources they would require if all potential outcomes ought to be calculated. But human beings simply do not have enough cognitive resources to think through the many options and consequences relating to each potential outcome of a choice (Reed et al. 2011). What is more, individuals also lack the time and the energy to calculate all, or even a significant set of different pay-offs for many choices. Herbert Simon introduced the term 'bounded rationality' (or 'procedural rationality') to pinpoint the limitations set on humans' capacity to reason and choose (Selten 2001; Simon 1955, 1972).

Furthermore, individuals often do not have consistent preferences – what they prefer in one situation might not be preferable in another, or what they prefer at one time in their lives they may not find preferable at another time. This entails that they need to rethink their preferences and the choices they make across situations and over time, continuously spending valuable cognitive resources on this task, and potentially experiencing even more dissatisfaction and anguish about the burden of choice or the consequences of specific decisions.

Lastly and most importantly, research has revealed that what people choose is not just the result of processes of rational thinking and calculation, but that all sorts of other faculties and factors are involved as well. People choose on the basis of their emotions, and on the basis of biases or stereotypes. This means that individuals make decisions based on a range of motivations that cannot be called rational (exactly), and it also means that individuals can easily make 'bad' choices, or make 'mistakes' in choosing. For example, they may be overly optimistic or overly confident in their decisions, they may prefer what they have over what they could potentially gain ('loss aversion' and the 'endowment effect'),[5] they may suffer from all sorts of framing mistakes,[6] they may be inclined to stick with their current situation ('status quo bias')[7], they may suffer from weakness of will (akrasia) or inertia,[8] they may focus on the wrong aspects of a choice or they may be guided (too much) by social pressures.[9] What's more, research has also revealed that individuals use a variety of heuristics when making choices, for example 'anchoring',[10] the 'availability heuristic'[11] or the 'omission bias'.[12] As with the biases and stereotypes discussed above, using such heuristics entails that decisions are hardly a matter of purely rational calculation.

We may conclude that research in different scientific domains has consistently revealed that the idea of maximizing the freedom to choose, so dominant in Western culture, is in need of urgent revision. Human beings, in fact, are not utility maximizing, rational choosers – the classical image of the homo economicus does not do justice to the ways in which human beings operate when they make decisions. Therefore, this image has been revised in the past decades on the basis of the empirical findings in social psychology and behavioural economics.

Our collective thinking about freedom of choice and its prominent role has also started to shift, gradually yet fundamentally, in light of these scientific findings. Perhaps there are situations in which individuals ought to be helped or supported in making choices, especially in light of the growing number of choices available to them in their roles as, for example, consumers, citizens, or end users on the internet. Two domains in which this line of thinking has firmly taken root are that of technology development on the one hand, and public policy making on the other hand. As I show, both domains have come to believe in the value of offering end users and citizens 'decision support' to help alleviate their burden to choose (Botti and Iyengar 2006; Hanoch and Rice 2006).

Behavioural data analytics

Unlocking the informational potential of the internet is one of the great challenges of the second generation of the internet. As we have seen, so much information is available today that channelling it, and making it available to the right audiences in the right ways and at the right time has become a vital issue for technology developers and designers. In that light, several solutions have been developed. For one, search engines such as Google use a mixture of complex algorithms to optimize their engines' performance and to ensure that end users can easily and effortlessly find the information they are looking for. The most well known of these algorithms is *Google PageRank*, which orders search results:

> by counting the number and quality of links to a page to determine a rough estimate of how important the website is. The underlying assumption is that more important websites are likely to receive more links from other websites.[13]

This is no trivial affair: the order in which search results are provided to end users can have a significant impact[14] on the number of visitors that website owners will attract to their sites, and hence on, for example, business revenues, on news and knowledge dissemination, and on political popularity (cf. Hannak et al. 2013). Aside from the *PageRank* algorithm Google also claims that it uses *Personalized Search*.[15] This technique uses the browser cookies on end users' computers, which store their preferences and search history, to order search results in such a way that the most interesting ones will appear on the first page(s), while the ones that the end user will likely find less interesting will appear further down.[16] The idea is that each end user will receive his or her own personalized version of search results, aligned with his or her (admittedly, guesstimated) informational wishes. The use of both algorithms combined entails that, contrary to what many end users implicitly or even explicitly believe (Hannak et al. 2013; Pan et al. 2007), search engines are not mere conduits, neutral in their information retrieval and presentation. Rather, the information that is made accessible is invisibly adjusted, sorted, by the search engines' algorithms.

While optimizing and personalizing search may greatly increase the ease with which end users can find information that suits them, at the same time there are some concerns over this development. Reshuffling and sorting search results on the basis of our personal preferences and search histories, one could argue, will 'create a unique universe of information for each of us [. . . a] a filter bubble [. . .] which fundamentally alters the way we encounter ideas and information' (Pariser 2011: 9). What is problematic about living in such a bubble, according to Pariser, is the fact that its workings and effects remain hidden from view to the end user. We do not know how information is filtered, on which grounds and when, and we do not know which information does *not* reach us, since we only see what is offered to each and every one of us inside our own bubble:

> Google doesn't tell you who it thinks you are or why it's showing you the results you're seeing. You don't know if its assumptions about you are right or wrong – and you might not even know it's making assumptions about you in the first place.
>
> (Pariser 2011: 10)

Personal search is part of a larger trend that we may call *behavioural data analytics*. This umbrella term captures a set of novel techniques including data mining, web intelligence and profiling (Custers et al. 2013; Han and Kamber 2006; Hildebrandt 2008a; Shroff 2013), all of which aim to automatically extract 'patterns representing knowledge implicitly stored [. . .] in large databases, data warehouses, the Web, other massive information repositories, or data streams' (Han and Kamber 2006: xxi). Businesses claim that using the outcomes of behavioural data analytics has great potential.[17] There is a wealth of data available today in databases and on the internet that can be used to find correlations and make predictions about the future behaviour and preferences of consumers. For example, businesses use behavioural data analytics to predict consumer behaviour with the intention of sending individuals targeted advertising, for the purpose of price discrimination and personalization, and to make decisions about, for instance, their credit-worthiness or the insurance risks individuals may pose (cf. Etzioni 2012; Hildebrandt and Van Dijk 2012; Leino and Räihä 2007).[18]

The main argument that businesses use to justify the application of behavioural data analytics and the creation of end user profiles is that these help them improve service levels for their customers.[19] After all, when customers receive targeted advertisements, tailored to their personal needs and wishes, they will not be burdened with information they are likely to find irrelevant or uninteresting – as is often the case with 'traditional' advertising's scattergun method. Similarly, when Google preselects and orders search results for end users to match their (presumed) informational desires, this will reduce the burden to choose and the risk of informational overload. And when Amazon.com offers us suggestions for books or other products on the basis of our past purchases and searches, combined with those of 'people like us', then this, too, is explained as a move to unburden the end user, to alleviate her burden to choose.[20] Thus, the deployment of this type of decision support by businesses is justified with reference to end users' limited capacities and/or willingness to find and process information, or to make choices in the vast stock of content that is available to them in the current online environment.

Nudging

A similar line of reasoning seems to underlie a trend in policy making that has become widely adopted in recent years: the rise of 'nudging'. This concept became wildly popular[21] after the publication of Richard Thaler and Cass Sunstein's book *Nudge: Improving Decisions about Health, Wealth, and Happiness* (2008). Thaler and Sunstein start with the idea of a 'choice architect': policy-makers, technology designers, regulators, architects, or anyone who has to design an environment in which individuals will (have to) make certain choices, must be aware of the fact that the design of such environments will affect the behaviours of the individuals who will use them. Choice architects have a responsibility, Thaler and Sunstein argue, to construct such settings so that individuals are gently stimulated ('nudged') to make choices that will benefit their (long-term) health, wealth, or happiness.

In order to bring this about choice architects must offer individuals what Thaler and Sunstein call a 'benign' default (Thaler and Sunstein 2008; also see Smith, Goldstein and Johnson 2013; Van den Berg 2014). As we have seen, when confronted with situations in which they have to make a choice, most individuals use shortcuts (biases, rules of thumb, etc.) to make a decision. One such shortcut is following the default that is offered. Individuals have a tendency:

> to be guided in their decision making by preset choices (such as automatic enrollment in a company pension scheme, or being charged on a particular tariff for [their] domestic energy use). Default options are often followed because[22] they require little effort on the part of the individual and provide the reassuring sense that they reflect a 'normal' choice to make.
>
> (Jones, Pykett and Whitehead 2013: viii)

Banking on the fact that most individuals, most of the time, will follow whatever default option is offered to them, if choice architects offer defaults that lead to beneficial choices, then they can contribute to improving (a small part of) the lives of choosers. They are 'agent[s] of design-led social change' (Jones, Pykett and Whitehead 2013: 18).

A nudge, then, is 'an aspect of choice architecture that alters people's behaviour in a predictable way' (Thaler and Sunstein 2008: 6). What sets nudges apart from other forms of regulation is that they are 'freedom-preserving', according to Sunstein and Thaler (cf. Sunstein 2013). This means that nudges will always enable individuals to 'opt out', to choose to *not* follow the default. A nudge will offer a path to follow, but will never forbid other options, or rearrange the set of choices in such a way that following another alternative is much more costly than following the default. Nudges work without 'forbidding any options or significantly changing their economic incentives' (Thaler and Sunstein 2008: 6).[23] This is considered to be the hallmark of what defines a nudge: 'To count as a mere nudge, the intervention must be easy or cheap to avoid. Nudges are not mandates' (Thaler and Sunstein 2008: 6). So nudges are paternalistic in the sense that the choice architect makes a decision with respect to the desired behaviour he or she wishes to invoke through the design of the environment. Yet at the same time, Thaler and Sunstein argue that nudges are 'libertarian' in the sense that they leave individuals with room to manoeuvre and freedom to choose.[24]

The idea behind nudging first emerged within the field of behavioural economics, where, as we have seen, experimental findings consistently revealed that the *homo economicus*, the rational calculating individual who weighs all possible outcomes and chooses the most beneficial outcome for himself, does not exist. Nudging can be understood as a way of acknowledging and respecting the fact that individuals are neither (entirely) rational in their reasoning nor very good at making choices – that is, not at making choices as defined by the rational choice paradigm. What is more, nudging has been sold as a policy instrument that explicitly taps into and builds on the experimental findings from behavioural economics. It takes the non-rational ways in which individuals make choices as a given rather than as something to be remedied, and it *exploits* the fact that most people, most of the time, will 'unthinkingly' follow a default that is offered to them to generate improvements in people's lives (cf. Bovens 2009; Hausman and Welch 2010).[25] One could argue that nudging is about lessening the burden to choose, about removing the amount of choices that individuals face. Choices are pre-structured or facilitated through the use of a default in such a way that certain automatic, unconscious psychological mechanisms will kick in, which will lead individuals towards 'options that are either thought to be in their own best interest or thought to be in society's best interest' (Bovens 2009: 208).[26]

Similar to what we encountered above when discussing the deployment of behavioural data analytics, here, too, we see that the wealth of information, and the wealth of potential choices this offers, is reduced to prevent individuals from choice overload and to help them make easier, 'better' choices. Just like the use of behavioural data analytics or the reordering of search results in search engines, nudging, too, can be labelled as a form of decision support. Note also that there is one other important similarity: the prevention of choice overload is brought about *through technology*, through the creation of defaults that gently push people in certain (desired/desirable) directions. When studying the numerous examples from the key literature on nudging one element stands out: true nudges are always about intervening in, or rearranging settings and environments, that is they work through *architecture*.[27] This is why we can label nudging as one of several forms of what I have called 'technological influencing' elsewhere (Van den Berg and Leenes 2013; Van den Berg 2014). Policy-makers can actively deploy architectures in the broadest sense of the word, to influence, steer and guide the behaviours of individuals, by implementing changes in the environment and using artefacts, spaces and technologies to elbow people in what they perceive to be the right direction.

With a little help from our friends . . .

The previous section discusses two forms of decision support from two different realms. It looks at behavioural data analytics and the ways in which search engines and data brokers profile our behaviours, so that businesses can provide us with personalized services or target us for 'special' prices. It also shows that policy-makers around the world now enthusiastically embrace the use of nudges to facilitate people's choices and to gently steer them towards healthier choices, or choices that positively impact their wealth or wellbeing, especially in the long run.

What links these two very different forms of behavioural influencing, first and foremost, is their acceptance, or even affirmation of the ways in which human cognition functions – part rationally, but also largely non-rationally, using emotions, biases, stereotypes, and so on and so forth to make choices in real-world, fuzzy contexts. The *homo economicus* in his purely rational form, we have seen, does not exist and never has. So therefore, the argument goes, why not acknowledge, and *use* human cognition as it *does* function. Why not work *with* humans' capacity to choose, and even with the risk of being overwhelmed by choice?

In both forms of decision support the risk of information and choice overload is taken as a given and solutions are developed to address that risk. The attempt here is not to *overcome* our limited abilities to make choices, but rather to put these limited abilities to use, or, to phrase it even more starkly, to *exploit* them. Rather than attempting to remedy the 'imperfections' of our rational cognitive faculties there is a strong appeal on policy-makers and technology developers in both forms of decision support to help the individual through lowering the burden to choose, in order to prevent anxiety or choice overload on his behalf:

> . . .policy makers should avoid situations in which people, uncertain about their preferences and impaired by cognitive overload and emotional concerns, do not choose or make choices that elicit unsatisfying results.
>
> (Botti and Iyengar 2006: 28)

What both examples that are discussed in the previous section share, moreover, is the solution space they choose to remedy the risk they address: both use technology or architecture in the broadest sense of the word to bring about their solutions to tackle the risk of information and choice overload. The underlying idea here is that individuals operate in their everyday environments in a largely automatic, unthinking way, following the social and material scripts that these environments offer them (cf. Akrich 1992; Van den Berg 2008, 2010; Schank and Abelson 1977). These environments afford or constrain their actions in certain ways in the way they are designed, they provide individuals with opportunities and limitations for action (Gaver 1991, 1996; Gibson 1986; McGrenere and Ho 2000). Decision support uses this as the key driver for offering personalized services or guidance towards the 'right' choices.

Lastly, one can argue that both supporters of behavioural data analytics and advocates of nudging feel that technology developers and governments can and should play a role in improving people's choices and information provision through regulatory interventions. After all, while individuals must be offered the freedom to shape their own lives as much as possible, at the same time 'people may err and [. . .], in some cases, most of us can use a little help' (Sunstein 2013: 9). That is precisely where decision support systems ought to come in, according to their proponents.

Thanks, but no thanks?

In the past years the use of behavioural data analytics and optimizing/personalizing online search engines has been critiqued on several grounds. The same applies to the use of nudges in public policy. What's interesting is that there is significant overlap in the arguments on the limitations of these two forms of decision support, just like there was overlap in the arguments in their favour, as we have seen in the previous section.

First of all, both forms of decision support have been labelled as manipulative and overly intrusive (cf. Etzioni 2012; Goodwin 2012; Hansen and Jespersen 2013; Hildebrandt and Van Dijk 2012; Hildebrandt 2008a, 2008b; Smith, Goldstein and Johnson 2013; Tucker 2014). As we have seen above, reordering search results for optimization or personalization purposes generates a filter bubble that remains largely outside the awareness of end users. Even worse, even if end users know that such a bubble exists, they still cannot see what information exists outside of that bubble – simply because that information is not made accessible to them. Similarly, when targeted advertisements or price discrimination are used on the basis of findings from behavioural data analytics, individuals have no way of knowing that this is the case, and even if they know or suspect that this is the case, they have no way of acting against it. Nudging runs into similar problems. As we see above, nudging works best when individuals are left in the dark about the fact that they are being shoved in a certain direction. As a matter of fact, transparency undermines, or in all likelihood even obliterates the working of nudges. Nudging is all about exploiting certain patterns of 'irrationality' (Bovens 2009: 209). Most importantly, it is about following defaults in an unthinking way. We can safely assume that such patterns will cease to operate when individuals are made aware of the implicit influencing that is at work, and engage in conscious, deliberate thought about it. This reveals a difficult Catch-22 in the use of nudges. When one *does not* inform individuals that they are being nudged, nudges work very well – banking on individuals' cognitive biases and bounded rationality – but they can be considered manipulative. But when one *does* inform individuals that they are being nudged, the nudge will be much less effective, or will not work at all anymore. After all, when individuals are informed about the fact that they are gently pushed in a certain direction, they will no longer *automatically* respond on the basis of their cognitive biases, and hence such biases may be (temporarily, situationally) overcome. If we would inform individuals that they are being nudged towards, for example, making a healthier choice in a cafeteria or towards driving more carefully around sharp bends, then we may safely assume that at least a portion of these individuals would, at least some of the time, return to finding the greasy foods hidden around the corner instead or driving just a tad too fast for their own good.

Transparency and information provision thus undermine the effective workings of both forms of decision support, and this raises the question if, and to what degree, they actually differ from other forms of manipulation, such as advertising or subliminal messaging.[28] And if they do not differ from these forms of manipulation in fundamental ways, this raises the question of whether or not the (widespread) use of these forms of decision support can be considered an improper or unwarranted intrusion into the private lives of individuals. Especially when manipulations take place at low levels or even outside the awareness of end users, the step from offering 'benign' defaults and 'personalized' services to various forms of abuse is easily conceivable. This is why Hausman and Welch conclude that 'shaping people's choices for their own benefit seems to us to be alarmingly intrusive' (Hausman and Welch 2010: 131).

Related to this first critique is a second one, namely, the fact that the influencing and persuading powers of decision support systems such as the ones discussed in this chapter undermine autonomous choice, or, more broadly, negatively impact autonomy in general (cf. Bovens 2009; Hildebrandt 2008b; Smith, Goldstein and Johnson 2013; Yeung 2012; Zarsky 2003). According to Dworkin, autonomy is:

> a second-order capacity of persons to reflect critically upon their first-order preferences, desires, wishes, and so forth and the capacity to accept or attempt to change these in light of higher-order preferences and values. By exercising such a capacity, persons define their nature, give meaning and coherence to their lives, and take responsibility for the kind of person they are.
>
> (Dworkin 1988: 20)

As Dworkin's definition reveals, in order for individuals to be able to exercise this second-order capacity they must be aware of the first-order preferences, desires, wishes and so forth that they have, and be able to reflect on them. This is precisely where different forms of decision support, including nudging and the use of behavioural data analytics, are problematic. By using a 'subtle form of manipulation [and] taking advantage of the human tendency to act unreflectively, [they] are inconsistent with demonstrating respect for individual autonomy' (Yeung 2012: 136). They debilitate individuals' capacities to critically reflect on their wishes and desires, because they invoke these through subtle, implicit means. Thus, individuals lack the control and consciousness to critically reflect on their actions and on the motivations that gave rise to them, thereby curbing their autonomy.

Now, of course one could argue that *any* form of decision support runs the risk of undermining autonomy, and that in some cases it is necessary to limit the autonomous choices of individuals, simply because the choices to be made are too many, too complicated, and too emotionally complex to make. Think for instance about many of the choices that patients face in the healthcare domain. Decisions about one's health, for example choosing between different treatments that all have their benefits and risks, is very difficult, especially when patients have to factor in the consequences to their health in the longer run. There is increasing evidence that patients find it very difficult to make such decisions autonomously (Botti and Iyengar 2006). This is why we have doctors and healthcare practitioners to help us make such choices, to provide decision support, and in some cases even to delegate decision-making to. However, there is one big difference between human decision support, as it is provided for instance by doctors in healthcare contexts or by financial specialists in matters of money, and the kind of decision support that is provided by search engines and through nudges. The former build on providing individuals with knowledge and information, and openly discussing the possible courses of action available to them. While the information provided by doctors and financial specialists is structured for the individual according to their expertise and insights, and may be coloured by, for example, their past experiences or preferences, in most cases such experts will provide individuals with different scenarios and options and help them choose by discussing the pros and cons of each. Moreover, individuals retain their autonomy in the sense that they can ask questions and probe for more information when things remain unclear.

In contrast, the decision support systems that are under review in this chapter preselect and predefine the desired outcome for individuals and offer them a default, a single preferred path to walk down, rather than a set of options. The amount of information here is limited rather than merely structured, and one main option is presented as the most favourable one. No option to challenge the default exists other than opting out of it entirely – which considering the implicit working of these mechanisms is awfully hard to do.

This brings us to the last line of criticism: the use of decision support is not liberty-preserving. Quite the contrary, it undermines our freedom (cf. Amir and Lobel 2009; Colander and Chong 2009; Hansen and Jespersen 2013; Hildebrandt 2011; Yeung 2012). When search engines reorder search results according to invisible rules, we lose informational freedom in the sense that search results may be made inaccessible to us, or are accessible only in such an inconvenient way (i.e. on the umpteenth page of search results) that our chances of finding it are negligible. Similarly, when businesses decide to charge us with a higher fee for a health insurance package because we have been profiled as belonging to a high-risk category for some disease, this affects our freedom to choose and obtain the services we desire under the same conditions as everyone else. And when a cafeteria gently pushes us towards eating healthier lunches through the presentation of the foods it offers, this, too, affects our abilities to choose autonomously and freely.

Having said that, one could argue that such impairments to our freedom of choice *always* exist. If a search engine offers its search results in an entirely random fashion, some of the most desirable information may still end up on a page number that is so high we are unlikely to check it. And if a cafeteria offers its foods, both healthy and not, side by side and equally accessible, we might still be influenced implicitly by other factors, for example the price or the choices of our fellow diners. Therefore, claiming that decision support undermines freedom of choice in the strictest sense falls short – our freedom to choose is never complete, and decision support systems do not fundamentally alter that fact. Quite the contrary: as we see above their explicit goal is to make it easier for individuals to make choices, to combat the risk of information and choice overload and to help individuals navigate the dense informational forests of today's high tech reality.

However, even if nudges and consumer profiles do not negatively impact freedom of choice in the strictest sense, as Karen Yeung rightly points out freedom of choice is only one element of liberty, and a rather small element at that. Instead, she argues, we need to look at the deeper

> value of individual freedom. Liberty can also be understood in a thicker, richer sense, incorporating an understanding of the value that liberty occupies within our moral and political framework. On this view, liberty is understood as respect for individual autonomy rather than simply freedom of choice
>
> (Yeung 2012: 135)

This brings us back to the risk that using decision support entails for the erosion of our autonomy. Thus, despite the fact that nudges and other forms of decision support can be said to be 'liberty-preserving', they may still have a negative impact on individuals' autonomy:

> [People's] freedom, in the sense of what alternatives can be chosen, is virtually unaffected, but when this 'pushing' does not take the form of rational persuasion, their autonomy – the extent to which they have control over their own evaluations and deliberation – is diminished. Their actions reflect the tactics of the choice architect rather than exclusively their own evaluation of alternatives.
>
> (Hausman and Welch 2010: 128)

Running through all of these critiques we can distil a common thread that exposes two opposing hypotheses (also see Jones, Pykett and Whitehead 2013: 61) underlying the application of nudging, of behavioural data analytics, and other behaviour change programmes, whether instigated by policy-makers attempting to tackle thorny societal challenges, or by businesses attempting to improve customer services, lower company risks and increase revenue.

On the one hand behaviour change programmes, and the decision support systems that result from them, explicitly argue that they aim to empower people, to make them 'better' at making decisions for themselves, to provide them with information of better quality or more relevance, or easier defaults, so that these individuals themselves can improve their own lives. The argument is that through the use of decision support, individuals can be turned into more capable, personally responsible individuals.

On the other hand, though, the means for doing so focus on *removing responsibility* from people, and placing it in the hands of others, in this case of policy-makers and technology designers who allegedly know what is best for individuals and help us make the right choices. By building on the predictability of individuals' 'irrationality', or at least the limits to individuals' rationality, and preselecting or pre-ordering the most desirable information or the best choice for them, these decision support systems do not contribute to increasing individuals' capabilities and personal responsibilities at all. In fact, quite the reverse is true. Offering individuals pre-ordered information or predefined defaults may lead to 'better' *outcomes* because of individuals' predictable irrationality, but it deprives these individuals of training with respect to the *path* to get to such outcomes. If individuals are not challenged to think about the choices they make, are not tasked with weighing options and deliberating about the consequences of each, then true empowerment cannot come to bloom.

Hemming in freedom of information

We started this chapter with the observation that the rise of the internet has provided us with unprecedented access to and opportunities for finding information. Never before has the abundance of sources and content been this great – so great, in fact, that according to some we are at the risk of being overwhelmed by it. In this chapter, we have seen that different strategies have been developed to cope with this abundance of information, to facilitate individuals in making choices and to provide them with the 'right information' at the right time. We have also seen that this happens in widely differing areas: from public policy making to the corporate world – all using the power of technologies and architecture to code the behaviours of individuals. We have concluded that in both areas the means that is used to curb the risk of information overload is that of decision support, helping individuals make ('better') choices by reordering and reprioritizing information for them.

What has become apparent from the description of how such decision support systems work, and what critiques have been formulated against them, is that by removing the burden to choose from end users these systems run the risk of hemming in our freedom of information. Search engines use optimization techniques and our personal search history to offer us their best guess of our informational needs, and businesses across the spectrum use profiles generated with the help of behavioural data analytics to make predictions on what we may wish to buy, what we would be willing to pay, and whether or not we are a risk to them. This entails that these businesses actively shape the informational space they offer us, and actively adjust the content we receive. Through such practices,[29] the internet is not a free, open space where information is simply made available to whomever has the means of access and the will to find it. Rather, our informational freedom is hemmed in by the decision support systems that these businesses have implemented, on a massive scale, with the argument of lessening our burden to search and choose.

Policy-makers who embrace nudging as a novel strategy to remedy societal issues do something similar. They, too, hem in our informational freedom, but from a different direction. Nudging, we have seen, builds on the exploitation of the limitations of our capacities to choose rationally. It literally takes the burden of having to choose from the hands of individuals – or at least the vast majority of choosers, namely, those who unthinkingly follow the default offered – and places it squarely in the hands of the regulator, i.e. the choice architect who designs the default. Nudges not only reduce the burden to choose, but also decrease the amount and variety of information available to end users. After all, that is what offering a default is all about. We have also seen that offering (more) information is detrimental to the practical effectiveness of nudges; it effectively undermines their working. These two facts combined may lead us to conclude, therefore, that the use of nudges hems in our informational freedom as well, albeit from a different direction than the deployment of behavioural data analytics.

Why is this problematic? Considering the fact that there is overwhelming scientific evidence from various fields (see the introductory section) that individuals have difficulties in making (rational) choices, and may suffer from anxiety and other psychological tribulations when offered (too many) options, is not offering up some degree of our freedom of information justified to remedy the threat of choice overload?

Choice overload, information underload and Floridi's infraethics

The answer, to my mind, is no. This is so for several reasons. First, in their eagerness to combat the risk of choice overload the proponents of these forms of decision support may run the risk of depriving individuals of information they might like, find interesting, or deem worthwhile. To put it more starkly, in their attempts to prevent *choice overload* they run the risk of effectively creating *information underload*, of removing liberty, and the ability to critically reflect and autonomously choose from the end user. At face value this may not seem like a big problem. As we have seen, choices are always structured by whomever offers them, and structuring choices always involves rearranging, ordering, selecting and leaving out information.

But there is a second, deeper concern about information underload. And that is that it deprives people of the ability to reflect on the choices they have, and in the process of doing so, over a lifetime, grow into responsible, (self-)aware human beings, to transform into morally competent, reflexive individuals (also see Keymolen 2014). As Jonathan Rowson remarks about nudging:

> The deepest problem with nudge is that it is not transformative. Indeed, darkly, this may be why it is so popular. Nudge changes the environment in such a way that people change their behaviour, but it doesn't change people at any deeper level in terms of attitudes, values, motivations etc.. [. . .] We also need an approach that is *reflexive* because [. . .] engaging with knowledge about our brains and behaviour literally changes the subject.
>
> (Rowson 2011: 16, original emphasis)

The same applies to the use of other forms of decision support, including search engine optimization and behavioural data analytics. If individuals are not invited to think about the choices they make, they lack the power to structure their lives, to take charge not only of the decision-making itself but also of its consequences, and they will not be encouraged to grow and change. Reflexivity is a key element of what makes us human (cf. Giddens 1991; De Mul 2003), and therefore it is vital that the structures, architectures and systems around us *invite* reflexivity rather than decrease it.

It is in this light that I read Luciano Floridi's chapter on infraethics in this volume (Chapter 7). One of the key elements of this perspective is a plea for the relevance of choice in our (moral) actions. Importantly, Floridi is not out to promote *some forms* of choosing, nor does he aim to stimulate *certain outcomes* from choice processes (as does, for example, nudging), but rather he emphasizes the importance, and even the necessity of *being able to choose*. In order for us to develop, to mature as moral individuals, Floridi argues, we must, at specific moments in our lives, make choices that involve moral deliberation, that involve taking a stance in a moral dilemma, and hence that force us to take a stance on a moral matter. By doing so we grow, become empowered, mature.

Interestingly, Floridi feels so strongly about this idea that he even takes a paternalistic position with respect to its application: he proposes to *make* people choose if they are unwilling to do so of their own volition. Floridi appears to reject the reduction of (possible) choices that is the result of nudging and other forms of decision support and the paternalism this involves: that there are 'choice architects' who decide for others when and what the 'best' choices are. But at the same time he provides us with an equally paternalistic idea when he states we must force individuals to choose so that they will become moral(ly mature) human beings. While decision support is said to be paternalistic in determining for individuals which choices to remove from their lives, Floridi's infraethics, in turn, is paternalistic in deciding for individuals that they *must choose*.

At the same time, one can argue that Floridi's paternalism is of a different kind than that expressed in decision support such as nudging of search engine optimization. This is not paternalism that focuses on changing *behaviour* but on changing *attitudes* and *values* instead, on increasing *reflexivity*. It aims to empower individuals and to enhance their autonomy, rather than tapping into their 'limitations' to make them behave 'better' or make choices more easily. It is not paternalism *per se* that is problematic, as any parent will attest to, but paternalism that disempowers, that deprives and removes responsibility. Instead, when paternalism feeds growth and transformation it is, ultimately, a mere aid in enhancing the autonomy of the individual, and hence increasing their freedom. To choose, to act. To access, to find, to absorb . . . information. This, then, ought to be the aim of any form of decision support, both online and offline. To increase reflexivity and provide more freedom, not less. The forms for decision support under review in this chapter do not meet that criterion, and hence should be deployed with restraint.

Notes

1 Of course, establishing the difference between knowledge and opinion is, and always has been, a thorny issue, not only on the internet but in the offline world as well. This is one of the fundamental questions in epistemology and philosophy of science. It is not easy to answer where one begins and the other ends. On the one hand, criteria such as the use of specific methods, sampling, conformation, falsification and other reliability requirements play a role in establishing whether or not an inquiry can be considered as leading to the establishment or validation of facts, and hence knowledge. At the same time, a set of attributes of the speaker (i.e. the person presenting the knowledge) also plays a role in valuing a piece of information as 'knowledge' rather than 'opinion'. This relates to – admittedly fuzzy – concepts such as expertise, training, and institutional embedding or representation. 'Epistemic trust', i.e. trusting a specific person 'in her capacity as provider of information' (Wilholt 2013: 233), plays a vital role in choosing to define a piece of information as knowledge or opinion. Epistemic trust also entails that 'knowledge and trust are fundamentally entangled. [. . .] At a certain point, [we] have to stop searching for further confirmation [of a presented fact] and start trusting' (Simon 2010: 344). What I am arguing here is not that there is a definitive distinction, or a clear demarcation, between what we generally consider to be 'knowledge' and 'opinions'. What I am after is that in the real world there are pointers, or rules of thumb, that we use (correctly or not) to distinguish facts from fiction, and knowledge from opinions, for example by looking at the speaker's expertise or the (scientific) methods used to come by the claim this speaker is making. On the internet, using the same kinds of rules of thumb does not always work (cf. Simon 2010). We cannot always establish easily whether sources are creditable and trustworthy, or at least not in the same ways that we do in the offline world. Hence, different mechanisms to (re)establish epistemic trust on the internet may be required.

2 It is important to add the qualifier of 'rational' choice here. Many of the theories discussed in this section aim to address weaknesses in rational choice theory and the image of the *homo economicus* that has been so prevalent in Western society, not only in economics but also in politics. As we see below in more detail, human beings, they argue, are not so much bad at choosing *per se* (most of us are quite capable of making choices in our everyday lives), but the *mechanisms* we use to make such choices do not align with the central tenet of rational choice theories: that we choose on the basis of maximizing best possible outcomes for ourselves through the rational processing of all possible options. Instead, human beings use all sorts of shortcuts when choosing. They use rules of thumb, let their emotions speak, follow stereotypes and biases, and so on and so forth.

3 The term 'choice overload' is attributed to the futurist Alvin Toffler, who in his book *Future Shock* (1970) used the term 'overchoice' to describe the same phenomenon. Toffler argued that changes in culture and the development of various information technologies would lead to what he called 'future shock', a version of 'distress, both physical and psychological, that arises from an overload of the human organism's physical adaptive systems and its decision-making processes. Put more simply, future shock is the human response to overstimulation' (Toffler 1970: 326). Toffler already pointed out that human beings in our modern world must make an ever increasing amount of decisions in their everyday lives, yet have limited capabilities to process information. Combined with the rise in information streams, and the destabilization of the environments in which they operate, this could lead to mental and physical overload.

4 See also Botti and Iyengar (2006); Iyengar and Kamenica (2010).

5 See e.g. Camerer and Loewenstein (2004); Camerer (2005); Cartwright (2011); Jolls, Sunstein and Thaler (1997); Jolls and Sunstein (2006); Sunstein and Reisch (2014); Sunstein (1997a), (1997b).

6 See e.g. Camerer and Loewenstein (2004); DellaVigna (2009); Jolls, Sunstein and Thaler (1997); Selten (2001); Sunstein (2002).

7 See e.g. Botti and Iyengar (2006); DellaVigna (2009); Kesan and Shah (2006); Schlag (2010); Sunstein (1997a).

8 See e.g. Heilmann (2014); Sunstein (2013); Yeung (2012).

9 See e.g. Cartwright (2011); Hausman and Welch (2010).

10 This means that individuals rely (too) heavily on information that is already available to them. In the words of Sunstein: 'Often people make probability judgments on the basis of an initial value, or 'anchor', for which they make insufficient adjustments. The initial value may have an arbitrary or irrational source. When this is so, the probability assessment may go badly wrong' (Sunstein 1997b: 2651).

11 The availability heuristic entails that 'the probability of an event is estimated after an assessment of how easily examples of the event can be called to mind' (Jolls and Sunstein 2006: 203–204).

12 The omission bias entails that:

> individuals prefer to be hurt because some action was not taken rather than equally hurt because some action was taken. In the realm of software, the omission bias suggests people will avoid changing a setting because they fear it might 'break' the computer more than they fear 'breaking' the computer by not taking any action.
>
> (Kesan and Shah 2006: 602)

13 See http://en.wikipedia.org/wiki/PageRank (accessed 19 January 2016).

14 Research consistently shows that end users only look at the first page of search results when they look up information using a search engine, and oftentimes even look at the first (few) results only (cf. Pan et al. 2007: 811). This has led to the fact that appearing high in the list of an end user's search results now has significant economic value, and hence companies can bid for, or buy, high rankings in many search engines.

15 See http://googleblog.blogspot.nl/2009/12/personalized-search-for-everyone.html (accessed 19 January 2016).

16 As a matter of fact, how Google's algorithms and search engine optimization systems work exactly is not clear. This is, of course, a well-kept business secret (cf. Hannak et al. 2013).

17 As a matter of fact, so do governments. Since the focus of this chapter is on the use of behavioural data analytics by businesses, I do not discuss its application, and the reasons for doing so in the main text. However, in order to provide the reader with a more complete picture, I mention these matters in the next two notes.

18 On their part, governments use the power of behavioural data analytics for various purposes as well, for example to create political or racial profiles, to reveal anomalies in tax returns or to make predictions on terrorist and criminal activities (cf. Brown and Korff 2009; Hildebrandt 2006, 2008a, 2008b; Rubinstein, Lee and Schwartz 2008).

19 Governments predominantly justify their use of behavioural data analytics with reference to attempts to increase (national) security and/or to prevent crimes and other subversive behaviours.

20 Of course, underneath businesses' goal to improve service levels for their customers there is an economic reason: personalized services (presumably) will make customers happy and increase the chance that they will buy (more) products (Amazon) or return for future services (Google).

21 Cass Sunstein, one of the originators behind the idea of nudging, served as an administrator to the Office of Information and Regulatory Affairs in the first Obama administration (2009–12), where his main task was to oversee the implementation of new regulations in a wide variety of domains, and to investigate, in each case, whether regulation through nudging was a viable regulatory solution. The Cameron administration in the UK has installed a 'Behavioural Insights Team' (also known as the 'Nudge Unit') within the Cabinet Office to apply:

> insights from academic research in behavioural economics and psychology to public policy and services. [They work] with almost every government department, [but also] with local authorities, charities, NGOs, private sector partners and foreign government, developing proposals and testing them empirically across the full spectrum of government policy.
>
> (Behavioural Insights Team nd; also see Jones,
> Pykett and Whitehead 2013: 35–42)

Following their British counterparts, several Ministries in the Netherlands have also instigated such 'nudge units' to investigate whether new and existing forms of regulation can be (re)designed into nudges.

22 More specifically, three reasons are offered to explain *why* people tend to follow the defaults they are offered (Smith, Goldstein and Johnson 2013: 161). First, individuals may perceive the default option as an endorsement by the designers or by policy makers, or interpret it to be the preferred option that the majority would follow. Second, following defaults can be explained with reference to people's limited capabilities for rational choice and the biases that inform their choice-making, most importantly loss aversion (see also the second section of this chapter). Lastly, individuals' tendency to stick with the default they are offered may be explained with reference to the effort it takes to avoid that default.

23 In the fourth section we critically assess whether this is actually the case.

24 As a matter of fact, according to Sunstein and Thaler, interventions can *not* be labelled a nudge when there is no alternative course of action open to the individual, as is the case, for example, in the deployment of 'techno-regulation', whereby rules are implemented into artefacts, which then steer the behaviours of individuals in such a way that avoidance or non-compliance of the rule is impossible (Van den Berg and Leenes 2013; Van den Berg 2011, 2014; Brownsword and Yeung 2008; Brownsword 2008; Dommering and Asscher 2006; Hildebrandt 2011; Leenes 2011; Lessig 2006; Nissenbaum 2011; Yeung 2011).

25 In the fourth section we critically evaluate this strategy.

26 Ideally, nudges not only help the individual make 'better' choices, but also benefit the collective: when fewer people smoke or are overweight, healthcare costs for society may go down. Similarly, when more people save up more money in their retirement plans,

fewer people will turn to state aid when their pensions turn out to be insufficient. 'Good' nudges, then, benefit not only the individual but also society as a whole.

27 Some often discussed examples include: (1) rearranging (school) cafeterias so that healthy foods are easily accessible, placed at eye level and at the beginning of the restaurant, whereas less healthy foods are hidden in the back, preferably (almost) removed from view – this is said to encourage individuals to choose the healthy options over the not-so-healthy ones (Thaler and Sunstein 2008: 1–4); (2) redesigning staircases to look like giant pianos to nudge people towards taking the stairs rather than the elevator or the escalator (Jones, Pykett and Whitehead 2013: 81); and (3) painting the white stripes on roads closer together in sharp bends to create an illusion of high speed – this will nudge drivers to slow down (Thaler and Sunstein 2008: 41; see also Yeung 2012: 123).

28 Thaler and Sunstein also address the issue of manipulation and subliminal messaging in *Nudge*. They argue that there is an easy way to ensure that nudging does not lapse into outright manipulation through the 'publicity principle' (Thaler and Sunstein 2008: 245): if policy makers inform individuals that they are being nudged, no subliminal or unconscious influencing will take place. However, as we have seen, transparency is diametrically opposed to the effective working of nudges. There does not appear to be a compromise between (properly) informing people of the fact that they are being nudged and applying nudges in a productive way.

29 And others, which fall outside the scope of this chapter.

References

Akrich, M. (1992) 'The De-Scription of Technical Objects'. In W. Bijker and J. Law (eds) *Shaping Technology/Building Society: Studies in Sociotechnical Change.* Cambridge, MA: MIT Press: 205–224.

Amir, O. and Lobel, O. (2009) 'Stumble, Predict, Nudge: How Behavioral Economics Informs Law and Policy'. *Columbia Law Review* 108: 2098–2139.

Behavioural Insights Team (nd) 'Behavioural Insights Team', available at www.behaviouralinsights.co.uk/wp-content/uploads/2015/07/BIT_Update-Report-Final-2013-2015.pdf (accessed 19 January 2016).

Botti, S. and Iyengar S. (2006) 'The Dark Side of Choice: When Choice Impairs Social Welfare'. *American Marketing Association* 25(1): 24–38.

Bovens, L. (2009). 'The Ethics of Nudge'. In T. Grüne-Yanoff and S.O. Hansson (eds) *Preference Change: Approaches from Philosophy, Economics and Psychology.* Dordrecht: Springer: 207–219.

Brown, I. and Korff, D. (2009) 'Terrorism and the Proportionality of Internet Surveillance'. *European Journal of Criminology* 6(2): 119–134.

Brownsword, R. (2008) 'So What Does the World Need Now? Reflections on Regulating Technologies'. In R. Brownsword and K. Yeung (eds) *Regulating Technologies: Legal Futures, Regulatory Frames and Technological Fixes.* Oxford: Hart Publishing: 23–49.

Brownsword, R. and Yeung, K. (2008) 'Regulating Technologies: Tools, Targets and Thematics'. In R. Brownsword and K. Yeung (eds) *Regulating Technologies: Legal Futures, Regulatory Frames and Technological Fixes.* Oxford: Hart Publishing: 3–23.

Camerer, C.F. (2005) 'Behavioral Economics'. Paper presented at the *World Congress of the Econometric Society* 2005, London, available at http://people.hss.caltech.edu/~camerer/worldcongress05v18.pdf (accessed 19 January 2016).

Camerer, C.F. and Loewenstein, G. (2004) 'Behavioral Economics: Past, Present, Future'. In C.F. Camerer, G. Loewenstein and M. Rabin (eds) *Advances in Behavioral Economics*. Princeton, NJ: Princeton University Press: 3–51.

Cartwright, E. (2011) *Behavioral Economics*. London and New York, NY: Routledge.

Chandler, J.A. (2007) 'A Right to Reach an Audience: An Approach to Intermediary Bias on the Internet'. *Hofstra Law Review* 35(3): 1095–1137.

Colander, D. and Chong, A.Q.L. (2009) 'The Choice Architecture of Choice Architecture: Toward a Nonpaternalistic Nudge Policy'. *Middlebury College Working Paper Series* Number 1036. Middlebury, VT.

Custers, B., Calders, T., Schermer, B. and Zarsky, T.Z. (2013) *Discrimination and Privacy in the Information Society: Data Mining and Profiling in Large Databases*. Dordrecht: Springer.

DellaVigna, S. (2009) 'Psychology and Economics: Evidence from the Field'. *Journal of Economic Literature* 47(2): 315–372.

De Mul, J. (2003) *Cyberspace Odyssee*. 2nd edn. Kampen: Klement.

Dommering, E. and Asscher, L. (2006) *Coding Regulation: Essays on the Normative Role of Information Technology*. The Hague West Nyack, NY: TMC Asser.

Dworkin, G. (1988) *The Theory and Practice of Autonomy*. Cambridge and New York, NY: Cambridge University Press.

Etzioni, A. (2012) 'The Privacy Merchants: What Is to Be Done?' *University of Pennsylvania Journal of Constitutional Law* 14(4): 929–951.

Gaver, W.W. (1991) 'Technology Affordances'. In *SIGCHI Conference on Human Factors in Computing Systems: Reaching Through Technology*. New Orleans: ACM: 79–85.

——. (1996) 'Affordances for Interaction: The Social Is Material for Design'. *Ecological Psychology* 8(2): 111–129.

Gibson, J.J. (1986) *The Ecological Approach to Visual Perception*. Hillsdale, NJ: L. Erlbaum Associates.

Giddens, A. (1991) *Modernity and Self-Identity: Self and Society in the Late Modern Age*. Stanford, CA: Stanford University Press.

Goodwin, T. (2012) 'Why We Should Reject "Nudge"'. *Politics* 32(2): 85–92.

Han, J. and Kamber, M. (2006) *Data Mining: Concepts and Techniques*. 2nd edn. Amsterdam and Boston, MA: Elsevier.

Hannak, A. et al. (2013) 'Measuring Personalization of Web Search'. In *Proceedings of the 22nd International World Wide Web Conference (WWW'13)*. Rio de Janeiro: 527–537.

Hanoch, Y. and Rice, T. (2006) 'Can Limiting Choice Increase Social Welfare? The Elderly and Health Insurance'. *The Milbank Quarterly* 84(1): 37–73.

Hansen, P.G. and Jespersen, A.M. (2013) 'Nudge and the Manipulation of Choice: A Framework for the Responsible Use of the Nudge Approach'. *European Journal of Risk Regulation* 1: 3–28.

Hausman, D.M. and Welch, B. (2010) 'Debate: To Nudge or Not to Nudge'. *Journal of Political Philosophy* 18(1): 123–136.

Heilmann, C. (2014) 'Success Conditions for Nudges: A Methodological Critique of Libertarian Paternalism'. *European Journal for Philosophy of Science* 4(1): 75–94.

Hildebrandt, M. (2006) 'From Data to Knowledge: The Challenges of a Crucial Technology'. *Datenschutz und Datensicherheit* 30: 548–552.

——. (2008a) 'Defining Profiling: A New Type of Knowledge?' In M. Hildebrandt and S. Gutwirth (eds) *Profiling the European Citizen: Cross-Disciplinary Perspectives*. Dordrecht: Springer: 17–45.

——. (2008b) 'Profiling and the Rule of Law'. *Identity in the Information Society (IDIS)*: 55–70.

——. (2011) 'Legal Protection by Design: Objections and Refutations'. *Legisprudence* 5(2): 223–249.

Hildebrandt, M. and Van Dijk, N. (2012) 'Customer Profiles: The Invisible Hand of the Internet'. In G. Munnichs, M. Schuijff and M. Besters (eds) *Databases: The Promises of ICT, the Hunger for Information, and Digital Autonomy*. The Hague: Rathenau Instituut: 62–72.

Howe, J. (2008) *Crowdsourcing: Why the Power of the Crowd Is Driving the Future of Business*. New York, NY: Crown Business.

Iyengar, S. and Kamenica, E. (2010) 'Choice Proliferation, Simplicity Seeking, and Asset Allocation'. *Journal of Public Economics* 94(7–8): 530–539.

Iyengar, S. and Lepper, M.R. (2000) 'When Choice Is Demotivating: Can One Desire Too Much of a Good Thing?' *Journal of Personality and Social Psychology* 79(6): 995–1006.

Jolls, C. and Sunstein, C.R. (2006) 'Debiasing through Law'. *Journal for Legal Studies* 35: 199–241.

Jolls, C., Sunstein, C.R. and Thaler, R.H. (1997) 'A Behavioral Approach to Law and Economics'. *Stanford Law Review* 50: 1471–1550.

Jones, R., Pykett, J. and Whitehead, M. (2013) *Changing Behaviours: On the Rise of the Psychological State*. Northampton, MA: Edward Elgar Publishing.

Kesan, J.P. and Shah, R.C. (2006) 'Setting Software Defaults: Perspectives from Law, Computer Science and Behavioral Economics'. *Notre Dame Law Review* 82(2): 583–634.

Keymolen, E. (2014) 'A Moral Bubble: The Influence of Online Personalization on Moral Repositioning'. In J. de Mul (ed.) *Plessner's Philosophical Anthropology: Perspectives and Prospects*. Amsterdam: Amsterdam University Press: 387–406.

Leadbeater, C. (2008) *We-Think: Mass Innovation, Not Mass Production*. London: Profile.

Leenes, R. (2011) 'Framing Techno-Regulation: An Exploration of State and Non-State Regulation by Technology'. *Legisprudence* 5(2): 143–169.

Leino, J. and Räihä, K.J. (2007) 'Case Amazon: Ratings and Reviews as Part of Recommendations'. In *RecSys'07*. Minneapolis, MN: ACM.

Lessig, L. (2006) *Code: Version 2.0*. 2nd edn. New York, NY: Basic Books.

McGrenere, J. and Ho, W. (2000) 'Affordances: Clarifying and Evolving a Concept'. In *Graphics Interface Conference*. Montreal, Quebec: 179–186.

Nissenbaum, H. (2011) 'From Preemption to Circumvention: If Technology Regulates, Why Do We Need Regulation (and Vice Versa)?' *Berkeley Tech. LJ* 26(11): 1367–1386.

Nordenson, B. (2008) 'Overload!' *Columbia Journalism Review*, available at www.cjr.org/feature/overload_1.php (accessed 19 January 2016).

O'Reilly, T. (2007) 'What Is Web 2.0: Design Patterns and Business Models for the Next Generation of Software'. *Communications & Strategies* 65(1): 17–37.

Pan, B. et al. (2007) 'In Google We Trust: Users' Decisions on Rank, Position, and Relevance'. *Journal of Computer-Mediated Communication* 12(3): 801–823.

Pariser, E. (2011) *The Filter Bubble: What the Internet Is Hiding from You*. New York, NY: Penguin Press.

Reed, D.D., DiGennaro-Reed, F.D., Chok, J. and Brozyna, G.A. (2011) 'The "Tyranny of Choice": Choice Overload as a Possible Instance of Effort Discounting'. *The Psychological Record* 61: 547–60.

Rowson, J. (2011) *Transforming Behaviour Change: Beyond Nudge and Neuromania*. London: RSA.

Rubinstein, I.S., Lee, R.D. and Schwartz, P.M. (2008) 'Data Mining and Internet Profiling: Emerging Regulatory and Technological Approaches'. *University of Chicago Law Review* 75: 261–285.

Salecl, R. (2011) *The Tyranny of Choice*. London: Profile.

Schank, R.C. and Abelson, R.P. (1977) 'Scripts'. In R.C. Schank and R.P. Abelson *Scripts, Plans, Goals, and Understanding: An Inquiry into Human Knowledge Structures*. Hillsdale, NJ and New York, NY: L. Erlbaum Associates.

Schlag, P. (2010) 'Nudge, Choice Architecture, and Libertarian Paternalism'. *Michigan Law Review* 108: 913–924.

Scholz, T. (2008) 'Market Ideology and the Myths of Web 2.0'. *First Monday* 13(3), available at http://firstmonday.org/article/view/2138/1945 (accessed 19 January 2016).

Schwartz, B. (2000) 'Self-Determination: The Tyranny of Freedom'. *The American Psychologist* 55(1): 79–88.

Schwartz, B. and Kliban, K. (2005) *The Paradox of Choice: Why More Is Less*. New York, NY: Harper Perennial.

Selten, R. (2001) 'What Is Bounded Rationality?' In G. Gigerenzer and R. Selten (eds) *Bounded Rationality: The Adaptive Toolbox*. Cambridge, MA: MIT Press: 13–36.

Shakespeare, W. (1993) *As You Like It*. Ware: Wordsworth Editions Ltd.

Shroff, G. (2013) *The Intelligent Web: Search, Smart Algorithms, and Big Data*. Oxford: Oxford University Press.

Simon, H.A. (1955) 'A Behavioral Model of Rational Choice'. *The Quarterly Journal of Economics* 69(1): 99–118.

——. (1972) 'Theories of Bounded Rationality'. In C.B. McGuire and R. Radner (eds) *Decision and Organization*. Amsterdam: North-Holland Publishing Company: 161–176.

——. (1978) 'On How to Decide What to Do'. *The Bell Journal of Economics* 9(2): 494–507.

Simon, J. (2010) 'The Entanglement of Trust and Knowledge on the Web'. *Ethics and Information Technology* 12(4): 343–355.

Smith, N.C., Goldstein, D.G. and Johnson, E.J. (2013) 'Choice without Awareness: Ethical and Policy Implications of Defaults'. *Journal of Public Policy & Marketing* 32(2): 159–172.

Sunstein, C.R. (1997a) 'Behavioral Analysis of Law'. *The University of Chicago Law Review* 64(4): 1175–1195.

——. (1997b) 'How Law Constructs Preferences'. *Geo LJ* 86: 2637–2652.

——. (2002) 'What's Available: Social Influences and Behavioral Economics'. *Nw UL Rev* 97(3): 1295–1314.

——. (2013) *Simple(r): The Future of Government*. New York, NY: Simon & Schuster.

Sunstein, C.R. and Reisch, L.A. (2014) 'Automatically Green: Behavioral Economics and Environmental Protection'. *Harvard Environmental Law Review* 38(1): 128–158.

Thaler, R.H. and Sunstein, C.R. (2008) *Nudge: Improving Decisions about Health, Wealth, and Happiness*. New Haven, CT: Yale University Press.

Toffler, A. (1970) *Future Shock*. 2nd edn. New York, NY: Random House.

Tucker, P. (2014) *The Naked Future: What Happens in a World That Anticipates Your Every Move?* New York, NY: Penguin.

Van den Berg, B. (2008) 'Self, Script, and Situation: Identity in a World of ICTs'. In S. Fischer-Hübner, P. Duquenoy, A. Zuccato and L. Martucci (eds) *The Future of Identity in the Information Society*. Boston, MA: Springer: 63–76.

——. (2010) *The Situated Self: Identity in a World of Ambient Intelligence*. Nijmegen: Wolf Legal Publishers.

——. (2011) 'Techno-Elicitation: Regulating Behaviour through the Design of Robots'. In B. van den Berg and L. Klaming (eds) *Technologies on the Stand: Legal and Ethical Questions*. Nijmegen: Wolf Legal Publishers: 403–422.

——. (2014) 'Colouring Inside the Lines: Using Technology to Regulate Children's Behaviour Online'. In S. van der Hof, B. van den Berg and B. Schermer (eds) *Minding Minors Wandering the Web: Regulating Online Child Safety*. The Hague: TCM Asser Press: 67–90.

Van den Berg, B. and Leenes, R. (2013) 'Abort, Retry, Fail: Scoping Techno-Regulation and Other Techno-Effects'. In M. Hildebrandt and J. Gaakeer (eds) *Human Law and Computer Law: Comparative Perspectives*. Dordrecht: Springer: 67–87.

Wilholt, T. (2013) 'Epistemic Trust in Science'. *British Journal for the Philosophy of Science* 64(2): 233–253.

Yeung, K. (2011) 'Can We Employ Design-Based Regulation While Avoiding Brave New World?' *Law, Innovation and Technology* 3(1): 1–29.

——. (2012) 'Nudge as Fudge'. *The Modern Law Review* 75(1): 122–148.

Zarsky, T.Z. (2003) '"Mine Your Own Business!": Making the Case for the Implications of the Data Mining of Personal Information in the Forum of Public Opinion'. *Yale Journal of Law Technology* 5(1): 1–57.

Index